# A Corporate Form of Freedom

**New Perspectives on Law, Culture, and Society**

*Robert W. Gordon and Margaret Jane Radin, series editors*

# A Corporate
# Form of Freedom

## The Emergence of the Modern
## Nonprofit Sector

### Norman I. Silber

A Member of the Perseus Books Group

Copyright © 2001 by Westview Press, A Member of the Perseus Books Group

Published in 2001 in the United States of America by Westview Press, 5500 Central Avenue, Boulder, Colorado 80301-2877, and in the United Kingdom by Westview Press, 12 Hid's Copse Road, Cumnor Hill, Oxford OX2 9JJ

Find us on the World Wide Web at www.westviewpress.com


Library of Congress Cataloging-in-Publication Data
Silber, Norman Isaac.
    A corporate form of freedom : the emergence of the modern nonprofit sector / Norman I. Silber.
        p.   cm.—(New Perspectives on law, culture, and society)
    Includes bibliographical references and index.
    IBSN 0-8133-9762-6 (pbk.)
    1. Nonprofit organizations—Law and legislation—United States—History—20th century.   2. Nonprofit organizations—Political aspects—United States—History—20th century.   I. Title.   II Series

KF1388.S55  2000
346.73'064—dc21

                                                            00-043999


The paper used in this publication meets the requirements of the American National Standard for Permanence of Paper for Printed Library Materials Z39.48-1984.

10    9    8    7    6    5    4    3    2    1

*For Nancy and Meeka,*
*Jeffrey and Jack,*
*whose profitable enterprises are*
*learning, loving, and commitment*

# Contents

# Acknowledgments

Helpful suggestions about earlier drafts, by Eugene Aleinikoff, John Morton Blum, William Buzbee, Victor Futter, Thomas Greene, David Hammack, Mary Heen, Robert Kagan, James Kainen, William McKeown, Marie Morgan, Subha Narasimhan, William E. Nelson, Robert Post, Edward Rubin, Jill Schatman, and John Simon have been greatly appreciated. Editors of the *Yale Journal of Law and the Humanities*, members of the NYU Legal History Colloquium and the Jurisprudence and Social Policy Seminar at the University of California at Berkeley provided valuable comments on earlier versions of the manuscript.

Among many supportive colleagues at Hofstra Law School who have helped me in this project I would like to thank in particular Robin Charlow, Linda Galler, Bill Ginsberg, John Gregory, Eric Freedman, Bernard Jacob, Lawrence Kessler, Cheryl Wade, and Vern Walker.

Thanks to research assistants Michael Anderson, Matt Camardella, Brian Dillon, Alex Fear, Larry Glick, Cristi Luckow, and Eliana Schonberg; to students in my Hofstra Nonprofit Corporations seminars, and to the Hofstra University Law Librarians, as well as to Dean Stuart Rabinowitz and Hofstra University for financial research support.

# 1

# Introduction

Newspapers in 1996 reported that a self-made billionaire and naturalized citizen had decided to spend $50 million to establish a foundation to support immigrants applying to become naturalized U.S. citizens and to assist community organizations providing English-language classes and other aid to immigrants.[1] When asked why he was making this gift, the benefactor replied that he was "appalled by Congress' recent action to deny vital public assistance to noncitizens who are lawfully resident in this country."[2] A public interest organization whose purpose was to improve immigration policies called this gift—the largest grant ever made for this purpose—a magnificent and courageous act of generosity.[3]

A few months later the evening television news broadcast a story about a prominent political leader who admitted to several wrongdoings and agreed to pay a large fine rather than face further disgrace. Using funds from a political action committee (PAC), which had been created for the purpose of helping the members of his party gain control of the U.S. Congress, he broadcast lectures and other messages on the subject of "renewing American Civilization" over "American Citizen's Television." His actions, he said, were calculated to enlarge his "citizen's movement" and to recruit to his political party "non-voters and people who were apolitical." To obtain needed money for his plan, he ran the program under the auspices of a previously defunct legal shell called the Abraham Lincoln Opportunity Foundation, whose originally stated purpose was to help inner-city youth improve their education, but whose legal virtue was that donations to it allowed donors to claim deductions on their tax returns.[4]

These reports suggest a few of the ways in which organizations and individuals have pursued social, political, and economic purposes by joining, maneuvering within, and sometimes exploiting an unusual set of legal rules. The rules help those who take advantage of them solicit money, recruit employees, and do many other kinds of routine business. The

rules equip them with financial inducements to attract contracts, investments, and donations. They encourage them—even the least important
or efficient of them—to divert sums—collectively amounting to billions
of dollars—from treasuries of the federal, state, and local governments.
Remarkably, the rules allow anyone to organize a group for almost any
desired purpose and then obtain many associated privileges by passing
tests that often are cursory or perfunctory in their nature.

These legal rules, of course, are those that govern the nonprofit sector.[5]
The groups in question are organized under laws that govern the nation's nonprofit corporations, foundations, nonprofit associations, charitable trusts, and the like.[6] Collectively, these groups have become integral
to the national economy and a valued part of the social fabric. By 1995,
the assets of nonprofit organizations amounted to approximately $1.9
trillion, and their revenues were estimated to be in the neighborhood of
$899 billion.[7] The annual revenues of the most popular federal classifica-
tion of nonprofits, those called § 501(c)(3) charities,[8] reached $406 billion
in 1990, which amounted to more than 7 percent of the gross domestic
product that year—even without including the product contributed by
unpaid volunteers. In 1996, Americans claimed $150.7 billion dollars in
charitable contributions to qualifying groups.[9] Although the U.S. gross
domestic product grew 52 percent between 1975 and 1990, assets of tax-
exempt organizations increased in real terms by over 150 percent.[10] The
nonprofit sector, and especially the nonprofit corporations that make up
a substantial part of it, have risen in their economic, cultural, and political importance over the past decades.

The altruism and social commitment of most who work in and donate
to the nonprofit sector is well-known. Indeed, it embodies the philanthropic goodness, conviviality, cultural excitement, and democratic spirit
of the American people.[11] It is not unusual to learn about community-
spirited projects made possible by the contributions of generous members of a fraternal club or the outreach efforts of employees of a community health clinic; or about an environmental group that purchased a
piece of abandoned property in the inner-city to turn into an urban park.
The nonprofit sector has provided a valued social location in which
groups can operate without pecuniary obsessions and with measures of
success that are not necessarily related to financial profitability.

Instances of exemplary conduct by nonprofit corporations, however,
appear increasingly pale in comparison to accounts of misdeeds. A powerful public skepticism has developed about whether most nonprofit organizations operate honestly and serve worthwhile social objectives that
justify their special treatment. In the profit-oriented world, a certain
amount of misbehavior is anticipated and forgiven as the natural, or even
the necessary, by-product of human nature bent by market incentives.

Abuses in the nonprofit world, however, can provoke a response of disillusionment because altruism, or at least a commitment to social betterment, is often assumed to be a prerequisite for operating with the not-for-profit designation. Governmental bodies are presumed to be responsible for selecting and monitoring organizations that enjoy advantages which are made available to them by government. Expressions of shock and outrage are common reactions to accounts of abuse of privileges in the nonprofit world.

It is partly a testament to the good faith of most who establish nonprofit groups and work within the nonprofit sector that so much of value emanates from it, since nonprofit groups are generally not well supervised. The regulators who are charged with enforcing laws intended to prevent nonprofit groups from misusing or wasting public resources, misleading the community about their objectives, or operating for private benefit are greatly overburdened. The design of the regulatory structures leads regulators to accept many assertions that are made by nonprofit groups at face value—and rarely to inquire affirmatively about whether an organization is well regarded, useful, efficient, purposeful, sincere, or even honest. The regulators don't know—and often can't know—who truly funds and operates nonprofit organizations. Very few operators of organizations governed by the nonprofit legal regime are routinely held accountable for their success or failure.[12]

The vulnerability of the nonprofit legal regime to abuse is not simply the product of inept regulators or shady operators. The requirements set out in applicable statutes are for the most part subject to variable interpretations, and the procedures for their enforcement are not straightforward. Accounting and disclosure requirements are laced with holes. Charges of class bias, arbitrariness, unfair competition, partisanship, rampant cheating, and the abuse of privilege by officers and employees are levied by critics and rival groups. Persons and groups with an economic interest in litigating to establish more responsible behavior by nonprofit rivals are frequently prevented by law from maintaining a lawsuit.[13]

The excesses and institutional weaknesses of several nonprofits have become more apparent than ever.[14] It is no longer unusual to learn about some group availing itself of nonprofit status to promote a ridiculous, frivolous, or hedonistic purpose; or about a locality reeling under the weight of the property tax exemptions that it is required to accord to relatively broad and indiscriminate categories of nonprofits; or about an abuse of trust by officers and employees of a nonprofit or by donors to it. Discussions documenting inequity and inefficiency, as well as stories describing outright fraud, are common.[15]

Sagging public confidence in the nonprofit sector has been examined in different places and from diverse perspectives.[16] Those who question the magnitude of the problem or suggest that the marketplace provides adequate information to allow consumers to police nonprofits might consider the work of two investigative reporters, Gilbert Gaul and Neil Borowski, who wrote an award-winning seven-part series of articles which excoriate the economy and laws that govern nonprofits.[17] In it they denigrate thousands of nonprofit organizations, including hospitals, sports organizations, motion picture societies, and other groups, that act extravagantly in their own self-interest and place the comfort of their officers and their employees foremost. They describe large areas of nonprofit activity in which nonprofit groups accomplish no more than *taxable, shareholder accountable,* or *unsubsidized* organizations are doing or might be doing to solve social problems or serve charitable, artistic, scientific, or cultural purposes. Many of the greatest philanthropic foundations are portrayed as "warehouses of wealth" that spend far less money on programmatic expenditures than would be spent if their investments yielded taxes paid to the government and spent on democratically sanctioned expenditures.[18] "Thanks to the remarkable largesse of the nation's lawmakers," they state, "an ever-expanding definition of charity and a near-total collapse of government supervision, America's nonprofit economy has become a huge, virtually unregulated industry."[19]

Not surprisingly, the self-reflective leaders of the more responsible organizations recognize that they have lost esteem, status, support, and popularity as a result of the legal regime's shortcomings. They have advocated and sometimes accomplished notable reforms.[20] But even the most responsible beneficiaries are prone to oppose higher levels of scrutiny or other changes that threaten to disturb their operations, and they have mobilized to defend their existing benefits.[21]

Calls for regulating nonprofits become louder every year. And because the outside perception of abuse is great, political agencies are likely to overreact. Some state and federal legislators threaten to eliminate *all* of the important privileges for *all* organizations, not just the abusers.[22] Fear of indiscriminate retribution by a disillusioned public spreads into the marketplace where services are employed and donations are made. Many of those involved understand that more trouble is coming unless broad changes arrive. Consequently, alarms have been sounded about the types of organizations that are permitted to occupy the nonprofit sector, as well as about their supervision and accountability.[23]

\*     \*     \*

Why has the nonprofit sector grown so spectacularly and not been supervised adequately? Knowledge about the historical evolution of the nonprofit sector and its related laws can help explain why today's nonprofit sector is governed as it is.

A full assessment of the historic role of nonprofit organizations—of the effect they have exerted on society, the economy, and culture—transcends the scope of this, or perhaps any single, work.[24] An examination of an important part of the story, however—the history of efforts to control the creation and permissible purposes for nonprofit corporations by states, and of the relocation of these efforts to the Internal Revenue Service—should illuminate both positive and negative dimensions of the larger picture.

For most of the nation's history, fewer advantages were accorded to the nonprofit sector than are available today. Tax advantages of all kinds, for example, were relatively minor or nonexistent for a long time.[25] Government supervised the nonprofit sector mainly by restricting access to it. The legislators and officials who supervised the formation and operation of nonprofits were more direct and arbitrary in their determinations and were less concerned than now about whether they were being evenhanded or "objective" or "neutral" in their decisionmaking.[26]

State legislatures at first exercised direct control over access by individually chartering charitable, educational, and other nonprofit organizations and by imposing limits on the administration of charitable trusts. Later, and for more than a century, legislatures gave judges in some states and bureaucrats in others the primary authority to stand guard at the main entrance to the sector and to monitor organizational changes to existing groups. The record of court opinions in a leading jurisdiction, New York, in particular, contains an unusually rich set of cases about nonprofit organizations.[27] New York judges reflected local traditions about voluntarism and about the support of charities in their opinions, but there is little reason to believe that their perspective about the appropriate role of voluntary groups, including nonprofit corporations, differed from perspectives in different regions of the country. Indeed, comparable views were expressed by other courts in other parts of the nation.[28] For a considerable part of American history, therefore, the thought of officials about what was a proper role for nonprofits can be illuminated by analyzing the actions of common law judges in New York, Pennsylvania, and the other states in which reported opinions can be found.

In New York and several other states,[29] judges vigorously expanded their power to grant or to withhold their approval of certificates of nonprofit incorporation. They held onto a discretion[30] which became so strong that their personal reservations—religious, political, class, cultural, racial, and social—as a matter of legal doctrine were sufficient to sanction disapproval. Remarkably, their orders were viewed as proper expressions of judicial authority, notwithstanding the fact that neither rules nor doctrine nor higher courts restrained their actions. They dispensed justice routinely and without controversy or even minor challenge from the public, the legislature, the bar, the bench, the academic community, or nonprofits themselves. They used their control to promote the causes they believed in, and even to advance their own careers. In states where judges did not receive authority to exercise such strong discretion, the law still regarded the incorporation of nonprofit corporations as a privilege to be dispensed by a legislature or a state official,[31] not as a right.[32] Groups around the country consequently confronted the possibility that their applications for nonprofit charters would be denied, regardless of the lawful nature of the purposes they hoped to pursue, because of the actions of courts or of administrative officials acting under the aegis of general incorporation laws.[33]

This all changed abruptly in the 1950s, when the process for approving certificates of incorporation took a broadside attack from law students and young lawyers. Assailing the common law tradition, these revisionists utterly routed the discretionary tradition. Within less than a decade, the system of judicial discretion—which state legislatures supposedly instituted to limit the number and kind of nonprofit corporations in order to check abuses of the public's money and trust—had been recast and converted into an improper judicial usurpation that spurned newly cherished legal values.[34]

The newly elevated legal priorities of the younger generation of law students remarkably sound familiar to us today. They incorporated greater anxiety about using state power to suppress minority viewpoints with less enthusiasm for using state power to promote social cohesion. They incorporated greater concern about distributing government largesse according to impartial procedures with less apprehension about wasting some of it.[35] They embraced greater fear of the abuse of state power with less eagerness to have officials reflect community values in their decisions. They presumed little faith in the ability of regulators and judges to protect consumers and promote economic welfare—and they relied more heavily on the accountability of nonprofit groups to forces in the marketplace. The older assumptions, which had been accepted as commonplace and reasonable, were rejected. The older assumptions became known collectively as incompatible with modern constitutional principles. Scholars came to label the line of judicial disapproval cases a serious embarrassment to their recently amended theories of judicial decisionmaking and review.[36] The old theoretical framework for substantive pre-incorporation scrutiny crumbled as a new jurisprudence about equality and pluralism emerged.[37] The postwar generation played a particularly large role in accomplishing this transformation—challenging the previous doctrine of nonprofit incorporation and prodding courts and legislatures to create a new one: to establish a broad right for any group of persons willing to abide by simple governance and distribution rules to incorporate as nonprofits in furtherance of virtually any lawful cause.[38] Constitutional doctrine would resolve the tension between unbounded discretion and undifferentiated largesse by constraining discretion severely.

In harmony with pervasive intellectual currents and social movements—which not coincidentally helped to validate other sorts of entitlement programs including Medicaid, social assistance, and other components of the "Great Society"—courts stopped asking if a group deserved a subsidy because of a socially beneficial purpose. They turned instead toward a less exacting sort of analysis. They now asked whether a nonprofit corporation would further the expressive aspirations and avowed purposes of its founders. Free expression and a more perfect democratic pluralism became legal objectives of a higher order. Eventually, the process of nonprofit incorporation was refashioned into nothing more than the official acknowledgment of an entitlement to do business as a nonprofit corporation. The affirmative participation of judges in the incorporation process became inconsequential in shaping the social contours of the nonprofit sector.

Refashioning the gatekeeping process for nonprofits occurred as part of a broader transformation of the nation's communal understanding of what constituted valuable nonprofit activity. At the same time, limits on taxing bodies and regulators reduced the public and private accountability of most nonprofit organizations.[39] In the main, courts, administrative agencies, and legislatures now embraced expansive views about the social, economic, and political value of a diversity of viewpoints and players in a nonprofit sector that was composed of large corporate associations as much as smaller community groups. These views invited the expansion of tax exemptions, lobbying privileges, immunities from suit, fees for service contracts, government grants, special postal rates, and other forms of assistance and largesse.[40]

What follows is an investigation of the relationship between the currents of jurisprudence, legal rules, and social and economic change. It asserts that as a consequence of doctrinal transformation, nonprofit legal entities and the nonprofit sector broadly considered flourished economically and enriched the social discourse as never before. The sector experienced extraordinary growth and diversification; it generated impressive economic activity and extensive social benefits. Enriched discourse about public policy, cultural and social values, art, and of course philanthropy flowed from previously ineligible corporate groups operating increasingly within a nonprofit form. The same story also goes a distance toward helping understand the darker side of recent experiences with nonprofit activity. It explains many of the problems confronted by those who would try to improve the supervision of the modern nonprofit sector.

Confusion enveloped the theory of nonprofit organizations and the criteria that were used to bestow entitlements and privileges upon them. From many different directions, the essential premises for drawing distinctions between nonprofit organizations and others came into question. Criticism of undeserved benefits and unfair competition grew. Unfavorable court rulings multiplied. Restrictive federal and state regulations increased. Tax benefits diminished. Public confidence in the efficiency and constructiveness of the sector deteriorated. The reconception invited abuse by some new entrants and some existing players. With respect to public confidence in the way benefits and advantages were being administered, charities and many other nonprofit groups found themselves "irretrievably in big trouble" at the beginning of the millennium.[41]

Six chapters follow in this book. Chapter 2 discusses the advantages of nonprofit status and the historical divergence of profit and nonprofit gatekeeping. Chapter 3 takes advantage of the record left by case law—primarily in New York but also in other states—to tell a story about the cultural prejudices and political and economic theories that have shaped the nonprofit sector. It explains how judges built a doctrinal platform for themselves that let them shape the nonprofit sector to reinforce the values of social consensus and to reflect dominant political and social conventions.

Chapter 4 examines the corrosion of the traditional structure of supervision after World War II. As nonprofit status became more than ever before capable of delivering substantial benefits, opposition by a new generation of students to the traditional scheme for the supervision of nonprofits grew quickly during the 1950s and 1960s. The convergence of four intellectual and social constructions propelled this opposition. (1) New judicial theories looked unfavorably on strong forms of judicial power. (2) Scholars examining the legislation of the Great Society encouraged lawmakers to treat several forms of government largesse as fundamental entitlements. (3) The civil rights movement powerfully articulated a norm of nondiscriminatory treatment between majority and minority groups throughout the law. (4) Constitutional guarantees of individual free expression were interpreted to require adjustment and expansion to meet the challenges of a corporate environment. These ideas about law and justice converged to destroy—annihilate might be a better word—the viability of a legal regime built on discretion. This destruction took some time, however, and Chapter 5 discusses the transition to the new incorporation regime, as well as the difficulty that judges and bureaucrats had in accepting it.

Chapter 6 traces the impact of the reconception on the growth of the nonprofit sector and on the effectiveness of its supervision. It considers ways in which overthrowing the discretionary conception signaled an important triumph for the freedom of expression and for American expressive pluralism, but at the expense of seeking to hold nonprofit groups accountable for serving consensus social and philanthropic values. It redefined the permissible boundaries of civic discourse and the national understanding of diversity. It deprived judges of some small amount of their enormous cultural power.

The collapse of the older perspective about the nonprofit sector produced new ideas about how to assure a minimal degree of supervision of nonprofits. New disclosure remedies and specialized types of enforcement were developed, along with special attention to using tax authorities more effectively. The new conception postulated that tax exemption was the "true" subsidy by the state, and so it seemed possible for supervision to be handled effectively through post-incorporation determinations of eligibility for exemptions. The assumption that these mechanisms would be satisfactory replacements for state supervision went largely untested and proved mistaken.

Having tamed discretionary review of nonprofits at the gatekeeping phase of the supervision process, lawmakers and legal reformers made a cultural and political mistake in assuming that the insertion of powerful discretionary authority at other points of contact between government and nonprofits would be substantially more palatable to courts or to society generally. As the final chapter, Chapter 7, suggests, the problem for the next generation of lawmakers and policymakers would be to find a way to redraw the line between privilege and entitlement to the advantages of nonprofit organization without allowing inappropriate actors to make objectionable, discretionary value judgments.

Looking at who the judges and officials were and how they defined the permissible purposes of nonprofit corporations may produce a clearer picture of traditional ideas about what nonprofit corporations were supposed to do, and of the impact of the emergence of newer views.

## Notes

1. *See* Eric Schmitt, *Philanthropist [George Soros] Pledges Help to Immigrants*, N.Y. Times, Oct. 1, 1996, at A22 col. 1.

2. *Id.*

3. *Id.*

4. *See* CNN Transcript, *Ethics Committee Hearing into Alleged Violations of Newt Gingrich, Speaker, US House of Representatives*, no. 97011701V00 (CNN special event transcript, Jan. 17, 1997, 3:15 P.M.).

5. The term "nonprofit sector" throughout this study refers to the large body of private groups, including nonprofit corporations, associations, trusts, foundations, schools, and religious groups, that are neither government entities nor business firms organized for profit. The variety of purposes to which these

groups devote themselves is great. See the discussion of the variety of types of groups that today organize under the nonprofit laws, *infra* ch. 4. Many but not all such groups (as well as some other groups) obtain advantageous treatment under governmental laws and regulations, including exemption from certain taxes, including income, sales, and property taxes. Among the benefits that some nonprofit, tax-exempt organizations enjoy—principally those entitled under §501(c)(3) and §170 of the Internal Revenue Code—is the qualification of contributions made by their donors as deductions from taxable income on income tax returns. Although federal tax law distinguishes between "charitable organizations" and "private foundations," in this study unless otherwise indicated the word "charity" is used broadly to refer to philanthropic organizations generally. *See* James M. Ferris and Richard W. Graddy, *Fading Distinctions Among the Nonprofit, Government, and For-Profit Sectors*, in THE FUTURE OF THE NONPROFIT SECTOR (ed. Virginia A. Hodgkinson and Richard W. Lyman 1989); Bruce R. Hopkins, THE LAW OF TAX EXEMPT ORGANIZATIONS 3–6 (1992). What constitutes "philanthropy" has long been a matter for philosophical and also technical discussion. *See, e.g.,* Robert L. Payton, PHILANTHROPY: VOLUNTARY ACTION FOR THE PUBLIC GOOD (1988).

6. *Id.*

7. *See* Information Access Company, *There's Gold in Nonprofits*, 1999 WL 24407502, Mar. 1, 1999.

8. *See* IRS report, WALL ST. J., Feb. 8, 1995, at 1 col. 5. Organizations that are classified as exempt under I.R.C. §501 (c)(3) benefit in two principal ways. The organizations themselves enjoy federal tax exemption (usually state tax exemption as well), and those who donate money to these organizations may deduct a portion of the contribution on personal federal tax returns. A careful empirical effort to describe the current breadth and working of the charitable nonprofits is presented in William G. Bowen et al., THE CHARITABLE NONPROFITS (1994).

9. Adam Bryant, *Companies Oppose Disclosure of Detail on Gifts to Charity*, N.Y. TIMES, Apr. 3, 1998, at A1.

10. Daniel F. Skelly, *Tax-Based Research and Data on Nonprofit Organizations, 1975–1990*, INT'L J. VOLUNTARY & NON-PROFIT ORG. (1993).

11. *See* Ben A. Franklin, *Profligate Nonprofits*, WASHINGTON SPECTATOR, vol. 19, no. 11 (1993).

12. *See* Geoffrey A. Manne, *Agency Costs and the Oversight of Charitable* Organizations, 1999 WISC. L. REV. 227 (1999); Regina E. Herzlinger, *Can Public Trust in Nonprofits and Governments Be Restored?*, HARV. BUS. REV., Mar.-Apr. 1996 at 97; John Kimelman, *Too Charitable to Charities?*, FINANCIAL WORLD, Sept. 1, 1994 at 46; Kevin P. Kearns, *The Strategic Management of Accountability in Nonprofit Organizations: An Analytical Framework*, 54 PUB. ADMIN. REV. 185 (1994).

13. *See* Rob Atkinson, *Unsettled Standing: Who (Else) Should Enforce the Duties of Charitable Fiduciaries*, 23 J. CORP. L. 655 (1998); MARY G. Blasko et al., *Standing to Sue in the Charitable Sector*, 28 U.S.F.L. REV. 37 (1993).

14. *See, e.g.,* Regina E. Herzlinger, *Can Public Trust in Nonprofits and Governments Be Restored?*, HARV. BUS. REV., Mar.-Apr. 1996 at 97. (Nonprofits do not "have the self-interest that comes with ownership and helps to ensure that managers do not receive excessive compensation, that the business accomplishes its goals effi-

ciently, and that risks are appropriately evaluated. Second, they often lack the competition that would force efficiency. Finally, they lack the ultimate barometer of success, the profit measure.") *Id.; see also* William G. Bowen et al., THE CHARITA-BLE NONPROFITS (1994). ("At least some nonprofits may lead lives which are simultaneously undistinguished and largely unnoticed. . . . It is fair to say that nonprofits as a group are far less closely monitored externally than are for-profit organizations. . . . representatives of the public interest are, ultimately the owners in the nonprofit world of the underlying assets, but they exercise a far different degree of oversight than do owners and their surrogates in the for-profit world.") *Id.* at xix–xx.

15. Following are a few examples of results that have provoked popular and/or scholarly criticism:

The president of a large university, along with all but one of its trustees, is forced to resign as the result of findings that the president abused his authority and received unreasonably large amounts of compensation. *See, e.g.*, Bruce Lambert, *New Trustees of Adelphi U. Dismiss Embattled President*, N.Y. TIMES, Feb. 21, 1997, at A1 col. 5.

Under attack by the mayor of a major city for displaying sacrilegious art, a city art museum is accused of using its exhibit space to showcase privately owned works and thereby to augment the private wealth of one of the museum's largest donors. *See* Michael Kimmelman, *After Long Silence, Biggest Museums Joined Fight*, N.Y. TIMES, Sept. 29, 1999, at B5 col. 4.

A coven of witches gets treated as a nonprofit church, and it thereby obtains lenient accounting rules, tax exemption for the coven, and charitable contribution deductions for witches who donate to it. *See* Donitry N. Feofanolv, *Defining Religion: An Innocent Proposal*, 23 HOFSTRA L. REV. 309 (1994). The Ku Klux Klan and the Big Mama Rag both get nonprofit corporate charters, tax exemptions, and benefits. *See* Big Mama Rag v. U.S., 631 F.2d 1030 (1980); Michael J. Klarman, *Rethinking the Civil Rights and Civil Liberties Revolutions*, 82 VA. L. REV. 1 (1996).

After bleeding the largest nonprofit corporation of more than a million dollars, its president goes to prison. *See, e.g.*, *United Way Chief Sentenced: Aramony Gets 7 Years, Told to Repay $552G for Embezzlement*, NEWSDAY, June 23, 1995; *United Way Faced with Fewer Donors Giving Less Money*, N.Y. TIMES, Nov. 11, 1997 at A1.

After turning over $332,000 of the organization's funds to an employee who had alleged sexual harassment, the executive director of the country's oldest nonprofit civil rights organization resigns under pressure. Investing hundreds of millions of dollars in the bogus Foundation for New Era Philanthropy, the leading nonprofit cultural and civic organizations of Philadelphia totter on the edge of bankruptcy. *See* BARRON'S, Sept. 16, 1996.

Evidence of backlash also has accumulated. A city in upstate New York debates denying real estate property exemptions to all of its nonprofit institutions. *See* William Glaberson, *In an Era of Fiscal Damage Control, Cities Fight Idea of Tax Exempt*, N.Y. TIMES, Feb. 21, 1996. (The mayor proposes charging tax-exempt entities a "core service fee.") Year after year, Congress considers ways to eliminate many of the privileges of nonprofit organizations—including postal subsidies, income tax exemptions, legal immunities, and many other benefits. *See, e.g.*, *Charities Face New Scrutiny by Congress*, NON-PROFIT LEGAL & TAX LETTER, Jan. 13, 1997 (indicating the likelihood that lawmakers would debate creating different classes of charities, limiting lobbying by charities, and placing restrictions on charities offering products and services). Lawsuits by small businesses that complain about tax-exempt rivals are on the rise: *More Small Firms Complain About Tax-Exempt Rivals*, WALL ST. J., Aug. 8, 1995, at B1 col. 3. Public giving to all nonprofits on a per capita basis has risen somewhat in recent years, largely because of the value of gifts of appreciated stocks, much of it to private foundations, especially those in health care. *See* Robert Franklin, *US Charitable Contributions Increased by 7.3% Last Year*, STAR TRIB.: NEWSPAPER OF THE TWIN CITIES, May 29, 1997, at 1997 WL 7568068 (reporting results of a survey commissioned by American Association of Fund-Raising Counsel Trust for Philanthropy); *United Way Faced with Fewer Donors Giving Less Money*, N.Y. TIMES, Nov. 11, 1997, at A1. Private giving of for-profit organizations to charitable nonprofits on a per capita basis also has declined in recent years, however. *See Survey: Charities' Feel-Good Figures Mask Income Shortfall*, INVESTORS CHRON., Mar. 22, 1996. Donations to social service charities and religious organizations have lagged well behind historic levels. *See* N.Y. TIMES, Nov. 11, 1997, *op. cit.*

For-profit corporations—ranging from phone companies to ice-cream purveyors—style themselves as humanitarian and public-spirited by promising to operate more efficiently and devote more funds to social causes than their nonprofit counterparts. *See* Africa Gordon, *Annual Donations Help Callers' Chats Do a World of Good*, USA TODAY, Feb. 24, 1997 at 1997 WL 6005339 ("peace, a cleaner environment, and of course, low rates are top priorities for San Francisco-based Working Assets Long Distance").

16. *See, e.g.*, Nina J. Crimm, *Why All Is Not Quiet on the "Home Front" for Charitable organizations*, 29 NEW MEXICO L. REV. 1 (1999); *see infra*, nn. 17–23 and accompanying text.

17. For their work on the subject of abuses in the nonprofit sector, Gilbert M. Gaul and Neil A. Borowski received among other honors the $25,000 Goldsmith Prize bestowed by the John F. Kennedy School of Government at Harvard University and were named finalists for the Pulitzer Prize. Their study examined the tax returns of 6,000 exempt organizations and reviewed compensation patterns among many of the largest nonprofit foundations and charities. *See* PHILADELPHIA INQUIRER, Mar. 12, 1994, at A02.

18. Editorial, *The Nonprofit Biz Tax Free Institutions Have Multiplied; Many Simply Aren't Worth the Cost*, PHILADELPHIA INQUIRER, Apr. 25, 1993, at E06.

19. *See, e.g.*, TACOMA WASH. MORNING NEWS TRIB., May 16, 1993, at 1. The examples and illustrations contained in the report are notable for their quantity and remarkable for their egregiousness. The National Football League spent less than 1 percent of its $35 million dollar budget on charitable activities while it leased seven floors of a Park Avenue Office Tower. The Motion Picture Academy was spending $6 million tax-free dollars to put on the Oscars show. Donors to the Salvation Army, the National Museum of Polo and Hall of Fame, and the Museum of Fine Arts were treated without discrimination for federal tax purposes. Foundations estimated to be worth $850 billion were giving about $9 billion in grants while costing $36 billion in taxes; taxes subsidized the purchase of a Jaguar for a nonprofit executive's expense paid office car; a tax-exempt hospital purchased a

duck hunting lodge; salaries of $1.5 million were paid to the director of the National Football League and $716,000 was paid in salary and benefits to the president of the nonprofit American Council on Life Insurance. In contrast to the tax treatment of for-profit broadcasting stations, Rev. Pat Robertson's Christian Broadcasting Network sold the Family Channel in 1989 for $55 million of CBN's $130 million "almost entirely tax-free revenue." At least $36 billion per year in federal tax revenues and many billions more in state and local tax revenues, they reported, are annually foregone for incommensurable benefits. *Id.*

20. *See, e.g.,* Alan S. Glazer and Henry R. Jaenicke et al., *New AICPA Audit and Accounting Guide for NPOs,* J. ACCT., Nov. 1, 1996, at 1996 WL 9175134.

21. *See, e.g., Foundations Lobby for Tax Incentives,* MONEY MANAGEMENT LETTER, Jan. 27, 1997, at 1 (Council on Foundations, with 1,391 member foundations and representing $115 billion in assets, lobbies for renewal of preferential tax treatment for donations of stock to exempt foundations); *Nonprofits Escape a Cloud,* LEGAL TIMES, July 15, 1996, at 4 (litigation preserves tax free exchange of mailing lists).

22. *See* Bruce D. Collins, *So You Say You Want a Revolution? It's Coming,* CORP. LEGAL TIMES, Sept. 1993, at 6; *see* hearings of the House Ways and Means Oversight Subcommittee (Pickle, Chr.)

23. PHILADELPHIA INQUIRER, Apr. 18–25, 1993.

24. An interesting and provocative anthology that captures constitutional, political, and economic developments is David C. Hammack, MAKING THE NONPROFIT SECTOR IN THE UNITED STATES (1998); for an effort to place the nonprofit sector in a larger social and political context through the use of interrelated historical and political essays, *see* Peter Hall, INVENTING THE NONPROFIT SECTOR (1992); *see also* Michael O'Neil, THE THIRD AMERICA (1989).

25. *See infra,* ch. 1.

26. *See infra,* ch. 1.

27. New York's nonprofit law contained a relatively unusual requirement that judges issue approvals of nonprofit charters, *see* ch. 3, *infra,* and so written judicial opinions are more plentiful in New York than other states. Regarding the importance and distinctiveness of New York, see the discussion at ch. 3 n. 2.

28. *Id.*

29. As of 1957, when legal doctrines began to change, the states that had special incorporation laws allowing the courts to exercise discretion included Georgia, Maine, Missouri, New York, Pennsylvania, and Virginia. *See* note, *State Control over Political Organizations: First Amendment Checks on Powers of Regulation,* 66 YALE L.J. 545 (1957).

30. *See infra* (discussion of discretion). There is a wide-ranging literature on the subject of discretion. *See, e.g.,* Edward Rubin, Discretion or Supervision, paper presented to the University of California Jurisprudence and Social Policy Workshop, Sept. 1997.

31. *See, e.g.,* IOWA CODE ANN. §504.1 (repealed by Acts 1990 (73 G.A.) c. 1164 §27); MASS. ANN. LAWS c. 180 et seq. (predecessor statutes dating back to 1857); MISS CODE ANN. §5310 (currently §79–11–101 – §79–11–403.)

32. *See* note, *Permissible Purposes for Nonprofit Corporations,* 51 COLUM. L. REV. 889 (1951); David Zeitzheim, *Refusal of Charter of a Non-Profit Corporation,* 15 CLEV.

MAR. L. REV. 162 n.1 (1966). In most states, commercial associations originally were subject to various public benefit tests in order to incorporate; these had fallen into widespread disuse by the twentieth century. *See generally* Herbert Hovenkamp, *The Classical Corporation in American Legal Thought*, 76 GEO. L.J. 1593 (1988) (discussing right of governments to impose charter restrictions on corporate behavior).

33. *See infra*, ch. 3.

34. *See infra*, ch. 3.

35. *See infra*, ch. 4.

36. *See infra*, ch. 4.

37. *See infra*, ch. 4. A related story, focusing on New York and tracing the marked transformation of jurisprudence and of the appropriate judicial role to be played to protect religious and ethnic equality over a similar time, is told by Professor William Nelson. *See* William E. Nelson, *The Changing Meaning of Equality in Twentieth Century Constitutional Law*, 52 WASH. & LEE L. REV. 3 (1995). Judging from Professor Nelson's portrait, very much the same considerations that weighed in favor of confining judicial discretion and relying on legislative action in the nonprofit area appear to have led to an expanding role for the judiciary, in relation to the legislature, in promoting equality. Nelson argues that "judges prior to the 1960s did not believe that an equal society required people with different cultural values to interact on an equal basis." *Id.* at 5–6.

38. *See infra*, ch. 4.

39. *See infra*, ch. 6. A major exception to the relaxed scrutiny indicated here resulted from the 1969 passage of amendments to the Internal Revenue Code designed to regulate the conduct of private foundations. *See* Peter Hall, INVENTING AMERICA 66–80 (1992); *see also* F. Emerson Andrews, FOUNDATION WATCHER (1973).

40. *See infra*, ch. 6. A partial catalog of the expansion of privileges and exemptions available to nonprofit organizations, and the ad hoc development of unrigorous supervision of their distribution in tax codes, antitrust laws, securities regulation exemptions, bankruptcy laws, postal regulations, labor regulations, copyright laws, criminal statutes, government assistance programs, and financial accounting rules, is contained in Bazil Facchina et al., *Privileges and Exemptions Enjoyed by Nonprofit Organizations*, 3 TOPICS IN PHILANTHROPY (1993).

41. *See* Bruce R. Hopkins, CHARITY, ADVOCACY, AND THE LAW 45 (1992) (providing special reference to tax-exempt organizations). *See also* John Kimelman, *Too Charitable to Charities?*, FINANCIAL WORLD, Sept. 1, 1994, at 46. ("In past years, foregone tax dollars were generally viewed as an appropriate sacrifice given the overall public-mindedness of charitable missions. But as reports in recent years have surfaced about charities running afoul of the law, many lawmakers are beginning to question whether they have coddled these institutions too long.")

# 2

## The Development of the
## Discretionary Model

### Advantages to Nonprofit Status

The discretionary model for chartering nonprofit corporations formed the original basis for parceling out nonprofit status and, more importantly, it rationalized the benefits that evolved along with it. Conferring nonprofit status in an arbitrary manner would have been of minor consequence if that status had cost nothing to others and had offered the organizations few advantages compared to different forms of enterprise. From the time the profit/not-for-profit distinction emerged, however, obtaining a not-for-profit charter or operating as a charitable trust[1] provided groups with a changing bundle of advantages compared to different ways to organize an enterprise.

Compared with the limitations of a for-profit corporation, the nonprofit form has offered various opportunities, subsidies, and reputational rewards. The only enduring characteristic of the nonprofit corporate form has been the fact that its legal personality includes a license for a group to operate with some central mission or purpose apart from, or in addition to, economic gain. Beyond this, to varying degrees at different times, it has offered an opportunity for securing private donations; for gaining access to categories of governmental funds and contracts; for attracting and retaining employees more highly motivated by charitable impulses; for price discrimination enabling the corporation to receive a willing premium from many customers; for more effectively immunizing officers and directors from suit; for garnering greater public goodwill and loyalty among regulators; for increasing the acceptance of its objectives among the public; for creating a membership concerned about the purposes of the corporation; for shedding reporting responsibilities;

and, not least, upon exemption, for reducing exposure to taxation or the imposition of costs, fees, and regulations.[2] It has also offered superior opportunities for founders to maintain control of their enterprises and compensate themselves without subsequent interference from share-holders and with little likelihood of close monitoring by the public or state authorities.[3]

Nonprofit incorporation has assured officers and members limited lia-bility from most of their corporate debts.[4] It has offered the right to sue and be sued in the corporate form. It has allowed officers and members the ability to readily enter into contracts and joint ventures with other corporate entities. It has provided a formal mechanism for institutional continuity—an important factor for actual and potential donors, mem-bers, and clients to consider in their planning.[5] Chartered nonprofit cor-porations have benefited from the public impression that the state has designated them as duly chartered not-for-profit organizations. In many states nonprofit status has allowed groups to benefit from the doctrine of charitable immunity from suit.

Among the most significant benefits of obtaining a charter or license permitting incorporation has been the greater probability that the group could then obtain a constellation of benefits from governmental entities, for whom a nonprofit corporate or trust form was the conventionally ac-ceptable legal vehicle. The group then could hold government grants, bid for government service contracts, hold government monopolies or privi-leges available principally or exclusively to nonprofit corporations; or it could enjoy some combination of these privileges.

Tax avoidance opportunities of many kinds—especially federal income tax exemptions and state and local property tax exemptions—are the fi-nancial advantages that today are most closely identified with nonprofit status. Obtaining a nonprofit charter or trust status has been the surest pathway to a variety of tax exemptions; including exemption from state and local property taxes, service fees, and sales taxes under applicable laws and regulations; exemption from employment and corporate in-come taxes; and exemption from surcharges and other occasional corpo-rate financial obligations. As already noted, nonprofit status attracts do-nations inasmuch as donors to qualifying nonprofits can avoid taxes through a deductible charitable contribution.

Today tax advantages often drive the decision to incorporate as a non-profit.[6] Nevertheless, a large number of nonprofit organizations neither start with nor focus on tax considerations.[7] Many have always incorpo-rated primarily for other reasons, knowing that they would never seek an exemption or that if they sought it the exemption would be of only a small benefit. Prior to the development of steep tax rates and withhold-ing schemes around World War II, in fact, tax considerations were secondary to legal personality in motivating the creation of the majority of nonprofits. Today there are thousands of chartered nonprofit organizations, for example, trade associations, hospitals, and medical groups, that have been taxed and have received few if any net tax advantages that would have been unavailable if they were organized under for-profit laws.

Many groups have preferred not-for-profit status because of the symbolic approval, or the favorable public image and favorable regulatory treatment, such as insulation from competition, they might receive. Anecdotal evidence even suggests that jury verdicts against nonprofit organizations have tended to be smaller on average than verdicts against for-profit organizations. As one attorney at the New York Bureau of Corporations stated, "one of the biggest advantages to nonprofit incorporation is the paradigm shift that occurs—the public perception that this [not-for-profit] is a 'good' corporation. From a legal perspective that may or may not matter, but when they get into trouble it certainly matters."[8]

There continues to be an official "imprimatur" of respectability attached to receiving a license to operate as a nonprofit organization. A charter signified to the donating and volunteering public that agencies of the State have reviewed the purposes of the association and determined them to be charitable, that the association operates for the public's benefit, that contributions of money and effort serve the public purposes of the organization, and that the assets of the organization were not being used to increase the personal well-being of individual officers and members. Possessing a charter implied to the public that appropriate state agencies monitor the corporation, subject it to regulatory supervision and control, and, potentially, subject it to dissolution according to rules that would distribute any remaining funds to groups that would use them for charitable purposes. Not-for-profit corporations have been able to advertise all of these attributes whenever they publicize and promote their views, whenever they solicit contributions and grants, whenever they seek business opportunities, whenever they advertise themselves, and whenever they try to get special waivers and exemptions.

The criteria for obtaining these various kinds of assistance has varied in difficulty by jurisdiction and by the nature of the support.[9] In some cases, a certificate of incorporation has been the only document required for the grant of the privilege.[10] Every state, for example, allows every group with a domestic nonprofit corporate status to operate there. Other types of assistance (e.g., property tax relief) have been more difficult to obtain.[11] There have always been some disadvantages to organizing as a nonprofit, as well.[12] Nonetheless, thousands of organizations, alone or together with associated privileges, have seen the certificate as more valuable than the right to do business as a traditional for-profit corporation.

## The Divergence of Commercial and Nonprofit
## Corporate Chartering Practices

Chartering both not-for-profit and for-profit enterprises as corporations became a common occurrence in *antebellum* America, but for many years the distinction between the groups was hardly noticed.[13] In the early republic, for-profit incorporation appears to have evolved from the earlier practice of incorporating charitable and religious bodies, and the two processes shared requirements and vocabulary during the early years of the republic.[14] During the constitutional period, the 1780s and 1790s, both not-for-profit and for-profit corporations were chartered individually by state legislatures, which looked for applicants who were dependable from a political, social, and religious point of view.[15] Legislatures tried to retain considerable control over shares of stock or the directors of the corporations they chartered on a case-by-case basis—both for-profit and not-for-profit.

The absence of a distinction between for-profit and not-for-profit ventures in early America is revealed in the leading Supreme Court case of the period, which deals with a charitable institution, *Dartmouth College v. Woodward* (1819).[16] In the *Dartmouth* decision, Justice Marshall's majority opinion held that an effort by the New Hampshire legislature to modify the college's charter violated the contract clause of the Constitution—a holding that modern constitutional law texts treat as a cornerstone of contracts law and of thinking about corporate governance. The importance of the case has endured because the significance of the distinction between profit and not-for-profit corporations was irrelevant to the outcome.[17] The legislature's capacity to revise the college's charter did not depend on any of what later would become the central characteristics of a nonprofit institution; the outcome rested neither on Dartmouth's sources of income (philanthropy) nor the extent of its benefits for the public or its students (educational purposes) nor the extent to which the Dartmouth Corporation restricted the distribution of its profits to its officers and employees ("pecuniary gain" restrictions).[18] At that time, *all* corporations, whether public or private, commercial or charitable, would *only* be chartered if they professed an intention to operate for the benefit of the public.[19]

### The Liberalization of Business Chartering

By the time of the *Dartmouth* case, questions had arisen about whether to expand the proposed purposes and structures that would permit the incorporation of for-profit corporations. Should access to the limited-liability corporate form be available without reference to public benefit?

Should business charters continue to be handed out individually after being considered by the state legislatures or as a matter of administrative routine?

Debates over the ease with which a state should grant special corporate charters divided the national parties of the day. In part it was posed as a contest between "Commerce" and "Virtue," with the Whig party "more interested in promoting economic development and territorial expansion than Democrats, and relatively less concerned that unfettered enterprise would compromise social values or exploit craftsmen, artisans and workers."[20] Democrats were identified as the enemies of chartered monopolies and favored state rather than federal chartering.[21] During the era of good feelings and later the Jacksonian era, the policy debates about chartering thus reflected contests between agrarian and merchant interests, poorer artisans and wealthier merchants, large banks and smaller ones, and between local and foreign competitors.[22]

Between 1810 and 1850, states greatly relaxed the tests that were created for privileging for-profit businesses with corporate existence.[23] There is a lively academic debate about how difficult it ever was to obtain a for-profit charter in most jurisdictions, and how important obtaining a charter actually was; however, obtaining a for-profit charter did seem necessary for many businesses. In some early cases courts denied charters to businesses because governments previously had granted charters to competing corporations; in some cases the government tried to reserve functions to itself.[24] State legislatures began to experiment with "general" rather than case-by-case incorporation of for-profit businesses. In 1811 New York authorized the general incorporation of most businesses.[25] In 1837 the Connecticut legislature passed an act that permitted the incorporation of "any lawful business," which became, for the for-profits, "the paradigm that would govern until 1896."[26] Legislatures in other states followed suit and replaced or supplemented their case-by-case chartering practices with generic ones.[27] These general incorporation statutes typically required a short application to do business, which was to be filed with state authorities. Such an application requested simple factual information, including the name and principal place of the business being conducted, the name of the incorporators, the names of initial stockholders, a statement of the nature of the business, and related information.[28] Although the general incorporation statutes continued to require that commercial corporations act "in the public interest" or "for benefit of the public," this was not a significant component of administrative review during the process of obtaining a certificate of incorporation.[29] There would be limits on businesses after they commenced operation, and rules for doing business that all corporations needed to obey, but by midcentury the incorporation of a business corporation had become, essentially, the recognition of "a private arrangement to achieve private ends for private gain."[30]

## The Selective Approach to Nonprofit Chartering

Obtaining a charter to operate a for-profit business became a matter of general entitlement by midcentury, but enterprises that would today be called charitable and not-for-profit groups did not share in the liberalization. Instead, those seeking to incorporate nonprofits had their mission, their structure, and their personnel scrutinized.[31]

The practice of obtaining corporate charters for nonprofit activities had begun in the colonial era, with public corporations and religious groups aiming to secure freedom from taxes and from interference by the state in educational activities.[32] Laws to govern the chartering of religious corporations were passed[33] as states tried to regulate the incorporation of "private associations that performed vital public services."[34]

During the 1780s and 1790s many states, particularly in the North, enacted general corporations laws for organizations with "literary, charitable or religious purposes."[35] Massachusetts, which had taken the lead in establishing stockholder-owned corporations, also chartered private groups to perform educational tasks. Harvard College, for example, was chartered as a corporation governed by ministers of the (state-supported) Congregational Church.[36] In Pennsylvania, Benjamin Franklin obtained charters for associations that he started for both benevolent and profit motives.[37]

In New York, the incorporation of religious corporations became permissible through the general incorporation statute of 1784,[38] although that law limited the amount that could be left at death to a religious corporation.[39] The New York legislature also began to charter nonreligious societies for a variety of literary, scientific, and benevolent purposes.[40] New York, like other states, incorporated them by issuing individualized or "special" charters. This meant dispensing them through the nineteenth-century political process of enacting private legislation, which in the fractious political climate of New York was particularly grueling.[41] This case-by-case legislative supervision not incidentally allowed individual legislators to exact fees or political debts from supplicants.[42]

Although business corporation charters were "few and of little importance" before the 1830s,[43] chartered charitable and religious corporations were highly visible and influential many years before then.[44] There was substantial popular enthusiasm for forming voluntary charitable, educational, and social associations as well as formal religious associations. In a rapidly growing nation with decentralized and underfunded community governments, important holes in the social fabric were going un-patched because government was poor, because worthy activities were unprofitable, and because necessary services were unaffordable.[45] As Alexis de Tocqueville commented in 1840 (in an often quoted passage from *Democracy in America*), the managery of voluntary associations pre-sented the most interesting and constructive aspect of American society:

> Americans of all ages, all conditions, and all dispositions constantly form as-sociations. They have not only commercial and manufacturing companies, in which all take part, but associations of a thousand other kinds, religious, moral, serious, futile, general or restricted, enormous or diminutive. The Americans make associations to give entertainments, to found seminaries, to build inns, to construct churches, to diffuse books, to send missionaries to the antipodes; in this manner they found hospitals, prisons and schools. If it is proposed to inculcate some truth or foster some feeling by the encourage-ment of a great example, they form a society.[46]

Most associations in the early republic operated without any legally recognized structure at all. Those that obtained legal recognition of their form did so mainly on the lines of the charitable trusts authorized by the English Statute of Charitable Uses of 1601, as it was received into the law of the different states.[47] The charitable use or trust permitted donors to dictate particular purposes and means for their bequests to be applied.[48]

By 1819, however, the enforceability of charitable bequests through trusts had come into question, growing out of suspicion that they would be used for the support of unpopular religious and political pur-poses.[49] Despite later cases upholding the enforceability of charitable trusts,[50] statutes authorizing their enforcement were repealed in several states in the years prior to the Civil War.[51] Later in the century some states exempted charitable trusts from many restrictions that were placed on private trusts; but even then, charitable trusts could be and were invalidated because their purposes were deemed impermissibly vague and uncertain.[52] Trusts came into disfavor after the Civil War as appropriate means of creating ongoing operating charities that might receive contributions of money and employ staff because of the tight and sometimes unpredictable judicial supervision of the trusts that were enforceable, the fiduciary liability that attached to those who ad-ministered such trusts, and their uncertain legal status.[53] In New York and most states, incorporation became the preferred manner for legiti-mating such activities.[54]

In states that did not establish special rules for nonprofit organizations, the standard business incorporation provisions equipped legislatures or state officials with the power to deny incorporation to unlisted associations.[55] Typically laws established general standards which required that proposed corporations express "lawful" or "publicly useful" purposes. Some denied incorporation to associations engaging in activities because they were not proposing a "a lawful business."[56] Some were simply denied a charter because they were not members of a favored economic class, political party, or religious group.

The 1848 New York law served as a prototype for the method of nonprofit incorporation adopted in many other states.[57] The statute passed by the legislature provided for the general incorporation of benevolent, charitable, scientific, and missionary societies, although the legislature retained the right to charter such corporations individually.[58] Those desiring to form corporations filed a certificate for any of the specified purposes listed in the title of the act.[59] A majority of the signers had to be citizens, and certificates had to be approved by justices of New York's Supreme Court (trial court).[60]

Applicants could expect to be required to provide information about matters such as the reputation of proposed officers and members, the nature of the intended enterprise, the likely effect of the enterprise on other charities or nonprofits, its likelihood of achieving its stated purposes, and the likely benefit, financial or developmental, that might accrue to the state from allowing the corporation to be chartered.[61]

From 1848 and for a century later, as commercial corporations burgeoned under a regime of relatively free incorporation, the number of chartered nonreligious nonprofits corporations grew more slowly.[62] The law was revised in 1895, when the New York Membership Corporation Law (NYMCL) consolidated the laws of charitable corporations relating to medical societies, veterinary societies, library corporations, and many other types of organizations.[63] It applied "to all corporations not organized for pecuniary profit except religious corporations and educational corporations."[64] For-profit corporations were governed by the New York General Corporation Law, unless the NYMCL or another specialized statute specifically applied.

In the years that followed the language of the statute was amended "to move the directors' responsibilities toward the business corporate model."[65] Section 41 of the NYMCL provided expansively that "five or more persons may become a membership corporation *for any lawful purpose*."[66] Nonetheless, the law demanded the approval of a judge before the corporation could be officially chartered: "every certificate of incorporation filed under this chapter," the law read, "shall have endorsed hereon or annexed thereto the approval of a justice of the supreme court of the judicial district in which the office of the corporation is to be located."[67] New York's statutory rules for creating nonprofit corporations remained fundamentally unchanged until the passage of the Not-for-Profit Corporation Law replaced it in 1970.[68]

### Accounting for the Divergence Between For-profit and Nonprofit Incorporation

Clearly, in antebellum America the process and substantive inquiries that characterized chartering diverged—but why? One explanation for the divergence is that compared to nonprofit associations, for-profits involved much less risk to the state: the foreseeable costs and benefits attached to incorporating for-profit businesses emerged as much more favorable to governments and to the public.[69] The lenient requirement for a business incorporation certificate as well as for the prerogatives it signified developed because incorporation served important entrepreneurial needs in a legally enforceable manner.[70] It permitted the holding of shares and limited liability for debt; it provided a vehicle through which entrepreneurs and stockholders could calibrate their exposure to potential risk and gain more precisely than previously. It made it easier for investors to pool their capital resources.[71]

Politicians of all persuasions during the antebellum period shared an interest in encouraging the creation of business and promoting economic investment through easy incorporation of for-profits.[72] A development-oriented social ethic tolerated the unregulated "private vice" of wealth seeking as a logical path to "public virtue" and prosperity.[73] Accordingly, many state legislatures competed with one another to create favorable conditions for businesses, without trying to predetermine their direction. Chartering limited liability corporations by general corporation laws offered an easy and inexpensive way to encourage development while permitting government to keep watch over, and perhaps to collect revenue from, businesses in the process.

The operation of nineteenth-century business corporations furthermore, unlike that of nonprofit corporations, apportioned to stockholders rather than to the state the responsibility for evaluating potential losses and gains of a venture. Some legislators recognized that inadequately capitalized or fraudulently designed for-profit corporations could have disastrous consequences for stockholders and the public, but the consequences to government of business failure did not appear sufficiently worrisome—or perhaps were not predictable enough—to warrant screening out businesses at the pre-incorporation stage.[74]

Allowing a nonprofit entity to incorporate involved different calculations. Although chartering new nonprofit associations as nonprofit corporations often enriched communities culturally and socially, they, unlike commercial associations, often appeared to come at substantial cost. They required a commitment of community resources and held little promise for stimulating economic development and prosperity.[75] Unlike most for-profit enterprises, the incorporators of not-for-profit associations usually wanted a charter to increase the likelihood that they would obtain volunteers, or so that they would be able to contribute less in property or other taxes or could solicit gifts or subsidies from private citizens, states, and local governments. In the absence of shareholders, the general citizenry would be providing necessary capital and support. Whether or not they succeeded, these corporations would certainly call for and perhaps put a strain on limited community resources.

Another reason for greater caution in chartering not-for-profits was the extent to which they complemented government services. Many nonprofits were proposing, in effect, to provide services that local government itself might have provided if the means or determination were present, for example, relief for the poor, education, or even road building.[76] Particularly when individuals of substantial wealth proposed to endow or create multipurpose charitable institutions, considerations of social status, tradition, and ideological control could come into play.[77] The quality of a chartered association or its mission and perspective would reflect beneficially or adversely on the values of a community and its leaders, or even on the effectiveness of government.

Many states sought to encourage the growth of new business enterprises, but few were equally interested in attracting a large number of not-for-profit enterprises that might cost more than they contributed. There was no general shortage of underfunded, unincorporated voluntary associations in search of the tangible symbol of approval for their good work and solicitations from the states and the general public that the state could provide—a charter. For these reasons, and in contrast to for-profit corporation statutes, the statutes that authorized the chartering of nonprofit corporations contemplated and imposed a level of pre-incorporation scrutiny that would reject unworthy applicants.

For these reasons, by the last decade of the nineteenth century, the law for the incorporation of nonprofits in New York having been adopted, for-profit and nonprofit enterprises had become differentiated in common and legal understanding. The two corporate forms filled different social requirements and satisfied different economic necessities. Until the post–World War II era, and in light of the advantages that nonprofit corporations enjoyed by virtue of charters, judges adopted the view that nonprofit status had been legislatively created as a greater privilege than for-profit corporate status. And they believed that they were entitled to exercise an extraordinarily wide freedom to decide whether the incorporators of a nonprofit group possessed "those qualifications which the law makes essential."[78]

## Notes

1. As indicated *infra*, nn. 51–58 and accompanying text, forming a charitable trust might sometimes provide a less burdensome alternative to forming a nonprofit corporation. The administration of trusts generally also operated under judicial supervision, however. On the distinction between charitable trusts and nonprofit corporations, *See* James Fishman and Stephen Schwarz, Nonprofit Organizations ch. 2 (1995).

2. *See* Bazil Facchina et al., *Privileges and Exemptions Enjoyed by Nonprofit Organizations: A Catalog and Some Thoughts on Nonprofit Policymaking*, *supra*. It should be noted that under some circumstances for-profit corporations may obtain tax exemptions if they demonstrate a public purpose and show that they operate functionally like a nonprofit.

3. *See* Evelyn Brody, *Agents Without Principals: The Economic Convergence of the Nonprofit and For-Profit Organizational Forms*, 40 N.Y.L. Sch. L. Rev. 457, 485 (1996).

4. *See, e.g.*, Frank Easterbrook and Daniel R. Fischel, *Limited Liability and the Corporation*, 52 U. Chi. L. Rev. 89 (1985); Easterbrook and Fischel, *The Corporate Contract*, 89 Colum. L. Rev. 1416 (1989).

5. *Id.*

6. *See generally* Peter Hall, Inventing the Nonprofit Sector (1992); Evelyn Brody, *Agents Without Principals: The Economic Convergence of the Nonprofit and For-Profit Organizational Forms*, 40 N.Y.L. Sch. L. Rev. 457, 480–90 (1996).

7. The typical benefit from sales, property, and income tax exemption was smaller during the nineteenth and early twentieth centuries than it was later on, when governmental units started to levy higher taxes to provide revenue to support educational, welfare, warfare, and income redistribution demands. *See* Burton Weisbrod, The Nonprofit Economy (1988).

8. Interview with Philip M. Sparkes, director, Legal Services Division, New York State Department of State, 1995.

9. State tax exemptions are ordinarily no harder to obtain than federal tax exemptions, but they are generally less difficult than real property tax exemptions in many areas. *See* William R. Ginsberg, *The Real Property Tax Exemption of Nonprofit Organizations: A Perspective*, 53 Temple L. Q. 291 (1980) (footnote regarding trusts).

10. *See* note, *Permissible Purposes for Nonprofit Incorporation*, 51 Colum. L. Rev. 889, 889–90 (1951).

11. *Id.*

12. Among the most significant disadvantages are the difficulty of raising capital that many nonprofits face, and the "non-distributional constraint"—the prohibition on private inurement. *See* Henry Hansmann, *infra*.

13. Not-for-profit enterprises in the middle nineteenth century embraced a range of activities that included charitable organizations such as hospitals and relief societies, improvement societies, educational organizations, religious bodies, musical and theatrical groups, fraternal organizations, and political clubs. Banks, turnpikes, and steamship companies were among those for-profit corporations that sought charters beginning in the 1830s. *See* J. W. Hurst, THE LEGITIMACY OF THE BUSINESS CORPORATION IN THE LAW OF THE UNITED STATES, 1780–1970; note, *Incorporating the Republic: The Corporation in Antebellum Political Culture*, 102 HARV. L. REV. 1883 (1989); Ronald Seavoy, THE ORIGINS OF THE AMERICAN BUSINESS CORPORATION 177–89 (1982); Ralph Nader et al., TAMING THE GIANT CORPORATION 33–62 (1976).

14. *See* Ronald E. Seavoy, THE ORIGINS OF THE AMERICAN BUSINESS CORPORATION (1982); *see* Hovenkamp, *supra* ch. 1 n. 32 at 1597.

15. *See* Peter Hall, INVENTING THE NONPROFIT SECTOR 21 (1992).

16. 17 U.S. (4 Wheat.) 517 (1819).

17. *See* Ronald D. Rotunda and John E. Nowak, 2 TREATISE ON CONSTITUTIONAL LAW: SUBSTANCE AND PRACTICE §15.8 nn. 26, 40 (1992, 2d ed.); *see generally* Peter Hall, INVENTING THE NONPROFIT SECTOR 16–35 (1992).

18. *Id.*

19. Indeed, for-profit corporations are still chartered under the nominal rationale that they serve the public interest, although the public interest requirements in corporate charters have rarely been enforced independently of other statutory requirements. *See* Ronald E. Seavoy, THE ORIGINS OF THE AMERICAN BUSINESS CORPORATION, 1784–1855 (1982).

20. Note, *Incorporating the Republic: The Corporation in Antebellum Political Culture*, 102 HARV. L. REV. 1883, 1889 (1989).

21. *Id.*

22. *Id.*

23. *Id.*

24. *See* Susan Pace Hamill, *From Special Privilege to General Utility: A Continuation of Willard Hurst's Study of Corporations*, 49 Am. U. L. REV. 81 (1999).

25. *See* Theodore H. Davis Jr., *Corporate Privileges for the Public Benefit: The Progressive Federal Incorporation Movement and the Modern Regulatory State*, 77 VA. L. REV. 603 (1991); *see also* Demetrious G. Kaouris, *Is Delaware Still a Haven for Incorporation?*, 20 DEL. J. CORP. L. 965, 969 (1995) (discussing competition to relax incorporation rules between Delaware and New Jersey in the 1890s).

26. *Id.*

27. *Id.*

28. *Id.*

29. Regarding criticism of weak state commercial charter requirements, *see, e.g.,* *Nader Report,* TAMING THE GIANT CORPORATION (1976).

30. Theodore H. Davis Jr., *Corporate Privileges for the Public Benefit, supra; but see* Susan Pace Hamill n. 28 (special chartering of business corporations continued longer than is generally believed).

31. *See* James J. Fishman, *The Development of Nonprofit Corporation Law and an Agenda for Reform,* 34 EMORY L.J. 617, 633 (1985).

32. *See id.* at 631.

33. *See* J. S. Davis, ESSAYS IN THE EARLIER HISTORY OF AMERICAN CORPORATIONS (1917) (state constitutions assured freedom of incorporation for religious purposes).

34. *See* Fishman, *supra* n. 31 at 631 (*citing* R. Seavoy, AMERICAN BUSINESS CORPORATIONS, 1784–1855 at 255 [1982]).

35. *Id.* at 632 (*citing* J. S. Davis, ESSAYS IN THE EARLIER HISTORY OF AMERICAN CORPORATIONS 16–17 [1917]). *See* 1784 N.Y. LAWS 18. *See generally* Savoy, *The Public Service Origins of the American Business Corporation*, 52 BUS. HIST. REV. 30, 38–39 (1978); J. CADMAN, THE CORPORATION IN NEW JERSEY, 1791–1875 at 5–6 (1949).

36. *See* Peter Hall, INVENTING THE NONPROFIT SECTOR 16–17 (1992).

37. *Id.* at 20 (1992).

38. *Id.* at 634; 1784 N.Y. LAWS 18.

39. *See* Fishman, *supra* n. 34 at 634; 1784 N.Y. LAWS 18.

40. *See* Fishman, *supra* n. 34 at 634.

41. *See* Edwin G. Burrows and Mike Wallace, GOTHAM (1999) 516, 932.

42. *Id.; see also* Abner J. Mikva and Eric Lane, THE LEGISLATIVE PROCESS pt. 1, ch. 1, 49–50 (1994); *see generally* Lawrence M. Friedman, A HISTORY OF AMERICAN LAW 346–62 (1985, 2d ed.).

43. *See* Fishman, *supra* n. 34 at 631.

44. *Id.* at 631–34.

45. *See* Robert A. Dahl, DILEMMAS OF PLURALIST DEMOCRACY: AUTONOMY V. CONTROL (1982).

46. Alexis de Tocqueville, DEMOCRACY IN AMERICA 114 (ed. P. Bradley 1959).

47. At least one commentator, Leslie G. Espinoza, believes that the supervision of trusts and trust accounting was poor from the outset. In *Straining the Quality of Mercy: Abandoning the Quest for Informed Charitable Giving*, 64 S. CAL. L. REV 605, 636–37 (1991) Espinoza states that "under English common law as it was received [by the American states] state attorneys general were charged with the duty to see to the due application of charitable funds. Their duty was to represent the public interest in the proper use of charitable funds by bringing supervisory actions to the courts." Because there was no counterpart to the Statute of Charitable Uses or the Charity Commission in the United States, "in reality, court supervision was minimal" *Id.* at 638. Nineteenth-century efforts to regulate public charities in the United States, through reporting statutes, she asserts, failed. Not until World War II did New Hampshire become the first state to provide the attorney general and probate courts with power to scrutinize trusts by the submission of accounting reports. *Id.* at 639. Much of the increased authority provided to supervise trusts grew out of concern about foundations and large national charities, leading in 1953 to the approval by the National Conference of Commissioners on Uniform State Laws of the Uniform Supervision of Charitable Trusts Act. *Id.* at 641. By the 1950s, however, three-quarters of the existing foundations were established as corporations and not as trusts. *Id.* at 642.

48. *See* Espinoza, *id.* at 638–39.

49. *See* Peter Hall, INVENTING THE NONPROFIT SECTOR 22–24 (1992). (originally pub. 1971)

50. *See* Vidal v. Girard's Executors, 43 U.S. (2 How.) 126 (1844).

51. *See* N.Y. REVISED STATUTES OF 1829, pt. II, ch. 1, tit. II, art. 2, sec. 45 at 727 (abolishing all except certain noncharitable trusts); MICH. REVISED STATUTES 1846,

ch. 63, secs. 1, 11 at 245–55 (same as N.Y.); Minn. Revised Statutes 1851, ch. 44, secs. 1, 11 at 202–3 (same as N.Y.); Wis. Revised Statutes 1849, pt. II, tit. 15, ch. 57, secs. 1, 11 at 318–19 (same as N.Y.); *See* also Fishman, *supra* n. 31.

52. Virginia, West Virginia, and Maryland began to restrict the use of charitable trusts after the decision in Trustees of the Philadelphia Baptist Assoc. v. Hart's Executors, 17 U.S. (4 Wheat.) 1 (1819). Michigan, New York, Wisconsin, and Minnesota began to restrict charitable trusts around 1829 by statute and accepted them again after the Tilden Act in New York and similar acts in other states, around 1893. *See The Enforcement of Charitable Trusts in America: A History of Evolving Social Attitudes*, 54 Va. L. Rev. 436 (1968).

53. *See, e.g.*, Green v. Dennis, 6 Conn. 293 (Ct. 1826) (refusing to enforce a vague charitable bequest); Gallego's Executors v. Attorney Gen., 30 Va. (3 Leigh) 450 (Va. 1832) (bequest held vague and uncertain); Trippe v. Frazier, 4 Harris & Johnson 44 (Md. 1819) (vague and uncertain); Dashiell v. Attorney *Gen.*, 5 Harris & Johnson 392, 398 (Md. 1822) (invalidating bequest for care and education of the poor); Owens v. Missionary Soc'y of the Methodist Episcopal Church, 14 N.Y. 380 (N.Y. 1856) (no definitive beneficiary); Bascom v. Albertson, 34 N.Y. 584 (N.Y.1866) (invalidating bequest to establish a girls school in Vermont).

54. Despite the fact that few nonprofit associations were organized as charitable trusts in the late nineteenth century and for much of the twentieth century, and that in New York the enforceability of charitable trusts was in doubt for much of the time, in theory it would have been possible to organize many (but not all) nonprofit corporations as such. But there were distinct disadvantages to the trust form that deterred most organizers and benefactors from desiring to use it. *See* Evelyn Brody, *Institutional Dissonance in the Nonprofit Sector*, 41 Vill. L. Rev. 433, 475 n. 209 (1996) (arguing that the corporate form is dominant in the United States because "nonprofit corporation law cedes a great deal of autonomy to founders and directors of charitable corporations, a level of discretion that trustees can match only if granted by the founder [of a trust] in a settlement instrument." Depending on the type of trust and the circumstances of its formation, however, a nineteenth- and twentieth-century charitable trust could be subject to no supervision or substantial supervision by civil authorities. *See* Fishman, *supra*; note, *The Enforcement of Charitable Trusts in America*, 54 Va. L. Rev. 436 (1968); *see also* Rob Atkinson, *Reforming Cy Pres Reform*, 44 Hast. L.J. 1112 (1993) (reviewing the extent to which cy pres doctrine added uncertainty to employment of charitable trust vehicles).

55. *See, e.g.*, People ex rel. Padula v. Hughes, 16 N.E.2d 922 (1938), discussed *infra*.

56. *See, e.g.*, Ala. Code Ann. tit. 10, §1; Conn. Gen. Stat. §5151 (incorporation available only to "any lawful business"); Mo. Rev. Stat. §352.060 (applicant's purpose for incorporating must be "lawful and useful"); S.C. Code 12–756 (applicant must not act in violation of the law).

57. *See* Fishman, *supra* n. 34.

58. *Id.*

59. *Id.*

60. *See* Fishman, *supra* n. 34 at 634 n. 88.

61. *Id.* at 633–36.

62. *See* Fishman, *supra* n. 34 at 633–35.

63. Mem. Corp. Law, §10. Later recodified with minor modifications as §41, Membership Corporation Law was derived from the 1848 enactment. 1848 N.Y. Laws 1848, ch. 319, §1.

64. *Id.*

65. *Id.*

66. *Id.*

67. *Id.*

68. *Id.*; N.Y. MEM. CORP. LAW §2, 1895 N.Y. LAWS 559 (repealed 1970). The New York Not-for-Profit Corporation Law, passed in 1970, replaced the Membership Corporation Law; *see* L. 1969, ch. 1066 §2 (repealer); L. 1969, ch. 1066 §3 (effective date of new law). Similar events occurred in the other states. California, for example, enacted a General Nonprofit Corporation Law in 1931. Cal. Civ. Code, tit. 12, art. 1 (1931). The California statute was based largely on an Ohio statute that had been modeled on the nonprofit statutes of New York, Maryland, Illinois, and Michigan. *See Id. (citing* H. W. Ballantine and R. Sterling, CALIFORNIA CORPORATION LAWS 529 (1949)).

69. *See* J. W. Hurst, THE LEGITIMACY OF THE BUSINESS CORPORATION IN THE UNITED STATES, 1780–1970 (1970); Walter Werner, *Corporation Law in Search of Its Future*, 81 COLUM. L. REV. 1611, 1615–17 (1981).

70. *See* Ronald E. Seavoy, THE ORIGINS OF THE AMERICAN BUSINESS CORPORATION (1982); Hovenkamp, *supra* ch. 1 n. 32. According to Hovenkamp, the form of the corporation began to take form in the mid–nineteenth century, reached its classical form in the 1880s and 1890s, and then began to fall apart. *Id.* at 1597.

71. A vigorous scholarly debate continues about whether the legal form of incorporation developed because of preexisting economic and social conditions or as the victory of special interests within the political culture of the day. *See* note, *Incorporating the Republic: The Corporation in Antebellum Political Culture*, 102 HARV. L. REV. 1883, 1889 (1989). Seavoy, *supra* n. 14; Oliver Zunz, MAKING AMERICA CORPORATE, 1870–1920 (1990); George Heberton Evans Jr., BUSINESS INCORPORATIONS IN THE UNITED STATES, 1800–1943 (1948); Merritt Ierley, WITH CHARITY FOR ALL: WELFARE AND SOCIETY: ANCIENT TIMES TO THE PRESENT (1984).

72. *See* Ralph Nader, TAMING THE GIANT CORPORATION (1976).

73. *See* Lawrence M. Friedman, A HISTORY OF AMERICAN LAW (1985, 2d ed.).

74. *Id.*

75. Advocates for nonprofits today have argued that spending money in support of charities is a superior way to stimulate the economy. *See, e.g.,* Avner Ben-Ner, *Who Benefits from the Nonprofit Sector: Reforming Law and Public Policy Towards Nonprofit Organizations*, 104 YALE L.J. 731 (1994); Dale F. Rubin, *The Public Pays, the Corporation Profits: The Emasculation of the Public Purpose Doctrine and a Not-for-Profit Solution*, 28 U. RICH. L. REV. 1311 (1994).

76. *See* John D. Colombo, *Why Is Harvard Tax-Exempt? (and Other Mysteries of Tax Exemptions for Private Educational Institutions)*, 35 ARIZ. L. REV. 841 (1993) (discussing surrogate theory).

77. *See* Peter Hall, INVENTING THE NONPROFIT SECTOR 36–49 (1992).

78. *In re* Wendover Athletic Ass'n, 70 Misc. 273, 128 N.Y.S. 561, 562 (Sup. Ct. 1911).

# 3

# Historic Excuses and Uses for Judicial Subjectivity in the Incorporation Process

*INCORPORATION, n. The act of uniting several persons into one fiction called a corporation, in order that they may be no longer responsible for their activities.*

**Ambrose Bierce (1911)[1]**

Nothing in the language of the statute in New York ordained it, but trial judges there—grandly titled the "justices" of the state's "supreme" court—developed original interpretations of their own authority, which let them issue binding decisions that rested only on their moral arguments and personal views. These were upheld on appeal, and thus a sustained jurisprudence of nonprofit incorporation developed that left a unique historical record.[2]

The judges discovered their authority within the language and the history of the legislative declaration that they should approve only organizations with "lawful" purposes. Their views about what was lawful, and therefore the circumstances in which incorporation of nonprofits would be permissible, depended to an extraordinary degree on their ethnic and social predispositions. These evolved with political events and social conditions and with the composition of the bench itself. Holders of great wealth and groups that reflected the views of mainstream America seldom were thwarted by these judges. But those on the fringes or without substantial means could be excluded. The judiciary was engaged in pushing social values toward the American center.

## The Emergence of Doctrinal
## Justifications for Special Treatment

Trial court justices began to exert greater substantive control over the formation of nonprofit corporations late in the nineteenth century. They first confronted and rejected the argument that they had an obligation to approve all nonprofit charters that proposed lawful conduct through lawful means. Then they developed a jurisprudence of privilege which required applicants further to demonstrate that their conduct would be socially beneficial, from the judge's perspective. Even for the conventional, the well respected, and the rich, demonstrating such benefit could on occasion be difficult.[3] For those on the wrong side of the cultural or income divide, as the cases demonstrate, it sometimes proved impossible.

During the winter of 1896 a group of Eastern European immigrants to New York, who had been meeting informally to provide social services and financial aid to other recent immigrants, determined to formalize their association as a not-for-profit membership corporation, to be called by the Hebrew name Augudath Hakehiloth. Under the 1895 General Laws[4] the group needed to prepare their certificate of incorporation and submit it to a justice of the New York Supreme Court—the trial level in the New York court system—for the justice's approval.[5] Justice Roger A. Pryor, a former Confederate general without a record of concern about immigrants, received the application.[6]

Analyzing his judicial responsibilities, Justice Pryor conceded that arbitrary or capricious disapproval would be inappropriate.[7] Nevertheless, he was disturbed that the proposed certificate indicated that meetings of Augudath Hakehiloth would occur on Sunday—the Lord's day. The question was not whether meetings on Sunday were illegal. They undoubtedly *were* legal. The issue was whether they should be approved by a Justice of the Supreme Court. "A thing may be lawful, and yet not laudable," the court reasoned.[8] In the state of New York, Justice Pryor pointed out, the Christian Sabbath existed as a day of rest by common law.[9] Previous courts, as well as the Penal Law of the State, called Sabbath "one of the civil institutions of the state, and the legislature, for the purpose of promoting the moral and physical well-being of the people . . . has authority to regulate its observance and prevent its desecration."[10] The application for a certificate nowhere indicated that the petitioners were Jewish, but the justice drew that inference. The fact that the Jewish Sabbath was on the seventh day might allow Jews some right to protect their own precious day, but it did not allow them to desecrate Sunday. Because holding corporate meetings on Sunday was contrary to the "public policy of the state, if not to [the] letter of its law,"[11] the justice declined to approve the certificate.

Possible transgression of the Sabbath could be determined from the factual information provided in the proposed charter. But that and other information supplied in a proposed certificate might or might not be accurately stated; and the truth about a group's nature was hard to ascertain from a facial review of an application alone. The ability to test the truthfulness of information supplied by an applicant was critical to discovering the inner truth about a proposed corporation.

When Justice John Goff of the New York Supreme Court considered the certificate of incorporation of the Wendover Athletic Association in 1911, therefore, he withheld approval because the information it provided—regarding the age and citizenship of the incorporators—was presented with only its "bare assumptions, without proof to support them." Although neither statutory language nor procedural rules required supporting affidavits, Justice Goff demanded them in order to dig further into the reputation and nature of the group.[12]

The juristic approaches taken by late-nineteenth-century judges encouraged them to offer an explicit justification whenever they engaged in such an unprovided-for fact-finding investigation, or when they created a new procedural step. One leading treatise on statutory interpretation, Sutherland's *Statutes and Statutory Construction* (1880), discouraged the taking of judicial liberty in the construction of unelaborated rules that would, ostensibly, further the intent of a statute.[13]

On the other hand, Justice Goff could search for a "rational construction" of the statute by inferring legislative intent to conduct a search even in the absence of language or history. The New York Court of Appeals would do that, for example, in the 1912 case of *Riggs v. Palmer*.[14] To prevent a murderous inheritor from benefiting from his crime, it invoked the "familiar canon of construction that a thing which is within the intention of the makers of a statute is as much within the statute as if it were within the letter; and a thing which is within the letter of the statute is not within the statute, unless it be within the intention of the makers."[15]

One of Goff's brethren on the bench, Platt Potter, directly addressed the problem of determining permissible ways to use discretion to establish the "boundaries" of legislation. In his 1885 annotation of Fortunatus Dwarris's *General Treatise on Statutes*,[16] Potter (using Dwarris) addressed how far judges should act when legislative guidance was minimal. In much the way in which critics of courts would pose it late in the twentieth century,[17] their treatise questioned just how far judges could go without clear statutory authority:

> Are courts to proceed upon established principles—to be governed by fixed rules; or, exercising a liberal discretion, to have recourse, in doubtful cases,

to natural principles—to aid and to moderate the law according to equitable considerations. . . .

The *General Treatise* asserted that to an English or an American lawyer, the choice of using rigid canons of construction or applying equitable discretion was not a hard one. In contrast to the French and Continental approaches to law, which mandated that judges decide cases no matter how inadequate the statutory guidance they were given, the *Treatise* encouraged American and English jurists not to travel far beyond the positive text of laws. The existence of serious doubt or ambiguity counseled a careful excursion into the intent of a law:

> It is the duty of judges, where a case occurs which was not foreseen by the legislature, to declare it casus omissus; or where the intention, if entertained, is not expressed, to say of the legislature, *quod voluit, non dixit* [what he intended he did not express]; or where the case, though within the mischief, is clearly within the meaning; or where the words fall short of intent,—or go beyond it;—in every such case it is held the duty of the judge, in a land jealous of its liberties, to give effect to the expressed sense, or words, of the law . . . according to their fair and ordinary import and understanding."[18]

The treatise compared this Anglo-American view of close construction and "plain meaning" to courts of equity and to courts that applied a natural law perspective. French law, for example, required that "in default of a precise direction for every case, judges should [search for] precedents and received maxims," and then, if there was nothing else to go on, the principles of natural law would be adequate:

> When we are directed by nothing that is established or known; when a case absolutely new occurs, we go back to the principles of natural law. For if the foresight of the legislator is limited, nature is infinite, and her rights apply to all that can interest men.[19]

The *Treatise*, on the other hand, approvingly quoted the aphorism of a less capacious Sir Francis Bacon: "the best law is the one that minimizes the arbitrariness of judges; the best judge does the same."[20] Where "so much is left to the discretion of the Judges," concluded the authors, it was important to try to investigate the intent of laws closely, apply appropriate maxims and principles, and then exercise judicial power cautiously.[21]

But what was the intent of the law? What was its "plain" meaning? The problem in Goff's case was justifying by the statute the imposition of a restrictive demand and a judicial power to investigate—a power that was nowhere stated in the statute. Was truth finding or mere paper sorting the responsibility of the courts? Despite the language in the 1895 Membership Corporations Law, which explicitly required judicial approval of certificates, the possibility existed that the legislature had only intended the requirement for judicial "approval" of certificates of incorporation of nonprofits to be formal or "ministerial" in nature.

The challenge was thus to seek a rational interpretation or an "equitable construction" of the phrase "any lawful purpose," which lay at the heart of the eligibility rule for the Membership Corporations Law.[22] It would be logical to be skeptical of a self-declaration of age, if substantive scrutiny of a declaration was proper. If the statutory responsibility was merely ministerial, on the other hand, Justice Goff's search for the underlying truth about the ages and citizenship of the incorporators might constitute an illegitimate usurpation of power.

The new Membership Corporations Law statute provided nothing explicit that directed Judge Goff to take the actions he had taken. Some justification for the very significant new procedural hurdle he had created and for his substantive inquiry into "lawfulness" therefore appeared to be necessary. Establishing the open texture of the statutory provision was necessary, as a matter of legitimacy, for permitting judicial discretion to evaluate the worthiness of a corporation.

Examining the statute,[23] Goff set out his theory that the legislative decision to rely on judges for their approval necessarily implied a request for them to probe for the substantial truth of formal assertions, as common law judges were traditionally expected to do. He posed and answered a thinly veiled rhetorical question: "Is the presentation of a certificate containing the bare formula prescribed by the statute sufficient," he asked, "or should there be proof of compliance with the elemental substance of the law?"[24] The legislature might have given *anyone* in government a merely ministerial authority to see that papers were in order. The legislative determination to use a judicial officer, Goff reasoned, implied the need for the application of a judicial temperament to the review of the certificate. A judge should be presumed to have been employed to review certificates in order to employ judicial skills, that is, to "apply those tests and rules to the certificate which are applied in judicial procedure in order to ascertain facts, as distinguished from mere assertion."[25]

The privileges of incorporation, moreover, were substantial, and the other requirements for obtaining them did not place anyone else in the process in a position to determine that an applicant was suitable to receive them. Under such circumstances, judicial entitlement to conduct substantive judicial review would be inferred:

The Legislature has prescribed simple means by which an artificial entity may be created, and, when created, endowed with certain powers and privileges. What more reasonable than that, before imparting legal life, there should be judicial scrutiny of those qualifications which the law makes essential, and not a mere perfunctory passing on what may be presented.[26]

Even in the absence of hard evidence that the legislature intended substantive review to occur, it seemed indisputable to Goff that as a matter of logic, substantive scrutiny of "essentials" by the judiciary had been presupposed.

Apart from the pragmatic argument that there were privileges that accrued to unincorporated nonprofits which received charters which justified substantive scrutiny of them, the authority of justices to probe the charter documents emanated from the bare fact that the legislature had provided an approval process which might be relied upon by the public:

the very act of approval imports that the justice sanctions and accepts as satisfactory the instrument which is required by law to receive his approbation, and this sanction and acceptance cannot be given, even to a ministerial act, unless there be applied to its performance judicial tests and principles.[27]

Goff's juristic perspective considered it self-evident that judicial approval would always constitute a thing of value to be coveted by any association. Since the legislature had created a system that asked judges to certify to the public, which would be consuming the products of nonprofit enterprises and donating to them, some associations deserved support and legal protection while others did not. It was, therefore, a matter of judicial duty to conduct a substantive review. In this context, exercises of judicial discretion would confer what the institutional economist Thorstein Veblen in a different context labeled signs of "reputability."[28] They would be acts of social protection.

## Applications of the Discretionary Conception by Judicial Progressives

The "search for order" that characterized many reform efforts during the era of progressivism—from approximately 1890 until 1916—involved a quest for subduing socioeconomic disorder using government as a "lever of change."[29] It manifested itself, for example, in efforts by entrepreneurs to seek governmental support for the consolidation of businesses and the development of professional associations and standards.[30] In the courts and the new regulatory commissions, these efforts included demands for legal protection from "unfair" competition and "unfair trade practices."[31]

The search for order in an increasingly chaotic marketplace was also reflected in judicial willingness to prevent nonprofit groups from competing too fiercely with one another.

As national markets for goods and services grew—fueled by national advertising—the importance of protecting business franchises became apparent. Goods and services were sold under brand names in which businesses had invested substantial sums, and federal trademark and service mark laws allowed them to be registered and protected.[32] Corporate names identified substantial business franchises to the consuming public and to other businesses. For-profit corporations, through trademark, copyright, and antitrust laws, sought and received legal protection from competitors' efforts to piggyback onto their own good reputation.[33]

Charities like the Red Cross, and fraternal orders like the Benevolent and Protective Order of Elks, also tried to protect themselves from "confusing substitutes." The logic of protecting businesses from other competitors, however, was not easily extended to nonprofit groups that "competed" for gifts and members against other entities that operated on a not-for-profit basis. For many years nonprofits depended mainly on the nonprofit incorporation laws to provide protection from imitators.[34]

One of the early groups to seek such legal protection in the New York courts was the "Benevolent & Protective Order of Elks," successfully chartered by a special act of the New York legislature in 1871.[35] The fraternal lodge members who created it intended it to be an exclusively white organization.[36] It had grown through promotional activities into a national organization that by 1912 could list branches throughout the country and a membership of about 280,000 persons.[37] "The Grand Lodge of the Improved Benevolent & Protective Order of Elks of the World," on the other hand, was incorporated under New York's Membership Corporations Law in 1907. Its membership consisted predominantly of "colored persons."[38] The African-American Elks' organization, which formed after the exclusion of African-Americans from the white organization, had grown by 1912 to about 80,000.[39] The white Elks now accused the black Elks of intentionally misleading and confusing the public by imitating the name, emblem, and titles of the white organization. The white Elks sued to restrain the black Elks from operating under their regularly chartered name.

Concerned about the public's inability to disassociate the exclusionary white organization from the predominantly black one, and disinclined to dilute the benefits associated with that most dignified of animals, the elk, the white Elks brought suit and based their case on the premise that the public might consider the two groups to be affiliated with each other.[40] And in this case an applicable rule was close at hand, since in 1908 the New York legislature had embraced this consumer protection rationale for nonprofit corporations.[41] It prevented "any person or group from adopting the name of a "benevolent, humane, or charitable organization incorporated under the laws of this state, or a name so nearly resembling it as to be calculated to deceive the public with respect to any such corporation."[42]

In the name of consumer protection, the New York Supreme Court in its 1912 decision in *Benevolent & Protective Order of Elks* granted standing to the white Elks organization to bring an action for revocation *quo warranto*.[43] Determining that the white Elks had become so well-known that the assumption of a title containing the word "Elk" would convey the false impression that there was some connection between them, the trial court enjoined the predominantly black group from the use of the word "Elk."[44] The court of appeals affirmed the injunction, remarking that if the black organization wanted the name of an animal, "there is a long list of beasts, birds, and fishes which have not yet been appropriated for such a purpose."[45] In subsequent decisions, New York courts would extend the consumer protection rationale for disapproving of an organization's application not only because of possible confusion with other groups but because a group's name might mislead the public as to its true function, or because the groups did not deserve the exclusive use of a word or phrase.[46]

Along with the consumer protection justification for the *Elks* decision, however, flowed a less admirable undercurrent of progressive judicial instrumentalism: the use of the law to keep black Americans separate from whites in social and fraternal settings.[47] The need to protect the general public from name confusion was weak, after all: the skin color of the members of the two organizations and the exclusionary policy of one of them rendered the possibility of deception in the course of any competition between the groups for members to be highly theoretical. But the courts at each level rejected this obvious argument and opted to allow the white organization to appropriate the word "Elk." The court of appeals embraced intentional color-blindness as the basis for ignoring the divergent racial composition of the organizations:

> While the question of color crops up in the evidence in this record, it does not appear to have any legal significance in the litigation. The rights of the parties . . . must be adjudicated here precisely as though the members of both corporations were all of the same color.[48]

Cloaking obtuseness as impartiality allowed the court to use the incorporation law to perpetuate the social and cultural separation of the races.

The judges of the Progressive Era used their authority not only to reinforce their views about race but also to strengthen norms which emphasized that America's culture must be assimilative and that its public discourse must not encourage extremism. Although Woodrow Wilson had promoted principles of self-determination for ethnic nationalities in Eastern Europe, millions of Americans worried about the disintegrative domestic effects that large numbers of unassimilated Eastern and Southern European immigrants would have on "American" culture. As an antidote, writers, artists, and opinion makers searched for a "usable" American past and tried to define what was "distinctively American" about the American character.[49]

At the close of World War I, disenchantment with foreign nationalistic fervor—which many Americans considered a primary cause for the conflict—quickly spread. In the wake of Communist revolution in Russia, antiradical suspicion led to violence and anti-immigrant hysteria throughout the country.[50] Alarmed by uninhibited manifestations of ethnic pride, and unsettled by the specter of violent class warfare, many state legislatures reacted with laws that, for example, mandated flying the American flag and imposed citizenship courses in elementary school curricula.[51]

State and federal judges diluted traditional protections of civil liberties through restrictive interpretations of First Amendment rights and their toleration of often brutal enforcement of alien and sedition laws during these years.[52] In deportation cases and cases concerning the distribution of allegedly subversive literature, courts limited protections under the First and Fourteenth Amendments. The broad discretion given to justices by the doctrine, which had emerged under the Membership Corporations Law, permitted similar antilibertarian tendencies to shape incorporation.

In 1920, the Catalonian Nationalist Club sought approval of its proposed certificate of incorporation in New York.[53] The club aspired to become a center for maintaining Catalonian culture and "the legitimate national aspirations of Catalonia."[54] It would promote "social intercourse and strengthen the bonds of solidarity and brotherhood among Catalonians and Catalonian-speaking persons."[55] In "lawful and proper ways" the incorporators promised to "promote the principles of self-determination of nationalities as applying to the emancipation of Catalonia."[56]

Justice Edward G. Whitaker had come from New York's social elite and rose through its political hierarchy.[57] He reflected New York's dominant religious and cultural perspectives[58] and did not support either ethnic nationalism or cultural diversity. Justice Whitaker did not believe that anything good for Americans would come from the incorporation of the Catalonian Nationalist Club. "It has, I think, been demonstrated in the recent past that the great need of the time is the teaching of American 'culture,'" he stated.[59] The result of fostering pride in their homeland among

immigrants was too often that "naturalized citizens to the second generation have retained a dual fealty."[60] Organizations that were formed for
the purpose of dividing people into racial groups retarded "homogene-
ity." They were helpful only to Catalonia.[61] Because such organizations
were undesirable for America, approving their certificates of incorporation would be contrary to public policy. Whitaker therefore rejected the
application.[62]

In addition to discouraging ethnic nationalism, discretionary chartering power also permitted judges to marginalize nontraditional expressions of political and social thought when it suited. With exceptional
good fortune, for example, the Lithuanian Workers' Literature Society
had obtained a nonprofit charter in 1918 as an organization consisting exclusively of members of the Socialist party and devoted to publishing
materials related to socialism and to promoting socialist causes.[63] Less
than two years later, however, the society apparently misstepped when it
decided to amend its charter to admit individuals who were "not opposed to the organization of the workers . . . in organizations which subscribe to Marxian principles."[64] Although a proposed certificate of incorporation allowed the court little except formal statements on which to
base a decision and although there was a presumption of continued existence that might have been applied to ongoing concerns like the Literature Society which sought to amend their charters, the court did not
make the distinction between the ongoing and proposed corporations
when it conducted its review.[65]

The judge who was presented with the application, Justice Isaac N.
Mills, had come to the bench after many years in private practice, in state
politics, and as a municipal court judge. The descendant of a long-estab-
lished Connecticut family, Mills exemplified many judges of the era in his
conservatism and his understanding of judicial authority.[66] He analyzed
the strong constraints he believed the federal and state constitutions
placed on his discretion, conceding that federal and state guarantees of
free expression limited his ability to restrict the expression of corporations. "However repugnant to our minds and consciences the Socialist
program may be," he stated, "we are not to stand in the way of organizations to promote its accomplishment, *provided only* . . . that the purpose
and intent of those organizations is to seek the accomplishment of that
program by lawful methods; that is to say, to change our form of government by amending the Constitution through constitutional methods."[67]

To Mills, the recent universal suffrage and prohibition amendments to
the Constitution demonstrated that there was in the United States "no
sort of moral excuse even for advocacy of a resort to any other means of
effecting such change [than through the electoral process]."[68] Alas, since
the organization's principal function appeared to be the dissemination of

"Socialist propaganda," an amendment to the charter might permit a new expanded membership to promote "Marxian principles" in their "broadest possible scope,"[69] which might embrace the promotion of unlawful conduct.[70] Justice Mills did not mention in his opinion that few if any other nonprofit corporations specifically prohibited their members from holding "Marxian" principles, either at the time or later.

To determine whether to allow the society's charter to be amended, Mills believed it was necessary to inquire into Marxist concepts of political economy—to determine whether the Lithuanian Workers' Society now could include "those who advocate or seek to accomplish . . . change by force after the manner in which the recent Russian so-called revolution was effected."[71] To answer this vexing question, Mills apparently visited the public library. Rather than read Marx in the original,[72] he located the book *Karl Marx: His Life and Work*, written by the journalist and author John Spargo, whom Justice Mills placed in the "lawful class of Socialists."[73]

For unexplained reasons Justice Mills gave considerable weight to Spargo's assessment of Marx's favorable description of the acts of the Paris Commune in 1871, declaring that "it clearly appears that Marx favored the several attempts to overthrow organized government by force." Mills quoted Spargo's quotation of Marx's description:

"[A]t page 335 of his book [Spargo] quotes Marx as having favored the acts of the Paris Commune in 1871 by writing of it in these laudatory terms:
    This insurrection is a glorious deed for our party . . . and the grandeur appears the greater when we think of all the vices of the old society, of its wolves, its swine, and its common hounds.

Having sustained his questionable inference with minimal proof, Justice Mills reached a predictably rigid conclusion. On the basis of this brief quotation he determined that the certificate of the Lithuanian Workers' Society as amended would permit as members persons whose sympathies would lead them to publish "propaganda which our Penal Law makes criminal and even felonious."[74] The court would therefore not approve the certificate, since it potentially embraced within the society socialists of the "forcible means" stripe.[75]

The racial, political, and ethnic presuppositions that informed the nonprofit incorporation process changed with the ethnic and social composition of the bench. By 1925, the swelling Jewish immigrant population included a large number of lawyers, from whom a small number of justices had been appointed to the bench. The first Jewish justice to discuss the previously answered question of appropriate standards for deciding whether a nonprofit corporation should be chartered was Justice Aaron J.

Levy, in *Daughters of Israel Orphan Aid Soc.*[76] Levy had been on the bench for only two years when the case came before him.[77] Not surprisingly, he agreed with earlier courts that his function in deciding to grant or deny approval of certificates was more than ministerial. In fact, Justice Levy held, an inquiry into whether an organization's purposes accorded with public policy was part of the larger duty to determine whether the proposed purposes of a corporation were lawful.[78]

No surprise either that Justice Levy disagreed with certain earlier views of his fellow justices as they affected Jewish customs and recent English-speaking immigrants.[79] Why, the justice asked, was it deemed necessary for organizations to be given English names, as long as they were transliterated from Hebrew or another language? No such requirement should be read into the statute, he believed.[80] Why should justices disapprove of certificates that tolerated meetings on Sundays? Previous judicial rulings, Levy believed, had misread the common law. "While at common law judicial proceedings were prohibited on that day of the week, all other transactions were held to be valid, except so far as forbidden by statute."[81] The work of charitable corporations was not "labor" in the sense contemplated by the Sabbath statutes, and so the statutes themselves were not applicable.[82] Certificates providing for Sunday meetings would no longer be rejected by his court.[83]

Unlike other legal proceedings, which were adversarial and permitted judicial bias to be confronted directly, these proceedings to approve charters were ex parte and generally concluded without a hearing. As contrasted with legal rulings that might be challenged on the basis of the absence of substantial evidence or for their unduly speculative nature, or because they were contrary to the law, these were appealable only on a claim of an abuse of discretion, which appeals never succeeded. As interpreted, the breadth of the statutory empowerment made the rulings of the judges virtually unreversible on appeal.

### Interwar Characterizations of
### Permissible Nonprofit Activity

When rules fail to offer a comprehensible guide to decision making, a philosophy of judicial restraint is impossible.[84] In the legal climate that had developed by the end of World War I, judges could not operate as anything *but* activists on behalf of their social order. Cultural, political, and ideological leanings informed their decisions. Between the wars, courts tried to allow nonprofits to ride the business expansion of the 1920s. During the Depression of the 1930s, they enforced their personal opinions of appropriate economic and social policy.

The expansion of economic activity and the increase of national wealth during the 1920s was at the time widely attributed to the entrepreneurial genius and self-improvement ethic of America's ambitious go-getters, and to a political and legal climate newly attuned to a business culture.[85] The culture that adored business exalted profitability as a measure of prosperity, and this outlook marginalized the value of nonprofit groups. If nonprofit activity only provided a refuge from the world of profit and only attracted persons who disdained the business culture, how could it continue to thrive? Perhaps the enthusiasm of the decade for profit making could be harnessed to the charitable impulse that had thrived in previous years. Perhaps it was not a contradiction in terms or a violation of fundamental philosophy to permit nonprofit organizations to engage in traditional business activities. There were entrepreneurs ready to explore the limits of entrepreneurship within the nonprofit sector.

Hugh B. Monjar founded the Decimo Club in 1924 in California as an unincorporated fraternal and social organization. He served as its chief officer.[86] In 1926, together with a group of other young men, he chartered the club as a Delaware membership corporation, without stock and not-for-profit, to "maintain . . . reading and club rooms . . . [to] promote social intercourse among its members, and [to provide for] the general advancement of its members through any honest and honorable methods that may later develop."[87] On a facial examination of the governing instruments, the organization appeared to operate as a gathering place where members would congregate to exchange information about getting ahead in business.

The Decimo Club's board amended its charter a year later to expand its corporate purposes: among other things, the club would buy and sell real property in order to establish subsidiary clubs to "cultivate the . . . business relations of the members . . . broaden their interests in . . . their occupations and professions; and to improve their standards of efficiency and productivity."[88] The club would limit its membership to "loyal American citizens of sound body and health" between twenty-one and forty-five years of age, who possessed "reasonable desire . . . to improve themselves and willingness to help others."[89] The club became popular and by 1928 included thirty-seven chapters and more than 60,000 members.[90]

At a slightly less obvious level, Monjar hoped that the clubs would operate as self-sustaining businesses. They were intended to grow wealthy on membership dues and members' purchases of club merchandise. Members paid an initiation fee and annual dues. Monjar set up two for-profit corporations, which he called Apasco Purchase and Sales Corporation ("Apasco") and Drew Tailoring Corporation ("Drew"). These for-profits sold goods and clothing to the Decimo Club, which the Decimo members would buy from the club "on favorable terms" and sell to others. Apasco grew to have assets of nearly $500,000 as a result of its sales to the club.[91]

At the least visible level, Monjar hoped to exploit the club for his own purposes. He was interested in using the nonprofit form to further his own enrichment. Monjar entered into a contract between himself as a recruiter and himself as an officer of Decimo. For his services in recruiting new members into Decimo, it paid him several hundred thousand dollars, which flowed from the $20 initiation fee the new members paid. Monjar also took dividends as owner of stock in Apasco and Drew.

Monjar's mantra of business as a spiritual calling struck a chord with ambitious younger people throughout the country. Unfortunately for Monjar, after complaints from some members, it struck district attorneys and other officials in several states, including California, Washington, Illinois, New Jersey, New York, and Wisconsin, as the hokum of a charlatan. Members of the clubs became aware that Monjar appeared to be taking profits from Decimo in the form of the Apasco and Drew corporation sales receipts.[92] At the 1927 annual membership meeting the rank and file in Decimo revolted. They ousted Monjar, replaced him, and received a settlement from him in the form of all the outstanding stock of Apasco. The new Decimo board devised a complicated plan for a new Decimo Club, which tied two nonprofit trusts, Decimo Club Inc. and Decimo Trust of America, to a for-profit business corporation called Decimo Industries.[93]

In several states, investigations of the legality of the old and new Decimo Clubs began. In Massachusetts, Attorney General Reading, a well-respected member of one of Boston's leading families, resigned after charges that he had been bribed by Monjar to avoid an investigation.[94] In New York, while the Bureau of Frauds began to investigate the club, lawyers for the leader of the Tammany Organization sought and received an injunction to prevent Monjar or other officers from removing assets, asserting that Monjar's contracts with Decimo were all invalid. "What did the members of this club get for their money?" asked the court. "Nothing but the 'blue sky,'" replied counsel for Tammany.[95] The treasurer of Decimo claimed the club was like other fraternal organizations, "except that its members had the right to buy anything they wanted through the Apasco Purchase and Sales Corporation."[96] Supreme Court Justice Riegelmann in New York declined to disqualify the club as a fraternal order.[97]

The attorney general of Delaware became convinced that the old Decimo Club as well as the newly forming Decimo nonprofits violated the law by allowing the nonprofit entities to engage in for-profit businesses. He sued to revoke the club's charter under authority granted in the

Delaware Membership Corporations Law.[98] Newspapers around the country followed the intriguing story of bribery, corruption, and a possibly fraudulent nonprofit scheme that had taken in thousands of unsuspecting (but perhaps less-than-humanitarian) members.[99]

The judge in Chancery was untroubled about the idea of a nonprofit corporation composed of a business fraternity of go-getters with their eyes on the main chance and anxious to make money on one another; and he did not find anything objectionable about the operation of the older Decimo Club.[100] Nonprofits could engage in business to *some* extent. The statute did not mean to prohibit them "absolutely and entirely" from doing business, and a membership corporation that engaged in business was not necessarily a corporation for profit within the meaning of the law. Only if circumstances showed that profit making was among the principal objects of the corporation would it be reasonable to revoke the not-for-profit certificate of incorporation.[101] He found no evidence that the Monjar management had turned the old Decimo corporation into a profit-making concern through his recruitment contract or his corporate side deals.[102]

It remained to examine the operating structure of the organization under the new plan of the board, which called for the members of the original Decimo Club to join the new club (a nonprofit corporation). At the same time they would pay a fee to the Decimo Trust of America (a nonprofit trust) to become holders of certificates of the trust as beneficial members of it. The Decimo Trust of America would purchase stock in Decimo Industries (for-profit), which made the supplies the members bought. Dividends on the stock of the for-profit business would be passed back to the trust and eventually, on dissolution, from the trust to the individual members of the Decimo Club. The new board of Decimo hoped that the plan would "save . . . the corporation and the benefits of the salient features of the Monjar idea, viz. . . . an appeal to the social and fraternal instincts of men together with an appeal to the individual desire for profit and gain."[103]

To the Court, the new board of governors of the Decimo Club seemed to understand the lucrative potential in turning moneymaking into a spiritual quest. The business fraternity idea was the core idea at the heart of Monjar's operation—and the court embraced the concept zealously:

> Monjar had demonstrated the ease with which business could be done with a group of men behind him who were welded together in the name of fraternity and brotherhood and who as a group could be exploited with the offer of opportunities of either making or saving money. Men organized on the basis of an appeal to the instincts of brotherhood were shown to be capable of a cohesive welding by the opportunity for business gain.[104]

Admiring the novel conception of a nonprofit endeavor on behalf of entrepreneurship, the judge wrote that the Decimo "movement" might be kept alive and withstand scrutiny if its profit-making and "fraternal and social phases" could be segregated among the two Decimo nonprofits and Decimo Industries.[105]

Despite the allegations and misgivings of the attorney general, the judge found nothing problematic about dividends from the trust's investments in Decimo industries stock being distributed by the trustees to individual certificate holders as beneficiaries of the trust. "If this were the end of the story," the court stated, "it is very doubtful if anything of an illegal nature could be charged against the club . . . because . . . the club . . . derives no benefit from the business which its members in another role as certificate holders hope to profit from."[106] The court ruled that the issuance of dividends by a for-profit corporation to a nonprofit trust did not automatically disqualify a group from nonprofit status.[107] The state would be protected against any scheming by the trust to avoid franchise taxes and dividend taxes after the corporation came into existence through the regulations of the secretary of state and through the threat of a *quo warranto* proceeding, through which the attorney general might revoke a corporate charter after it had been issued.[108]

Only in the provisions that allowed for the redemption of the members' equity in the assets of the trust on dissolution did the court find a problem. The Delaware Nonprofit Corporation Law prohibited an organization that was organized primarily for "pecuniary gain" from incorporation as a nonprofit.[109] The proposed charter of the trust indicated that upon termination, its property and assets would belong to all the Decimo Club members rather than to the holders of the certificates in the trust, contaminating the separation between the club and the trust. Considering that the club's statement of purposes reflected a self-image as "to some extent . . . a business enterprise," the court reluctantly concluded that the termination provisions established that the Club was primarily a profit-making venture. "From its organization to date, the appeal [of Decimo Club] has been more to the instinct of men for profit than to the instincts for social and fraternal development."[110]

Allowing a for-profit organization to operate under nonprofit laws was wrongful, the judge explained, because the legislature was lenient with nonprofits relative to for-profits:

> [The Legislature did not mean] to allow the easy and liberal provisions of the corporation and revenue statutes applicable to corporations organized not for profit to be enjoyed by corporations whose purpose is in fact to engage in business for profit to such an extent that the desire for profits constitutes a conspicuous object of its existence.[111]

Professing personal admiration for the concept of harnessing the profit motive to a nonprofit cause, the judge indicated that Decimo had gotten it precisely backward. Without penalizing any of the officers or directors of the club personally, he entered a decree for revocation of the club's charter.[112]

The facts of the Decimo case, and reports of the judicial opinions, found their way into newspapers around the country. In 1930 Monjar was convicted of committing fraud in connection with the Decimo matter and was barred from selling stock in the for-profit entities.[113] Monjar's troubles with various attorney generals on account of several other such schemes continued for years, and he eventually wound up in prison. [114]

The possibilities for stretching traditional ideas about voluntarism and charity to include the promotion of profit-making skills were captivating because they were quite new to the public. In the culture of the 1920s, however, promoting a compatibility between the world of public virtue and private interests once more seemed logical and innovative. And in the course of ruling on the revocation, the Delaware court had asserted its own role in determining the boundaries for nonprofit corporate activity and widened those boundaries to allow new opportunities for business activities, provided they were technically compliant with established rules.

The onset of the Depression brought judges, along with almost everyone else, down to earth. New social, political, and economic realities affected those who were forming groups and those who were evaluating permissible nonprofit activity. Within the Depression environment courts considered the business possibilities of nonprofit enterprise more restrictively than earlier.

In a Depression world of shrinking resources and deteriorating quality, a commitment to older standards sometimes led judges to impose unreasonable expectations at the expense of the poor.[115] In 1934 Rox County, located in western Pennsylvania, there existed a small, unincorporated athletic association. Although the association claimed eighty members, it operated without a clubhouse, a headquarters, or a meeting room big enough to accommodate them all. The Rox County Athletic Association hoped to grow and enlarge its facilities, the association's president testified later, and it applied for a charter because that might help it to grow. "The place is too small," the president testified. "We will have to get a larger place."[116] The encouragement of athletics was a proper function for nonprofit organizations according to Pennsylvania Nonprofit Corporation Law. So also was the chartering of social clubs.[117]

The Common Pleas judge in Allegheny County denied the association's application nevertheless, with a short written opinion.[118] "We do not think that we should grant Club charters to such an organization to

help them get proper rooms," the trial court judge explained rather pa-
ternalistically.[119] "With the preposterous initiation fee of 25 cents and the
equally preposterous monthly dues of 25 cents, it seems asking too much
to designate such a club as a[n] . . . Athletic Club."[120] The idea that an
athletic club could operate on such a small budget appeared ridiculous to
the judge, who thought it might take an unrealistically long period of
time to raise money for what the judge considered an adequate facility.

On the other hand, the judge's support for Prohibition may have been
at issue in this case. The Prohibition Amendment recently had been repealed, to the delight of many and the dismay of some. The judge contended that the athletic club could not continue to exist except by "passing the hat" or else (in the post-Prohibition environment) by getting a
liquor license and "adding one more drinking resort to those already
posing as Chartered Clubs."[121] It is impossible to know for certain
whether his suspicion that the club fronted for a "drinking resort" was
accurate, but if it was, the judge's ruling seems to fall within the tradition
of progressive moralism and paternalist consumer protection described
earlier.[122] The court prevented the incorporation of what he called a
"penny-ante" athletic association, and the Supreme Court of Pennsylvania affirmed the Common Pleas decision.[123]

Labor leaders too were compelled by the discretionary approval doctrine to confront the personal labor sympathies of the New York court
justices. Among the major political and social realignments that the New
Deal engineered was a new sense of legitimacy and respectability for the
labor movement. Prior to the Roosevelt administration's support for the
labor unions, their fundamental lawfulness came into question on numerous occasions.[124] Although a federal incorporation statute permitted
the incorporation of labor unions, they often operated as unincorporated
associations.[125] After the passage of the Norris-LaGuardia Act and the
Wagner Act,[126] however, all this changed. The organization of workers
into unions was actually encouraged, and John L. Lewis's organizing cry,
"The president wants you to join a union," became emblematic of the
new political accommodation. Unions in fact sought to organize themselves, when they could, under general nonprofit incorporation laws.[127]

The politicization of nonprofit incorporation rules during this period is
nowhere more evident than in their treatment of unions. Incorporation
under the nonprofit laws provided union members valuable protection
from lawsuits against individual members, who, as members of unincorporated associations, had on certain occasions been held personally liable
for antitrust violations and damages caused during strikes. To many
workers, furthermore, the acquisition of a charter would confer respectability and legitimacy on the union and test the bona fides of the
state.

In 1937 the Illinois legislature became concerned that its nonprofit incorporation laws were being used for inappropriate purposes, and it amended the language of the state's not-for-profit law to specify the purposes for which nonprofit corporations might be formed.[128] The previous language in the statute allowed "Societies, corporations and associations (not for pecuniary profit)" to be formed.[129] The new language permitted the formation of "Societies . . . for civic, educational, patriotic, agricultural, horticultural, soil, crop, livestock and poultry improvement, electrification on a cooperative basis, ownership of residential property on a co-operative basis, pleasure, social, athletic, political, benevolent, charitable, eleemosynary, research, or other similar purposes and commercial, industrial or trade associations . . . without pecuniary profit to the members thereof."[130] In the process, the legislature omitted labor unions from the list of acceptable societies.[131] When the Allied Federation of Labor tried to file a certificate of incorporation, the secretary of state rejected it, claiming the authority to do so because the incorporation of labor unions had been the subject of great controversy when the legislation was adopted, and the amendment had been intended to narrow the opportunities to take advantage of the not-for-profit corporation laws.[132]

The appellate court of Illinois agreed.[133] Notwithstanding the Federation of Labor's claim to be a "trade association," or else an organization for "similar purposes" to those enumerated, the court indicated that discretion resided with the secretary of state to make that determination.[134] The legislature, said the appellate court, was well accustomed to using the terms "labor organizations" or "labor unions" in statutes whenever it wanted such groups to be covered.[135] Canons of statutory interpretation provided an easy resolution of the case.

The same year the New York legislature moved in exactly the opposite political direction. It amended its General Corporations Law and Membership Corporations Law in a manner sympathetic to labor.[136] The legislature clarified the ability of labor unions to organize under the Membership Corporations Law and, to guard the genuineness of the labor sympathies of those who applied, required that the corporate charters of organizations concerned with labor, wages, or working conditions receive prior approval from the New York Board of Standards and Appeals, an administrative body.[137]

A test of the new law came when, in July 1937, the Empire Worsted Mills Shop Union submitted its proposed certificate to the Board of Standards and Appeals.[138] The approval immediately was opposed by many other labor organizations on the ground that Empire Worsted Mills had coerced its employees into forming a "company union" subservient to employer interests.[139] Finding evidence that the purpose of the organization was to prevent a true national labor union from organizing Empire

Worsted Mills—a purpose that contradicted the purpose of the National Labor Relations Act—the Board of Standards of Appeals disapproved of the certificate.[140]

On appeal to the New York Supreme Court, the question presented was whether the board had the discretion to withhold its consent to the incorporation of a labor organization because it was a company union.[141] After a lengthy rehearsal of the history of labor unions in the United States, Justice Schenck turned to the development of judicial review of nonprofit charters through case law. He analogized the duty of the Board of Standards and Appeals to the duty of justices of the Supreme Court to approve the charters of other nonprofit corporations. In both instances it was necessary to determine whether the objects and purposes of the corporation would accord with public policy, the justice stated.[142] The company ("shop") union argued that pre-incorporation review was tantamount to prejudging the union's good faith before it had a chance to prove itself. If the shop union behaved in violation of any law after it was incorporated, the shop union claimed, then appropriate enforcement bodies were in a position to enforce the labor laws and, if necessary, obtain revocation of the union's charter.

Asserting its own view of its discretionary power to determine a lawful purpose, the Court rejected the shop union's argument. Despite the fact that post-incorporation regulatory supervision by the Labor Relations Board might cure some of the shop union's deficiencies after it had come into existence, it was "more salutary that there be prevention rather than cure where that is practicable."[143] In other words, pre-incorporation screening, at least in the context of company unions, appeared essential to the effective regulation of nonprofit activity.[144]

The importance of screening not only proposed certificates of incorporation but also proposed *amendments* to charters was highlighted in cases where unscrupulous officers took control of legitimate organizations after they had formed. A society that organized in Colorado during the 1920s for the relief of tuberculosis victims, for example, received permission from New York to operate (as a foreign corporation) a sanitarium and solicit funds in New York. Much later, in 1949, it petitioned for an amendment to its certificate that would indicate that the sanitarium was actually in Colorado. [145] The amendment was approved by the Court because it was not objectionable on its face.[146]

It so happened that at the very same moment the amendment to the certificate was pending, the New York attorney general was in another court—bringing suit to restrain the corporation from operating there.[147] The corporation had been taken over illegally by a group of officers and directors who were mismanaging the sanitarium in Colorado—they were treating patients poorly and providing inadequate medical facilities.[148]

Having just approved the amendment to the charter of the Relief Society, the court now entertained and granted the request to revoke the charter entirely. "Had the court been informed of the pending action brought by the People of the State of New York against this foreign corporation, it would have, in the exercise of its discretion, refused to approve the proposed amended certificate," Justice Hecht fumed.[149] To prevent future mishaps the Membership Corporations Law subsequently was amended to provide the attorney general with advance written notice of applications for approval of certificates and amendments.[150] Again, preventative efforts to screen out corporations whose purposes were unlawful or whose officers were disreputable appeared preferable to subsequent remedial measures.

The system, which depended on the exercise of power to determine eligibility for access to the benefits of the nonprofit sector, had become well enough established to subdue lingering judicial self-consciousness about the ordinary jurisprudential limitations on discretion which had been evident in earlier years. Policy rationales, court doctrines, and personal sympathies toward the most controversial matters of the day—labor, economic policies, and prohibition among them—were intertwined.

## Wartime Applications

The treatment of immigrants, especially Jewish immigrants, continued to occupy the state courts of New York as problems in Europe spilled over into America. Several years before the burning of the Reichstag (1936) and the organized mob riot of Kristallnacht (1938) brought awareness to most Americans, some alert members of the Jewish community in New York realized that as the National Socialists (Nazis) rose to power, Jews living in Germany faced severe persecution. Newspapers, including the *New York Times* and the *New York Herald Tribune,* were closely following events in Germany as early as 1933. In the American Jewish community, charitable relief efforts began shortly afterward.[151]

In contrast to more than two hundred cases in which judicial approvals were *withheld* in New York, Pennsylvania, and other states, the record of judicial discretion contains few examples of trial court *approvals* of certificates of incorporation.[152] Justice Levy of New York,[153] however, used the application for incorporation made in 1934 by the German Jewish Children's Aid Society as an opportunity to record (and perhaps to publicize) the importance of making these and other such humanitarian efforts. The society was being established to facilitate the entry of Jewish children into the United States and to care for them afterward.[154] Justice Levy, as already noted,[155] had become adept at using his review of charter applications as a platform to gain political and community support for favored causes.

A state trial judge could hardly receive a better opportunity to promote himself in his own community. Levy praised the cause and those who organized efforts on its behalf. He extolled "the high sponsorship of this corporation," which included on its intended board an unnamed judge of the court of appeals, a former justice of the Appellate Division, and "a large number of persons well known in philanthropic activities."[156] He considered these persons of repute "a genuine guaranty of the sincerity of purpose."[157] The review Justice Levy conducted was ex parte and unopposed; nevertheless, he mounted a multipage defense against unnamed critics of his views. Did he believe his harshest critic would be isolationists? Or those who opposed immigration? More likely, he felt they would be—like himself—proponents of assimilation who in less dangerous times would have objected to the need for an organization proposed to help not American children in need or even all German children in need, but *exclusively Jewish* children in trouble. Anticipating the arguments of those unnamed critics, he recorded reports of the distinctions that Nazis made between the treatment of Jews and of others they considered undesirable; this compelled special treatment by the court in this case. Justice Levy quoted a non-Jewish observer who wrote that "from the other groups what is wanted is submission. But it is the aim [of the German Aryan brotherhood] to eliminate the Jews."[158] He repeated at length an address by Stefan Zweig, "Their Souls a Mass of Wounds":

> Many of the children who are growing up now in Germany, must, I fear, become embittered, and bitter, infected by the hatred which incomprehensible injustice will arouse in them. . . . [A]s many Jewish children as possible should at the present moment grow up not in Germany where they must be exposed to enmity . . . but . . . should either be planted in the native soil of Palestine, or for a time find a home among nations . . . that . . . elevate themselves by the liberty that they grant in matters of religion of every form to every race upon this earth.[159]

This discussion was quite extraordinary in a judicial opinion—even more so in a decision regarding nonprofit corporation law. Justice Levy undertook it, he said, because it was necessary to determine whether the purposes of the nonprofit corporation accorded with the objectives of public policy.[160]

Another problem with the society was that one of its principal stated missions was to post bonds with various jurisdictions to hold them harmless from German Jewish children who gained entry to the United States who might become wards.[161] Was this bonding function a banking or an insurance business impermissible for a nonprofit? No, the justice declared, it was not impermissible because the bonding activity was confined appropriately to that business which was necessary for the larger charitable mission.[162] He approved the certificate, declaring the society "obviously unselfish and altruistic."[163] His opinion was reported approvingly in the *New York Times*.[164]

Just as Justice Levy's horror of events in Germany shaped his approach to approving Children's Aid, it also led him to a dark view of the German Bunds (associations) in America. When the General Von Steuben Bund, Inc., presented its application in 1936, the justice found all the formal papers in order and the statement of purposes proper. Although the stated purposes seemed to be within the law, deeper examination, however, convinced him that approval of the Bund would not accord with public policy.[165]

Relying on his earlier opinion in *re Daughters of Israel Orphan Aid Soc'y*,[166] Levy observed that a proposed certificate of incorporation might well "conceal its true object while expressing its purposes in acceptable or, at least, innocuous form."[167] The Bund proposed "to unite persons of German birth or descent, and Christian faith, [and] . . . to preserve . . . ideals of the land of their nativity or ancestry and to harmonize the same with those of America."[168] These goals were not facially unlawful or unacceptable, but a review of the German language program sheet announcing the Bund's 1935 Steuben Day celebration in New York convinced the justice that the Bund intended to encourage immigrants to retain their "German ideals" and to shun American ones.[169]

If the true purpose of the organization were to act as a vehicle for establishing a dual or divided allegiance among its members, it would not be entitled "to the official blessing of our courts in the form of judicial approval."[170] Justice Levy examined the evidence he had obtained on his own for indications that there were ulterior purposes contained in the German language program of the unincorporated Bund:

> [W]e find a complete German program of fourteen numbers with speeches exclusively in German. The only American feature is the opening song, The Star Spangled Banner, the effect of which, however, is neutralized by the singing of the Horst Wessel song, the official hymn of the National Socialist dictatorship in Germany.[171]

Singing the Horst Wessel song and speaking only in German implied to Justice Levy that the motives of the Bund surpassed fraternal bonding and cultural support. An unincorporated society, furthermore, known as the Steuben Society of America, opposed the incorporation of the General Von Steuben Bund because the original Baron Von Steuben, the namesake and officer of the American Revolution, held principles that were inconsistent with German dictatorship.[172] The unincorporated Steuben group complained that it would be confused with the new Bund if the new Bund were incorporated. Condemning the society because it promoted "dual fealty"[173] and because it might be confused with the unincorporated association called the Steuben Society of America, Justice Levy withheld his approval of the Bund's charter.[174]

The court did not consider whether its actions had adversely affected the free speech of the Steuben Society.[175] Indeed, the approval process offered one of the few spaces in the law where First Amendment constitutional protections did not stand in the way of judicial condemnation of vastly unpopular political expression. The *New York Times* reported the opinion in detail and concluded with a tinge of glee that the opinion had effectively prevented the Bund from receiving a charter. "Under the law, the General von Steuben Bund has the right to appeal to another Supreme Court Justice for approval," the *Times* wrote, "but the fact that it has been turned down previously usually militates against future approval."[176] However thin the evidence may have been as a matter of the law of evidence and however biased the court's procedure, the outcome seemed to be the right one in the court of public opinion.[177]

Around the outbreak of the war, doctrinal justifications for disapproving of nonprofits swelled as the courts became ever more self-assured about their actions, and wartime exigency excused a less tolerant judicial approach to civil liberties. The popular and journalistic enthusiasm for denying nonprofit status to Bunds encouraged judges to pay special attention to German groups. When the German and Hungarian War Veteran's Post applied for a charter in 1939,[178] Justice Francis G. Hooley[179] expressed frustration with the difficulty of carrying out his responsibilities based on the information he had at hand. He described the problem of probing the true motives of these nonprofit fraternal groups in metaphorical terms.[180] Incorporation, he stated, dressed associations in a "cloak" of respectability.[181] In the garment of its nonprofit incorporation, a group might masquerade its true nature as one of the paramilitary Bunds that lately had sprouted up. These Bunds loudly proclaimed their Americanism. Secretly, however, they "worshiped the swastika" and sowed the "seeds of un-American religious and racial intolerance."[182] The Bunds promoted the Hitlerian view "that a man who was once a German continued to be a German subject, notwithstanding his oath of allegiance to any other country."[183] Courts needed to make a careful inquiry in these cases, the justice stated, to learn the true nature of the mysteriously garbed figure knocking at the door; if subterfuge was involved, approval of such a nonprofit corporation would be out of the question.[184]

During years of ideological warfare and rhetorical excess, courts tried to control the way the nonprofit sector used and monopolized language—to supplement intellectual property rules by using nonprofit law to save certain parts of vocabulary from monopolization. In 1938, for example, the outspoken president of the Borough of Queens, George Harvey, and other members of a veteran's organization called the Legion of Valor, decided to form a new organization to "stamp out 'isms.'" [185] The group intended to "combat communism and promote Americanism."[186] "Every group is organized except the Americans," Harvey asserted.[187] The incorporators proposed to call themselves "We Americans" and to incorporate in order to "combat by lawful means the advocacy and practice of Communism, Nazism, Fascism, or any other doctrine which may preach, teach, urge or practice hostility to or disrespect or modification of, by other than lawful or constitutional methods, the existing form of democratic government."[188] Although some officers of other veteran's groups believed that We Americans would be a valuable organization in the fight against subversion, others thought that Harvey merely sought to use the corporation to "fly his own kite" toward political office.[189] The announcement of the proposed creation of We Americans stirred commentary in the press. Prominent veterans and veterans' groups divided over whether to combat the isms or oppose combating them.

Justice Thomas C. Kadien, himself no stranger to politics,[190] did not like the group that proposed to take the name because, he said, all citizens should be able to use the name "We Americans." He ruled that no group should be permitted to incorporate the phrase as their exclusive designation.[191] Words in common usage already had been conscripted for ideological purposes, however, and expropriating the rhetoric of patriotism for political purposes was nothing new in the American experience. Conservative groups in the 1930s named themselves the Liberty Lobby and America First. A liberal group called itself The People's Lobby. Father Coughlin referred to his group as the National Union for Social Justice.[192] Kadien picked one group out of hundreds of equally guilty rhetorical offenders.[193]

Compared with the popular support judges received for rebuffing pro-German organizations during wartime, support for challenging the "unlawfulness" of pro-American patriotic societies was negligible. Zealous civilians had formed many new patriotic clubs in support of the armed services, but it appeared to Justice Frank E. Johnson that there were too many for them all to succeed. When the Victory Committee of Greenpoint Patriotic, Social, and Fraternal Club proposed to incorporate in order to support the troops still abroad and build "a spirit of friendship and good will among the returning men and women in the service,"[194] Justice Johnson withheld his approval based on his impression of the magnitude of the task compared with the parochialism of the group. Support for the troops was really a "countrywide undertaking," not to be restricted to Brooklyn, he declared.[195] Besides, there were "so many organizations already doing this kind of work, some of which need more money than they have been able to secure, that it seems unwise to add to the number of those who will make any demand upon such funds as are available."[196] Johnson's discretionary rationales were neither ideological, security-oriented, nor directed to protecting the tax base. Instead, he acted from paternalist assumptions about the neighborhood and his desire to protect the viability of already existing groups.

After World War II the use of the approval process to confine advocacy groups that the judges believed were irresponsible persisted and, if anything, increased. The exaggerated fear of subversion that took hold in many respects emanated from the fear of sabotage that first appeared on the home front during World War II. During the war, the media and the military persistently suggested that some disloyal Americans were trying to undermine the effort and that there were government secrets whose revelation could change the outcome of the war.[197] The Red Scare, which had begun to take shape shortly before World War II, resumed after the war ended, and self-styled patriotic organizations proposed to ferret out and punish disloyalty to American constitutional values.

In the furtherance of this ferreting out, new associations expressed their willingness to advocate the suspension or termination of constitutional guarantees of free expression. Ironically, even as the war came to an end and enthusiasm for the suppression of civil liberties grew, several prominent legal scholars were arguing that tolerance and respect for opposing views were the principal values of "Americanism," which distinguished American democracy from European fascism and communism.[198]

When a group calling itself the Patriotic Citizenship Association sought judicial approval of its charter in early 1945, liberal state Supreme Court justices twice withheld approval.[199] Justice Charles Froessel objected to language in the statement of the purposes of the Patriotic Citizenship Association asserting that the group would seek to amend the Constitution to suppress certain civil liberties and government benefits:

> [The Association will] promote . . . amendments to the Constitution . . . [to] provide that *all persons* who shall believe in, advise, advocate, or teach, or who are members of or affiliated with any organization . . . that . . . advocates the overthrow by force or violence of the Government . . . or who shall write, publish . . . or *who knowingly have in their possession for the purpose of circulation* [such materials] . . . *shall be deemed to have voluntarily relinquished and forfeited their rights of citizenship* . . . [and shall become] incapable of holding any office of trust . . . or of exercising any rights of citizens."[200]

The incorporators had taken patriotism too far, declared Justice Froessel, a Democrat.[201] They would destroy the meaning of freedom in the process of trying to save it. If they achieved their goals, the proposed amendments they wanted would constrict the liberties of well-intentioned citizens. What if the justice himself distributed copies of subversive materials to "leading patriotic citizens with a view to combating the subversive organization responsible for them," Froessel wanted to know?[202] The justice feared that he would have forfeited his rights of citizenship under the act.[203] It was "unthinkable that approval should be given on behalf of the people of the State of New York to anyone to incorporate for the purpose of advocating a constitutional amendment of this character."[204]

Another new test for lawfulness involved evaluating the dignity of a group's name. The outpouring of grief after the death of President Roosevelt led many groups to memorialize him in name, including the proposed "FDR Social and Civic Club," which by its name hoped "to aid in the perpetuation of the name of our beloved late leader and President of the United States of America."[205] Justice Hammer refused to allow the conversion of such an honorable name for such a common use:

> It clearly appears that to permit small scattered groups of individuals to appropriate the name [of Roosevelt] to their own peculiar uses and purposes can only result in detracting from the dignity and profound respect which should be accorded to it because of its potent meaning.[206]

There was already a Franklin D. Roosevelt Library and a Franklin D. Roosevelt Memorial Foundation organized under the membership corporation laws. The justice felt that these and other existing membership corporations were sufficient for the purposes of honor stated by the club. Who knew what the club would do or say once it had solicited support under the president's name? There was "grave danger that the vicarious use of the late President's name would be misleading and deceptive."[207] The name of Franklin Delano Roosevelt belonged, Justice Hammer stated, "to all the people of the United States, and, undoubtedly, of the world."[208]

## Protecting Consensus Values in the Postwar World[209]

After the war an ever broadening scope for inquiry into lawfulness of purpose gave room for judges to act vindictively toward the American relations of former enemies. Anti-immigrant sentiment persisted, tinged with a residue of wartime antagonism. In October 1945, Justice Johnson considered and turned down the application of nine residents of Brooklyn, "whose names would indicate that they are of Italian descent," [210] to incorporate the Mazzini Cultural Center, to foster "an appreciation of the musical arts, sponsoring musical productions, concerts and entertainments, encouraging musical education among under-privileged children ... and perpetuat[ing] ... '100 percent Americanism.'"[211]

Justice Johnson, regrettably, did not agree with the incorporators that Mazzini's name was suitable for such an organization. Mazzini stood among the most famous patriots and politicians in Italian history,[212] but Johnson found no "historical foundation" for assuming that Mazzini was "a musician or primarily interested in social intercourse."[213] He gratuitously offered the advice that if the group truly meant to foster American citizenship and preach "100 percent Americanism," there was "an abundance of American names that might be much more appropriate."[214]

Justice Hammer believed that one purpose of the approval process was to exclude groups insufficiently joyful about the American victory. Considering the recent triumph over the Axis, he believed that approval of the certificate of the Voters Alliance for Americans of German Ancestry should be withheld:

> In the present relations between this nation and Germany, when our military forces are still in occupation of that belligerent, with its leaders on trial as war criminals, and with peace not negotiated or agreed upon in treaty, it seems more than merely inadvisable to attempt organization under the name "Voters Alliance for Americans of German Ancestry."[215]

The membership of the society might consist of persons in a state of resentment about defeat, Hammer speculated, and their vituperative state of mind was sufficient to prevent incorporation.[216]

The sense that it was necessary to protect a fragile social order by supporting consensus values acquired considerable power after World War II. In their nonprofit cases, judges took an active role in trying to reinforce values that they believed were widely held and to strengthen institutions they believed worthy of support. In the religious sphere, for example, the perspective that there were "three *major* religious faiths" in America—Protestant, Catholic, and Jewish—took hold late in the 1940s as a defining characteristic of American society in distinction to the unitary religious states and godless countries under communist rule.[217] Survey data indicated that America had entered a new period of institutional religious commitment—a larger number and proportion of Americans indicated that they belonged to one denomination or another of these "major" faiths than ever before. Although laws regarding separation of church and state limited state sponsorship of religion, the three faiths alternated opening the sessions of Congress while the phrase "In God We Trust" became part of the national seal.[218] When governance disputes arose between different wings of churches, the courts sometimes became involved in interpreting nonprofit corporation laws.

Judicial involvement in supervising the creation of religiously affiliated nonprofits started earlier. In the 1920s, for example, differences between the urban and rural wings of the Pentecostal movement split the Church of God, the first formally organized Pentecostal denomination. The adherents of that church, led by Bishop A. J. Tomlinson, were once called Holy Rollers and claimed a national membership in excess of 100,000 people. In 1943 the bishop died and church overseers and ministers chose between Bishop Homer A. Tomlinson of Queens Village, Queens, and his brother Milton, who was living in Tennessee, to succeed him as general overseer. The schism between the two brothers was followed in the daily press. Milton prevailed; as part of a settlement, Homer departed from the Church of God of Prophecy and proposed to start the worldwide headquarters of the Church of God at his house on 224th St. in Queens.[219]

When the church applied for a not-for-profit certificate,[220] Justice Wenzel[221] turned the group down flat. Wenzel's justification was chiefly based on semantic considerations:

> I have before me for approval a certificate . . . offered by a group of co-religionists who wish to be known by the title "Church of God World Headquarters, Inc." The fact that all the incorporators but one are residents of Queens might seem to make the words "World Headquarters" a trifle grandiose, but these words might of course refer to the incorporators' ambitions rather than to their present sphere of influence. The appellation "Church of God," however, is one which the petitioners should not be permitted to arrogate to their own exclusive use by adoption as a corporate name. It is a generic term. Every church worthy of the name is a "Church of God" regardless of its sect or creed. We speak generally of "a House of God" and the "Church of God" in connection with every institution of divine worship. Application denied.[222]

Wenzel apparently knew little about the Church of God or its size. He understood, however, that the approval of a name such as "The Church of God" exclusively assigned to one group created a certain injustice to other faiths. He prevented the Pentecostal sect from adopting what he considered to be a grandiose corporate name based on the proprietary franchise that incorporation appeared to confer.

Federal and state constitutional protections for religious freedom limited judicial and administrative control over the formation, operation, and tax exemption of religious corporations more sharply than over other nonprofit groups that applied for charters.[223] Nonetheless, nonprofit associations that were not "primarily religious in nature" or were not otherwise subject to special laws for religious corporations faced the need to incorporate under ordinary incorporation rules, including in

New York the need to obtain judicial approval for their proposed corporate activity.[224]

Convinced that they were protecting the consumer against fraud and misrepresentation, justices sometimes demanded assurances of the success of religiously connected nonprofit ventures at the outset of their existence. In rejecting the certificate of the World Church of God, for example, the court commented on the grandiosity of that title, considering that the group consisted of five people living in Brooklyn.[225] Out of such dicta grew another test which, when invoked, called for a demonstration that the proposed purposes of a corporation could in fact be achieved.

The problem of whether to approve groups that were being organized to proselytize among other major faiths was troublesome. In 1944, two groups seeking to convert Jews to Christianity applied for approval of their certificates of incorporation. Although the religious affiliations of the incorporators were nowhere stated, the court observed that the signers had Jewish-sounding names.[226] Justice Frank E. Johnson[227] inferred that these incorporators had converted to Christianity and were "either connected with some Christian church or are desiring to independently do Christian missionary work."[228]

The state constitution, Justice Johnson wrote, mandated that "the free exercise and enjoyment of religious profession and worship, without discrimination or preference, shall forever be allowed in this state to all mankind."[229] The U.S. Supreme Court, furthermore, had not been sympathetic to the asserted rights of listeners to suppress conversion appeals.[230] The Supreme Court was too friendly, Justice Johnson suggested—to the Jehovah's Witnesses:

> [The Supreme Court] has gone very far in support of the right of Jehovah's Witnesses to try to convert others, and has even failed to come to the rescue of those who do not want to be converted and who insist that they are being annoyed by persistent, inconsiderate and fanatical missionaries who have no respect for privacy and who insist on interviewing people, who do not want to be interviewed, in trying to interest them in religious propaganda that they are bitterly opposed to being approached about.[231]

Although Justice Johnson acknowledged that these U.S. Supreme Court religious solicitation cases mandated deference toward the rights of missionaries, he distinguished them because they dealt with "clumsy local ordinances which violated fundamental principles."[232] He asserted that his designated role demanded that he review corporate purposes to determine whether they accorded with lawful public policy.[233]

Justice Johnson presented his own nonprofit sector corollary to First Amendment protection for missionary activities.[234] Prosletyzing, although lawful and protected, was not a purpose for which the privilege of incorporation would be available. In New York, at least, the right to the free exercise and enjoyment of a religious profession could not "be subjected to a state-approved corporate drive to interfere . . . with this very exercise and enjoyment."[235] The justice emphasized that incorporation was not necessary for the free expression of beliefs or the formation of associations. "What individuals may do," he stated, "is entirely different because they do not call upon the state to approve of their efforts."[236] Judicial approval and acceptance by the secretary of state of the certificate of incorporation would amount to approval of the proposed purposes:

> The decisions in the Jehovah's Witnesses cases therefore must not be misread to mean court approval of the right of one religious group to pursue another. No citizen ought to ask the state to give its indorsement to any corporate effort which is bound to result in an attempt to persuade citizens of a particular faith to abandon their faith for another.[237]

Turning persons of one faith toward another was something that groups could take up on their own, without any endorsement or support from the state. "Unincorporated associations, which do not ask the approval of the Supreme Court or the sanction and help of the state itself, ought to be just as able as any corporation to achieve the ends that these signers are aiming at," he decided, as he withheld his approval.[238] According to Johnson's understanding of constitutional rights, nonprofit incorporation was not a necessary condition for free expression; there could be no prejudice toward a group by withholding an incorporation charter.

Outside the context of religion, preserving social consensus meant insulating established social activities and causes from competition for clients and donors. This might call for the application of the same "confusion test" that had been used to protect groups a half century earlier.[239] In 1946, for example, the Boy Explorers of America submitted a proposed certificate to a New York state Supreme Court justice for approval. Justice Koch applauded the objectives, which were to provide boys with some of the experiences of professional explorers and "develop in each member the attitude that life is an expedition on which all unfamiliar fields are his to explore."[240]

The justice doubted that children or their parents would distinguish the Boy Explorers of America from the Boy Scouts of America Explorers program, however. Because the proceedings were ex parte in nature, he stated, the duty to proceed cautiously in approving a new group was greater, since applications for approval were free from opposition by other groups that might be affected by "the functioning of another organization of the same or similar name."[241] The bounds of discretion were defined in even broader terms than before: the justice stated that he was *required* to "draw freely on his own knowledge and experience as well as whatever other sources of information may be available to him in determining whether the proper exercise of judicial discretion dictates approval or disapproval in any particular case."[242]

Comparing the two organizations, Koch found that they were similar in essential respects. The Boy Scouts had a right to protection under the general rule against unfair competition first set out in *Benevolent & Protective Order of Elks*[243] because there appeared to be a "real danger that the general public might be misled and confused."[244] Justice Koch denied the application for approval of the Boy Explorers.[245]

At other times, protecting the status quo called for invoking a new test: requiring proof of a proposed enterprise's potential for success. One such occasion occurred when a group of New Yorkers proposed to establish an overseas hospital and solicit support in New York.[246] Justice Samuel M. Gold suggested that fund-raisers for the group would likely compete with similar charities.[247] The court doubted that the proposed corporation would succeed and supposed that it would "merely lead to confusion and misunderstanding and tend greatly to impair the work now being carried on by long established and well-known agencies. . . ."[248]

Justice James S. Brown was probably correct in applying the "potential for success" test to the application presented by five Brooklynites who all suffered from diarrhea. They proposed to incorporate the National Foundation for Diarrheal Diseases (NFDD).[249] Justice Brown assured the applicants that the court would not question the importance of devoting time and money to improving diarrhea treatments or the altruistic motives of the group. He suggested, however, that the NFDD was neither a "foundation" (suggesting a corporation with funds for contributing to the endowment of institutions) nor "national" (suggesting a nationwide scope). Although national associations for cancer, polio, and other diseases had probably begun on a shoestring too, the justice suggested that it would be necessary for a diarrheal organization to think small.[250]

The justices also privileged existing groups by claiming, without evidence of harm either to other organizations or to the public, that new organizations were impermissibly duplicative. Justice Stoddart refused to approve of the Waldemar Cancer Research Association because the American Cancer Society, a national organization, already solicited in New York and used its funds to support cancer research.[251] "I do not believe the public should have numerous groups soliciting funds when one well-recognized and well-operated organization is seeking their contributions," the justice concluded.[252] Justice Samuel M. Gold declined the certificate of the International Sports Foundation because "the court knows of its own knowledge that there are already in existence many organizations whose main purpose is to provide athletic and recreational advantages . . . for the boys and girls of America."[253] Without examining the question empirically, the court supposed that even if the organization lived up to its name, the competition itself might be harmful to the larger public good.[254]

Given the breadth of interpretive authority that had been read into the incorporation laws and the difficult standard for review on appeal, [255] appeals from a judicial disapproval were extremely rare. When in 1957 Justice Henry Clay Greenberg denied the Metropolitan Republican Club's petition to incorporate based on the refusal of the Republican county chairman to consent to the club's formation,[256] the club appealed.[257] The appellate division affirmed the disapproval, as did the court of appeals, which stated that the issue was whether withholding consent was "unreasonable" within the meaning of the Membership Corporations Law.[258] In the case of political parties, the law required the consent of county party chairmen before a certificate of incorporation could be filed with the secretary of state.[259]

Judge Desmond of the court of appeals dissented because he believed the refusal to charter a political organization violated democratic principles. The only legislative purpose for the imposed requirement of consent by party chairmen, he argued, was to "eliminate spurious political clubs . . . used for the conduct of gambling and vice."[260] There was no legislative purpose, he protested, to provide county chairmen with a veto power over the organization of political clubs by party members who happened to be rivals or critics, and yet "in this proceeding the statute is allowed to be used for just that latter purpose."[261] The trial court and the appellate division majority decisions, however, indicated that it was a sufficient basis for the county chairman's denial that he "thought there were already enough Republican clubs in New York City" and that petitioners, "concededly good party members, should carry on their political activities not independently but under the supervision of the county committee of which respondent is the chairman."[262] To the justices below and to a majority of the court of appeals it had seemed reasonable for the county chairman to use an established discretionary tool that allowed him to refrain from signing "a warrant for his and the organization's destruction."[263]

Although judges in New York and administrators in other states agonized over many hard cases, there were also cases that caused few qualms. The Ohio Supreme Court (Ohio's highest court) did not have to struggle to reach the conclusion that the secretary of state had the power to reject a proposed certificate of incorporation submitted by an association of nudists.[264] The association aimed to "promote and develop a strong nudist movement composed of member clubs and individual members" and to "provide private facilities where members of both sexes may congregate together and . . . practice nudism."[265] Provisions of the state's penal code prohibited the exposure of private parts in the presence of two or more persons of the opposite sex, and this part of the penal code had never been challenged as an intrusion on the constitutional right to free expression.[266] Forming a corporation to provide a place where both sexes could congregate together in the nude, the court held, "clearly would be violative [of the Ohio Code] . . . which prohibits the practice of nudism, regardless of the belief of those desiring to practice it as a doctrine of life, cult or sect."[267]

Here was one straightforward instance of a proposed nonprofit corporation disapproved because it was formed, at least in part, for a purpose that literally was unlawful.[268]

*          *          *

Examining the relation between the historical record of the judicial and administrative approvals and disapprovals and the larger pattern of social and political developments makes it clear that for better than half a century, those who exercised the authority to approve or withhold approval of nonprofit charters acted on the basis of an evolving concept of the public good. But this concept of good scarcely developed out of an autonomous, internally driven form of legal discourse among judges about public policy and legal doctrine.[269] Instead, it came from personal convictions, culturally derived. If it is true, as one scholar has put it, that "occidental law may accurately be described as a 'relatively autonomous' cultural form,"[270] then here was a glaring exception to that norm: here was an environment in which administrative, judicial, and statutory standards were open-ended and courts acted as their own bureaucrats.

In this environment judges found it easy to act on their convictions, since they had no reason to fear reversal or public derision by doing so. On the contrary, they viewed the approval process as an opportunity for receiving social approval and even acclaim, since they did what was expected of them: they preserved the privileges of the nonprofit sector for "worthy" groups.

In most of these cases tax benefits were no better than a secondary objective of the groups trying to incorporate. Almost always these "would-be nonprofits" hoped mainly to obtain recognition that they were, in the eyes of democratically chosen state officials and judges, acceptable voluntary associations entitled to corporate status, public support, legal protection, and community respect. Judges and other state officials believed they were entitled to exercise their discretion because they were elected or appointed through a form of democratic process, possessed of appropriate professional skills, and endowed with appropriate statutory power.[271] They believed that the legislatures and communities around them expected and wanted them to disapprove of nonprofit corporations that they themselves did not like.

Although constitutional controversies swirled around the action of the U.S. Supreme Court when it invalidated state legislative actions,[272] no concern was expressed about common law judges having excessive authority to interpret legislative enactments or create rules out of whole cloth. The judges expressed few doubts about the legitimacy of turning to whatever sources they wished and in whatever ways they wanted to make determinations about "lawfulness" or public usefulness.

There was in particular no great debate about whether common law judges generally were misapplying statutes or misinterpreting the constitutional rights of individuals or possibly groups. However personally troubled these judges might have been by the First Amendment associational or expressive rights of groups to incorporate,[273] their written opinions reflected little self-doubt about their authority or ability to deprive groups of the right to associate in corporate form. They ruled without attracting discernible opposition to their conduct.[274]

Their interpretive perspective was natural and legitimate; as they saw it, their common law approach had established a zone in which they could give free play to their social and political and economic values within the larger area of common law adjudication, in which a philosophy of judicial restraint applied.[275] Subjective evaluation and moral approbation entered judicial deliberation directly through evaluative concepts such as "lawfulness" or "public policy" that had been placed into the statute.[276] The doctrine they established appeared necessary to preserve American values or to protect consumers and the donating public from abuse. Exercising appropriate discretion meant conferring the privileges of nonprofit status only on exemplary groups.

How well did this system of supervision work? Some of the most important dimensions of this question can't be answered here. There is no proof available that the public was better protected against unscrupulous nonprofit organizations by the discretionary conception of nonprofit corporate formation than it would be in later years. There is no evidence that judicial gatekeeping worked efficiently in the sense that it served to allow an appropriate number of new nonprofits to be born or an appropriate number of new nonprofit missions to flourish, or that it deprived an appropriate number of charters to groups that should not have been chartered. There is no clear way to measure the harm that free speech suffered and/or the social cohesiveness gained by discretionary review. Nor is it possible to know whether groups that were denied nonprofit incorporation under the discretionary model continued to pursue identical goals and objectives through other legal forms.

It hardly shows that the discretionary model of nonprofit chartering "worked," furthermore, to state that there was no generalized uneasiness about the way the legal system dealt with nonprofit groups throughout the earlier period or to observe that scandals like the Decimo case were rare and that praise for charities and philanthropies was common. The fact that the number of nonprofit corporations did not grow rapidly or attract attention may reflect excessive supervision or insufficient resources devoted to important causes. There is thus no proof that the discretionary system worked particularly well—only a strong likelihood that it reinforced confidence in the good faith and value of existing voluntary associations and nonprofit groups.

Courts appeared best adapted to the task of sorting out worthy and unworthy purposes, useful and worthless causes by exercising a broad discretion under general grants of authority. "Even though economists and sociologists might differ irreconcilably as to whether any particular corporate purpose is injurious to the community," wrote one student of the nonprofit chartering system in 1940, "the judges of the various courts . . . are agencies well calculated to estimate the practical future effect of a proposed nonprofit corporation."[277] There might be "isolated cases" in which courts provided "unsound reasons in support of their action in refusing applications for corporate charters," but these were "few as compared with the great number of charters granted."[278]

Here was a situation in which the law unquestionably encouraged judges to embrace a cultural dynamic instead of the legal one. As Justice Cardozo otherwise had stated it more generally, law accepted "as the pattern of its justice the morality of the community whose conduct it assumes to regulate."[279]

### Notes

1. Ambrose Bierce, The Devil's Dictionary 152 (1911).
2. New York is in many respects a unique jurisdiction. Each region of the country reflected its own traditions of voluntarism and attitudes toward the support of charities through its laws. In the antebellum South, for example, Catholic associations sometimes faced particularly difficult obstacles to the formation of welfare organizations and educational institutions. Racial policies also left a permanent imprint on the creation of social and religiously oriented nonprofits. In New England, nonprofit corporations were popular vehicles to accomplish quasi-governmental ends, and "public tasks tended increasingly to be delegated to corporations—albeit ones closely controlled by the state." *See* Peter Hall, Inventing the Nonprofit Sector and Other Essays on Philanthropy, Voluntarism, and Nonprofit Organizations (1992).

Nonetheless, New York, for most of the history of the United States, has been among the most important states, if not the most important state, in which non-profit incorporation occurs. It is not possible to know precisely how New York's judicial supervision was dissimilar to the bureaucratic supervision that existed in states where no advance judicial approval was necessary for incorporation. Nonetheless, cases evaluating along similar lines the proposed purposes of non-profit charters or amendments to charters for pecuniary motives and lawfulness were reported occasionally in many states, including Alabama, Arkansas, California, Colorado, Delaware, Florida, Indiana, Iowa, Michigan, Minnesota, Mississippi, Missouri, Nebraska, Louisiana, New Jersey, Tennessee, Texas, Washington, and Wisconsin, and more numerously in Illinois, Ohio, and Pennsylvania. *See* 16 A.L.R.2D 1345 and supp. At least six states offered statutory grounds for judicial discretion to be exercised. *See* note, *State Control over Political Organizations: First Amendment Checks on Powers of Regulation*, 66 YALE L.J. 545 n. 41 (1957); *see also* note, *Judicial Approval As a Prerequisite to Incorporation of Non-Profit Organizations in New York and Pennsylvania*, 55 COLUM. L. REV. 380 (1955).

3. Individuals of great wealth usually had little trouble obtaining corporate charters for the establishment of private universities, libraries, or specific benevolent societies. But even Carnegie, Rockefeller, Vanderbilt, and other industrialists faced opposition to obtaining charters from courts and state legislatures for the establishment of general purpose charitable institutions, trusts, and "foundations." As Peter Hall has written, both legal uncertainties and the political climate contributed to the difficulty of obtaining charters for foundations designed for open-ended and vaguely defined charitable purposes such as "for the good of mankind" or "for the permanent improvement of social conditions." President Theodore Roosevelt, for instance, opposed the chartering of the Rockefeller foundations in 1910–1913 because he feared that they would serve his own private interests. Peter Hall, INVENTING THE NONPROFIT SECTOR 47–48 (1992).

4. 1895 N.Y. LAWS, ch. 559 §31.

5. *In re* Agudath Hakehiloth, 18 Misc. 717, 42 N.Y.S. 985 (Sup. Ct. 1896).

6. Pryor's background reveals a patrician southern upbringing disrupted by the Civil War, and some discomfort with immigrant life in urban New York. After graduating from Hampden and Sidney College and later taking several courses at the University of Virginia, Pryor was admitted to its bar, but he decided to turn to journalism instead. He became influential in Virginia politics and was elected to Congress in 1859. Upon secession he joined the Confederate army and was said to be the last survivor of the Confederate assault on Fort Sumter. Taken prisoner by Union soldiers, he was pardoned by President Lincoln, moved to New York, and took up writing for the *New York Daily News*. He studied New York law for a short while and in 1890 was appointed to the New York State Supreme Court at the request of one of his former Union enemies. See *Gen. Roger A. Pryor Dies in 91st Year*, N.Y. TIMES, Mar. 15, 1919, at 15 col.3.

7. Agudath Hakehiloth, 24 N.Y.S. at 985.

8. *Id.* at 986.

9. *Id.*

10. *Id.* (*quoting* People v. Moses, 140 N.Y. 215, 35 N.E. 499; *citing* N.Y. PENAL CODE §259).

11. *Id.* at 987.

12. *See In re* Wendover Athletic Ass'n, 70 Misc. 273, 128 N.Y.S. 561, 562 (Sup. Ct. 1911).

13. J. G. Sutherland, STATUTES AND STATUTORY CONSTRUCTION §364 (235) (1880, 1st ed.).

14. Riggs v. Palmer, 115 N.Y. 506, 509 (1889) (refusing to enforce a testimonial bequest to a murderous inheritor).

15. *Id.*

16. Platt Potter, A GENERAL TREATISE ON STATUTES: THEIR RULES OF CONSTRUCTION, AND THE PROPER BOUNDARIES OF LEGISLATION AND OF JUDICIAL INTERPRETATION. BY SIR FORTUNATUS DWARRIS, KNT., WITH AMERICAN NOTES AND ADDITIONS AND WITH NOTES AND MAXIMS OF CONSTITUTIONAL AND OF STATUTE CONSTRUCTION 296–329, 304 (1885).

17. *See infra,* ch. 4.

18. *Id.* at 313.

19. *Id.* at 311 (*citing* DeAgu. Scient lib. 8, c.3 aph 45).

20. *Id.* at 305 (*citing* BACON'S WORKS vol. 7, p. 148: "Optima est lex, quoe minimum relinquit arbitrio judis; optimus judex, qui minimum sibi"). *Id.*

21. *Id.* at 311.

22. *See* Kim Lane Scheppele, *Facing Facts in Legal Interpretation, in* LAW AND THE ORDER OF CULTURE 45–47 (1991) (*discussing* Riggs v. Palmer, 115 N.Y. 506 [1889]).

23. §41 of the Membership Corporations Law provided that five or more persons could become a membership corporation by making, acknowledging, and filing a certificate stating the name, object, location, and number and names of directors, and "such certificate shall not be filed without the written approval . . . of a justice of the Supreme Court."

24. *In re* Wendover Athletic Ass'n, 70 Misc. 273, 128 N.Y.S. 561, 562 (Sup. Ct. 1911).

25. *Id.* Justice Goff served as a New York State Supreme Court justice from 1906 until 1919; he was among the few justices who did not study law systematically at a law school. An Irish immigrant, he graduated from Cooper Union College and was admitted to the bar in 1879 after an apprenticeship with the U.S. attorney. *See Ex-Justice Goff,* N.Y. TIMES, Nov. 10, 1924, at 17 col. 3.

26. *In re* Wendover Athletic Ass'n.

27. Wendover Athletic Ass'n, 128 N.Y.S. at 561–62.

28. *See* Thorstein Veblen, THE THEORY OF THE LEISURE CLASS (1901).

29. *See* Arnold M. Paul, *Legal Progressivism, the Courts, and the Crisis of the 1890s,* 83 BUS. HIST. REV. 497 (1959); *reprinted* in Friedman and Scheiber, AMERICAN LAW AND THE CONSTITUTIONAL ORDER 283, 537 n. 2 (1988) (adopting the terms "progressivism" and "progressive" as descriptive of "a political point of view favoring substantial use of government as a lever of change upon existing socioeconomic patterns").

30. *See* Robert Wiebe, THE SEARCH FOR ORDER (1967); *see also* Martin Sklar, THE CORPORATE RECONSTRUCTION OF AMERICAN CAPITALISM, 1890–1916 (1988).

31. *See* Gerard C. Henderson, THE FEDERAL TRADE COMMISSION (1927).

32. *See* Norman Isaac Silber, TEST AND PROTEST: THE INFLUENCE OF CONSUMERS UNION (1983).

33. *See* Otis A. Pease, THE RESPONSIBILITIES OF AMERICAN ADVERTISING (1958).

34. Section 4 of the 1914 Federal Trade Commission Act, for example, included a definition of a "corporation" that meant "any company or association incorporated or unincorporated which is organized to carry on business for profit. . . ." Federal Trade Commission Act Pub. L. No. 203, 38 Stat. 311 (1914).

35. *See* Benevolent & Protective Order of Elks v. Improved Benevolent & Protective Order of Elks of the World, 98 N.E. 756, 757 (N.Y. 1912).

36. *Id.*

37. *Id.*

38. *Id.* at 757.

39. *Id.*

40. Misuse of corporate names had been actionable as a trade tort by business corporations for many years, but action by nonbusiness corporations was a recent development. It began in New York in 1897, when Major Asa Bird Gardiner asked the secretary of state and the attorney general to refuse to grant a charter to the Plattsburg Society of War of 1812 because it had taken the same name as his own Society of the War of 1812. This was "a monumental exhibition of cheek" and an "impertinent invasion" of the rights of club men, Major Gardiner insisted. *See* N.Y. TIMES, Feb. 26, 1897 at 4 col. 4; N.Y. TIMES, Feb. 28, 1897 at 10 col. 5.

After an adversarial hearing, the secretary of state approved the rival's charter and informed Gardiner that his only course of action would be a civil suit. N.Y. TIMES, Feb. 28, 1897 at 10 col. 5; Society of War of 1812 v. Society of War of 1812, 46 A.D. 568, 572, 62 N.Y.S. 355, 357–59 (App. Div. 1900). The rationale for prohibiting similarity in organizational names among for-profit businesses was rooted squarely on unfair competition terms, however, but nonprofit corporations were not by theory in competition with one another. Granting an injunction to the Society of War of 1812, therefore, depended on a more indirect line of reasoning related to consumer protection rather than unfair competition. This reasoning was adopted both in *Society of War of 1812* and in other cases. *See, e.g.,* International Committee Y.W.C.A. v. Young Women's C.A., 62 N.E. 551 (Ill. 1901) (Illinois Supreme Court enjoined a breakaway segment of the Young Women's Christian Association of Chicago [YWCA] from operating or soliciting funds under the name "International Committee Young Women's Christian Association" on the grounds that it might deceive or mislead the public).

41. 98 N.E. at 757–58 (explaining that N.Y. CORP. LAW, ch. 40 [Consol. 1909]) was originally enacted in 1908 yet it "did not take effect until after judgment was rendered in this action").

42. N.Y. CORP. LAW, ch. 40 (Consol. 1909); *see also* 98 N.E. at 758.

43. 136 A.D. 896, 120 N.Y.S. 1113; *see also Negro Elks Restrained*, N.Y. TIMES, May 23, 1912 at 10 cols. 3, 7. A *quo warranto* action challenged the usurpation of a franchise ("by what warrant?").

44. 98 N.E. at 758.

45. *Id.*

46. *See, e.g., In re* Incorporation of Howard Aid Society, 160 N.Y.S. 789 (Supreme Court, Kings County, Special Term 1916) ("the use of the word 'aid' in the name is not allowable, as that would clearly lead the general public to believe that some 'benefit' was to be derived from membership in the corporation"). *Id.*

47. Regarding courts and race during the Progressive Era, and the historiography thereof, *see* Randall Kennedy, *Race Relations Law and the Tradition of Celebration: The Case of Professor Schmidt*, 86 COLUM. L. REV. 1622 (1986).

48. Benevolent & Protective Order of Elks, 98 N.E. at 757. It is noteworthy that well before the U.S. Supreme Court determined that race-specific policies contained in private covenants warranted strict constitutional scrutiny, *see, e.g.*, Shelley v. Kramer, 334 U.S. 1 (1948), New York courts were using the doctrine of purposeful color blindness to the disadvantage of the black minority. *See* T. A. Aleinikoff, *A Case for Race-Consciousness*, 91 COLUM. L. REV. 1060 (1991).

49. *See, e.g.*, Constance Rourke, AMERICAN HUMOR (1931); Henry Steele Commager, THE SEARCH FOR A USABLE PAST, AND OTHER ESSAYS IN HISTORIOGRAPHY (1967).

50. *See, e.g.*, William Preston, ALIENS AND DISSENTERS: FEDERAL SUPPRESSION OF RADICALS, 1903–1933 (1963); Robert K. Murray, RED SCARE (1955).

51. Preston, *id.*

52. *See, e.g.*, Vincent Blasi, *The Pathological Perspective and the First Amendment*, 85 COLUM. L. REV. 449 (1985) (considering the post–World War I "red scare" cases to have eroded "core" constitutional values).

53. *See* Application of Catalonian Nationalist Club of New York, 112 Misc. 207, 184 N.Y.S. 132 (Sup. Ct. 1920).

54. *Id.*

55. *Id.* at 133.

56. *Id.*

57. Justice Edward G. Whitaker was born in New York and educated in Germany. He was admitted to the bar in 1876 and became deputy attorney general of the state in 1884. He served on the New York State Supreme Court from 1912 until 1926. For many years a prominent leader of the bar and a well-known social figure, Justice Whitaker was a president of the New York State Bar Association and a president of the Manhattan Country Club, as well as a president of the Long Island Country Club. *See Edward G. Whitaker, Ex-Justice, Is Dead*, N.Y. TIMES, July 26, 1931 at 4 col. 1.

58. *Id.*

59. 184 N.Y.S. 132.

60. *Id.*

61. *Id.*

62. *Id.*

63. Lithuanians of various religious affiliations immigrated to the United States in substantial numbers at the turn of the century. They quickly developed a diverse religious and political culture, forming numerous Lithuanian socialist newspapers, magazines, and publishing houses. By 1919 the Lithuanian Socialist Federation had close to 200 local lodges. By 1920, however, the Lithuanian socialist movement in the United States had lost much momentum as a result of its leaders being arrested or driven into hiding during the postwar red scare. Supporters of Bolshevism soon gained control of many of the local socialist clubs and formally affiliated themselves with the Communist Party of America. *See* HARVARD ENCYCLOPEDIA OF AMERICAN ETHNIC GROUPS 670–72 (1980).

64. *See In re* Lithuanian Workers' Literature Soc'y, 187 N.Y.S. 612, 614 (App. Div. 1921) (quoting appellant's petition).

65. *See id.* at 612–17.

66. Justice Isaac N. Mills was in the eighth generation of a family of Connecticut farmers who had come from England in 1630. He served on the New York State Supreme Court between 1906 and 1921, after six years in the state senate. He was a graduate of Amherst College and Columbia Law School, from which he graduated in 1876. Justice Mills was a member of conventional fraternal, nonideological, nonprofit organizations, including the Hiawatha Lodge, the Royal Arch Masons, the Bethlehem Commandery, the Knights Templar, hunting clubs, and fishing clubs, in addition to being active in Amherst College alumni affairs. *See Isaac N. Mills Dies: While in the Surf*, N.Y. TIMES, July 15, 1929, at 21.

67. 187 N.Y.S. at 614.

68. *Id.* at 614–15.

69. *Id.* at 614.

70. *Id.*

71. *Id.* at 615.

72. Why Justice Whitaker did not read a few of the writings of Karl Marx in the original is uncertain. Such reading might well have led him to affirm his conclusion that Marx theorized the inevitability of violent change under some economic and social circumstances and applauded actions by workers to overthrow those who dominated them. Marx and Engels made this plain, for example, in the *Communist Manifesto* (1848): "Communists disdain to conceal their views and aims. They openly declare that their ends can be attained only by the forcible overthrow all existing social conditions. Let the ruling classes tremble at a communist revolution. The proletarians have nothing to lose but their chains. They have a world to win." Karl Marx and Frederick Engels, THE COMMUNIST MANIFESTO (1848); Internet ed. <http://csf colorado.edu/psn/marx/-archive>. On the other hand, neither Marx nor American followers of Marx in Whitaker's day believed that the triumph of Marxism in the United States would or should occur in the violent manner of the French or Russian Revolutions; nor did many engage in violent struggle themselves. Many Marxists believed that the principles of Karl Marx would inevitably lead to a victory at the ballot box for Communists in America without revolutionary bloodshed and within the democratic system. *See, e.g.,* Louis B. Boudin, THE THEORETICAL SYSTEM OF KARL MARX IN THE LIGHT OF RECENT CRITICISM (1907) (1968 ed.); *see also* Marc Rohr, *Communists and the First Amendment: The Shaping of Freedom of Advocacy in the Cold War Era*, 28 SAN DIEGO L. REV. 1, 148 (1991) (judicial treatment of Communist ideology during the Cold War); Louis B. Boudin, *"Seditious Doctrines" and the "Clear and Present Danger" Rule (Part II)*, 38 VA. L. REV. 315, 354 (1952) (suggesting that the Russian version of violent overthrow was inapplicable to other contexts).

73. *See* John Spargo, KARL MARX: HIS LIFE AND WORK (1910); *see also* John Spargo, THE BITTER CRY OF CHILDREN (1903).

74. *In re* Lithuanian Workers' Literature Soc'y, 187 N.Y.S. 612, 616 (App. Div. 1921).

75. *Id.* at 617. When the *New York Times* reported the opinion, it suggested that the amendment had been intended to exclude socialists rather than admit Marxists. The *Times* headline read, *Marxian Socialists Defeated in Court; Literature Society Must Not Bar Those Opposed to Direct Action Principles. See* N.Y. TIMES, Apr. 1, 1921 at 18 col. 11.

76. *See In re* Daughters of Israel Orphan Aid Soc'y, Inc., 125 Misc. 217 (N.Y. Sup. Ct. 1925).

77. Justice Aaron J. Levy came to the New York State Supreme Court in 1923 after having been a majority leader (Democrat) of the New York Assembly. He was a graduate of Cooper Union and New York University Law School. In this way his ascendance to the bench—from practice to politics to the judiciary—fit the traditional pattern. His urban immigrant upbringing, however, could not be said to fit that of most of his fellow jurists. As can be seen in this case, as well as the rulings of Justice Levy discussed later in the work, his loyalties—ethnic or ideological or personal—counted more than theory or doctrine.

There were several challenges to Levy's fitness to serve during his career, including accusations of bribery and influence peddling on behalf of friends, operating a business while on the court, and "technical difficulties" that occurred while president of a boy's orphanage. He resigned in 1951, and in 1952 the State Crime Commission held hearings that revealed an unexplained excess of $80,561 in expenditures over Levy's known cash receipts for the period 1946–1951. *See Aaron J. Levy, 74, State Ex-Justice,* N.Y. TIMES, Nov. 22, 1955, at 35 col. 4.

78. *See In re* Daughters of Israel Orphan Aid Soc'y, Inc., 125 Misc. 217, 210 N.Y.S. 541, 543 (Sup. Ct. 1925).

79. *Id.*

80. *Id.* at 546.

81. *Id.* at 547.

82. *Id.*

83. *Id.*

84. *See* Antonin Scalia, *The Rule of Law As a Law of Rules,* 56 U. CHI. L. REV. 1175 (1989). Although there is general agreement with the above proposition, just what sources and analytical techniques should be used to assist judges in the comprehension of different types of rules is the subject of much discussion. *See, e.g.,* Robert C. Post, *Scalia's Originalism,* in NEW YORK REVIEW OF BOOKS (1998).

85. *See, e.g.,* William Leuchtenburg, THE PERILS OF PROSPERITY (1958); Loren Baritz, THE CULTURE OF THE TWENTIES (1978).

86. *See* Southerland ex rel. v. Decimo Club, Inc., 142 A. 786 (Del. Ch. 1928).

87. *Id.*

88. *Id.; See also Decimo Club Faces Boston Investigation,* N.Y. TIMES, May 17, 1927 at 26 col. 5.

89. 142 A.786.

90. *Id.* at 787.

91. *Id.*

92. *Id.; See Says Reading Took $25,000 Decimo Fee,* N.Y. TIMES, Feb. 15, 1928 at 7 col. 1.

93. Decimo Club, 142 A. at 787–88.

94. In an attempt to secure better treatment for himself, Monjar accused Attorney General Reading of Massachusetts of taking a bribe from him In return for discontinuing his own investigation and intervening with New York's Attorney General to discontinue the New York proceedings which had enjoined it from doing business there. Reading's career was ruined. *See Bay State Has Case Unique in Its Annals,* N.Y. TIMES, June 10, 1928, at 2 col. 4; *See Says Reading took $25,000 Decimo Fee,* N.Y. TIMES, Feb. 15, 1928, at 7 col. 1.

95. *See $1,020,000 Fraud Laid to the Decimo Club,* N.Y. TIMES, July 16, 1927, at 1 col. 13; *see also Ottinger to Get Decimo Suit Papers,* N.Y. TIMES, Mar. 1, 1928, at 16 col. 1.

96. *See $1,020,000 Fraud Laid to the Decimo Club,* N.Y. TIMES, July 16, 1927, at 1 col. 3.

97. *See Court Vacates Order Against Decimo Club,* N.Y. TIMES, Oct. 5, 1927, at 29 col. 6.

98. Decimo Club, 142 A. at 790.

99. *Id.*

100. *Id.*

101. *Id.*

102. *Id.*

103. Decimo Club, 142 A. at 787.

104. *Id.* at 791.

105. *Id.*

106. *Id.*

107. *Citing* Read v. Tidewater Coal Exchange, Inc., 13 Del. Ch. 195, 116 A. 898 (1922).

108. Decimo Club, 142 A. at 790 (*citing* Read v. Tidewater Coal Exchange, Inc., 13 Del. ch. 195, 116 A. 898 (1922).

109. *Id.* at 792.

110. *Id.*

111. *Id.*

112. *Id.* at 792–93; *see also In re* Henry County Mat. Burial Ass'n, 77 S.W.2d 124 (Mo. App. 1934) (affirming trial court's revocation of a nonprofit burial association where removal of the association to a different county promoted the funeral business of the association's president).

113. A U.S. attorney later filed a fraud complaint charging that the career success training offered was "merely a subterfuge . . . to win the confidence of these people and induce them to purchase securities of doubtful or no worth" and also presented evidence that Decimo misrepresented itself as having a "professional faculty," which in fact consisted of ordinary tailors. *See Grand Jury to Sift Monjar's Company,* N.Y. TIMES, Oct. 19, 1928, at 21 col. 6; *Stock Sales Take Monjar into Court,* N.Y. TIMES, Dec. 5, 1929, at 51 col. 1. Monjar agreed to a permanent injunction on the sale of his stock in 1930. *Monjar Accepts Ban on Sale of His Stock,* N.Y. TIMES, Apr. 24, 1930, at 13 col. 4.

114. Monjar's encounter with the law did not persuade him to cease in his schemes, however. A decade later, Monjar faced another indictment for another "gigantic money-making swindle," in connection with the Mantle Club, a "na-

tional social and fraternal association" that claimed of 60,000 persons nationwide. *See Mantle Club Is Accused*, N.Y. TIMES, Dec. 7, 1941. The Mantle Club board included persons previously on the board of the Decimo Club. *Id.; see also SEC Seeks Injunction*, N.Y. TIMES, Feb. 25, 1942 at 24 col. 3. In 1943, fifteen years after the Decimo scandal, Monjar and other Mantle Club officers were found guilty of mail fraud and violations of the 1933 Securities Act. He was sentenced to five years in prison and fined $49,000. *H.B. Monjar Guilty in Mail Case*, N.Y. TIMES, May 28, 1943 at 14 col. 4; *Monjar and 11 Aides Sentenced to Prison*, N.Y. TIMES, June 26, 1943, at 11 col. 3.

115. Many producers lowered the quality of the products and services that they sold in order to lower their prices, to find customers who had less to spend than before. Standards for hundreds of products declined. The code mechanism established by the National Recovery Administration (proposed in 1934) was in fact designed among other purposes, to diminish deteriorations in quality by getting producers to agree on common standards of quality. *See* Silber, *supra* n. 32.

116. *In re* Rox Athletic Ass'n of McKees Rocks, Pa., 178 A. 464, 465 (Pa. 1935).

117. *Id.*

118. *Id.*

119. *Id.*

120. *Id.*

121. *Id.*

122. *See supra* (illustrated in the case of the feuding Elks in 1912).

123. *Id.*

124. *See generally* William E. Forbath, LAW AND THE SHAPING OF THE AMERICAN LABOR MOVEMENT (1991); Melvyn Dubofsky, THE STATE AND LABOR IN MODERN AMERICA (1994).

125. *Id.; see also* Katherine Van Wezel Stone, Rethinking Labor Voluntarism, Legal Personality, the Enforcement of Trade Agreements, and the AFL's Attitude toward the State in the Progressive Era (Oct. 1996 draft).

126. Norris-LaGuardia Act, 29 U.S.C. §101 et seq. (1988); Wagner Act, 49 Stat. 449 (1935) (codified as amended at 29 U.S.C. §151–69 [1988]).

127. *See* Forbath, *supra* n. 124; Dubofsky, *supra* n. 124; *see also* Milton Meltzer, BREAD AND ROSES: THE STRUGGLE OF AMERICAN LABOR, 1865–1915 (1991); *see also* Howard L. Oleck, NONPROFIT CORPORATIONS, ORGANIZATIONS, AND ASSOCIATIONS (1988).

128. *See* NOT-FOR-PROFIT ACT OF ILL, §29 (as amended 1937); ILL. REV. STATS. 1937, ch. 32, §158.

129. People ex rel. Padula v. Hughes, 296 Ill. App. 587, 16 N.E.2d 922, 923 (1938).

130. *Id.*

131. *Id.*

132. *Id.* at 923. *See also In re* Incorporation of Philadelphia Labor's Non-Partisan League Club, 328 Pa. 465, 469, 196 A. 22, 24 (1938).

133. *Hughes*, 16 N.E.2d at 923.

134. *Id.* at 923–24.

135. *Id.*

136. *See* N.Y. GEN. CORP. LAW, ch. 820, sec. 1, §9-a (1937); MEM. CORP. LAW, sec. 2, §11, subdiv. 1-a.

137. *See* N.Y. GEN. CORP. LAW, ch. 820, sec. 1 §9-a (1937).

138. *See* Campbell v. Picard, 300 N.Y.S. 515, 517 (Sup. Ct. 1937).

139. *Id.*

140. *Id.* The application for an order reversing the determination of the Board of Standards and Appeals was made under article 78, sections 1283–1306 of the New York Civil Practice Act.

141. *See* Campbell v. Picard, 165 Misc. 148, 300 N.Y.S. 515, 517 (Sup. Ct. 1937).

142. *Id.* at 522 (*citing* Matter of Daughters of Israel Orphan Aid Soc'y, Inc., 125 Misc. 217, 210 N.Y.S. 541 [Sup. Ct. 1925]).

143. *Id.*

144. *See also Orders Charter Ruling*, N.Y. TIMES, Oct. 8, 1937 at 10 col. 2; *Union Charter Is Denied*, N.Y. TIMES, Oct. 15, 1937, at 5 col. 3 (reporting opinion).

145. *See In re* Jewish Consumptives' Relief Soc'y, 92 N.Y.S.2d 673, 674 (Sup. Ct. 1949).

146. *Id.*

147. *See* People v. Jewish Consumptives' Relief Soc'y, 196 Misc. 579, 92 N.Y.S.2d 157 (Sup. Ct. 1949).

148. Jewish Consumptives' Relief Soc'y, 92 N.Y.S.2d at 764.

149. *Id.* at 675.

150. N.Y. MEM. CORP. LAW §10 (amended by 1958 N.Y. LAWS, ch. 598, sec. 1) *See also In re* Excavating Machine Owners Ass'n, Inc., 205 N.Y.S.2d 265 (Sup. Ct. 1960) (evaluating attorney general's objections on antitrust grounds, as the result of notice and pursuant to authority in the N.Y. GEN. BUS. Law §343, to the incorporation of association of machinery owners).

151. *See* Arthur D. Morse, WHILE SIX MILLION DIED: A CHRONICLE OF AMERICAN APATHY (1968); Robert Michael Marrus, THE HOLOCAUST IN HISTORY (1987); Lucy S. Dawidowicz, THE WAR AGAINST THE JEWS, 1933–1945 (1975).

152. Cases in which certificates were denied are listed in note, *Judicial Approval As a Prerequisite to Incorporation of Non-Profit Organizations in New York and Pennsylvania*, 55 COLUM. L. REV. 380 (1955) and discussed *infra*. Note that this statement does not include appellate reversals that granted certificates initially denied.

153. *See supra,* n. 77.

154. *See In re* German Jewish Children's Aid, 151 Misc. 834, 272 N.Y.S. 540 (Sup. Ct. 1934).

155. *See supra,* n. 77 and accompanying text.

156. 272 N.Y.S. at 542.

157. *Id.*

158. *Id.* at 543 (*quoting* Dorothy Thompson in a symposium entitled "Nazism").

159. *Id.* at 544 (*quoting* address by Stefan Zweig delivered in London, Nov. 30, 1933).

160. *Id.* at 544–45.

161. *Id.* at 545.

162. *Id.*

163. *Id.* at 543.

164. *See To Aid Jewish Children*, N.Y. TIMES, June 10, 1934, at 27 col. 2. After its creation, the organization proceeded to bring hundreds of children to the United States. *See 250 Reich Children to Be Brought Here*, N.Y. TIMES, Sept. 7, 1934, at 12 col. 3; *9 Jewish Boys Here from Germany*, N.Y. TIMES, Nov. 10, 1934, at 5 col. 2.

165. *In re* General Von Steuben Bund, Inc., 159 Misc. 231; 287 N.Y.S. 527, 528 (Sup. Ct. 1936).

166. 125 Misc. 217, 210 N.Y.S. 541 (Sup. Ct. 1925).

167. General Von Steuben Bund, Inc., 287 N.Y.S. at 528.

168. *Id.*

169. *Id.* at 528–29.

170. *Id.* at 529.

171. *Id.*

172. *Id.* at 531.

173. *See* Matter of Catalonian Nationalist Club of New York, 112 Misc. 207, 208, 184 N.Y.S. 132, 133 (Sup. Ct. 1920), discussed *supra*.

174. *In re* General Von Steuben Bund, Inc., 159 Misc. 231, 287 N.Y.S. 527, 535 (Sup. Ct. 1936). In fact, there seems little doubt that the General Von Steuben Bund was in fact an organization sympathetic to Nazism and the political aims of the Nazi movement, seeking corporate status with an innocuous name for the protection such status might afford to its members, for symbolic legitimacy, and for the advantages it might obtain from doing business in corporate form. *See also Nazi Group's Plea for Charter Fails*, N.Y. TIMES, Feb. 12, 1936, at 9 col. 1.

175. *Id.*

176. *See Nazi Group's Plea for Charter Fails*, N.Y. TIMES, Feb. 21, 1936, at 9 col. 1.

177. *Id.*

178. *See In re* German and Austrian-Hungarian War Veterans Post No. 65 of Glendale, Queens, Inc., 13 N.Y.S.2d 207 (Sup. Ct. 1939).

179. *Id.* Justice Hooley served in the Second Judicial District (Brooklyn, Queens, Richmond, Nassau, and Suffolk) from 1935 to 1952. Hooley was a "Knight of the Holy Sepulcher" who supported Catholic social and philanthropic activities. *See Francis G. Hooley, 79, Former State Justice*, N.Y. TIMES, Apr. 25, 1962, at 39 col. 1.

180. *Id.*

181. *Id.*

182. *Id.*

183. *Id.*

184. *Id.* Cases testing the right of Nazi organizations to incorporate were among a series of cases in this period that arose in the New York courts concerning the rights of Nazis under libel, family, employment, contract, jury trial rules and other state laws. *See, e.g.*, Holzer v. Deutsche Reichsbahn Gesellschaft, 290 N.Y.S. 181 (1936) (wrongful discharge of Jewish employee); Long v. Somervell, 22 N.Y.S. 931 (1940) (refusal to sign renunciation affidavit); Levy v. Gelber, 25 N.Y.S.2d 148 (1941) (slander and libel); Kilroy v. News Syndicate Co., 32 N.Y.S.2d 210 (1941) (libel); Reimann v. Reimann, 39 N.Y.S.2d 485 (1942) (custody); Smith v. Smith, 39 N.Y.S.2d 485 (1943) (child support); Gruhn v. J. H. Taylor Constr. Co., 40

N.Y.S.2d 765 (1943) (jury prejudice); Grigorieff v. Winchell, 45 N.Y.S. 31 (1943) (slander and libel); Freund v. Laenderbank Vien Aktiengesellschaft, 46 N.Y.S.2d 393 (1943) (right to discharge Jewish employee).

185. *See Harvey's "We Americans" Turned Down by Court*, N.Y. TIMES, Feb. 11, 1938, at 17 col. 2; *Harvey Denounces Poletti As a "Red,"* N.Y. TIMES, Oct. 9, 1938, at 31 col. 2.

186. *See Harvey Red Drive Splits War Groups*, N.Y. TIMES, Jan. 14, 1938, at 7 col. 3.

187. *Id.*

188. *In re* We Americans, Inc., 166 Misc. 167, 2 N.Y.S.2d 235, 236 (Sup. Ct. 1938).

189. *See Harvey Red Drive Splits War Groups*, N.Y. TIMES, Jan. 14, 1938, at 7 col. 3.

190. *Id.; Harvey's "We Americans" Turned Down by Court*, N.Y. TIMES, Feb. 11, 1938, at 17 col. 2. Justice Thomas C. Kadien served on the New York State Supreme Court between 1934 and 1948. A graduate of New York School of Law, his career "spanned eighteen years in the judicial and political circles of Queens," until he was defeated for reelection to the bench. Mayor LaGuardia had threatened to "dim the lights in Brooklyn" if the justice upheld salary increases for court employees in that borough. The justice allowed the increases and the Appellate Division upheld the right of justices of the court to grant salary increases without approval from city authorities. *See T.C. Kadien, Jr., 60, Ex-State Justice*, N.Y. TIMES, Sept. 23, 1950, at 17.

191. *In re* We Americans, Inc., 166 Misc. 167, 2 N.Y.S.2d 235, 236 (Sup. Ct. 1938).

192. *See* Charles E. Coughlin, A SERIES OF LECTURES ON SOCIAL JUSTICE (1935).

193. Nonprofit statutes in most jurisdictions continue to restrict organizations from using certain words in their names. Some words, for example "Bank" or "Academy," require the consent of a state administrative body because they imply to consumers the provision of special services and regulatory oversight by certain agencies. *See* N.Y. NCPL §301 (1997); *see also* 18A AM JUR 2d Corporations 294.

194. *See In re* Victory Committee of Greenpoint of Patriotic, Social & Fraternal Club, Inc., 59 N.Y.S.2d 546 (Sup. Ct. 1945).

195. *Id.* at 547.

196. *Id.*

197. *See* Norman Isaac Silber and Geoffrey Miller, *Toward "Neutral Principles" in the Law: Selections from the Oral History of Herbert Wechsler*, 93 COLUM. L. REV. 854, 874–891 (1993).

198. *See* Edward Purcell, THE CRISIS OF DEMOCRATIC THEORY (1973); Morton Horwitz, THE TRANSFORMATION OF AMERICAN LAW (1993).

199. *See In re* Patriotic Citizenship Ass'n, Inc., 52 N.Y.S.2d 311 (1944); 53 N.Y.S.2d 595 (Sup. Ct. 1945).

200. *Id.* at 596–97 (emphasis in original).

201. *Id.* 53 N.Y.S.2d 595. Justice Charles Froessel served on the New York State Supreme Court between 1937 and 1949, when he was elected to the Court of Appeals, from which he retired in 1962. He graduated from New York Law School in 1919 and worked as an assistant to the U.S. attorney in charge of slum clearance in New York City before being appointed a justice by Governor Herbert H. Lehman. *See Charles Froessel, Ex-Judge, Is Dead*, N.Y. TIMES, May 3, 1982, at D13.

202. 53 N.Y.S.2d at 597.

203. *Id.*

204. *Id.*

205. Application of F.D.R. Social and Civic Club, 58 N.Y.S.2d 549, 550 (Sup. Ct. 1945).

206. *Id.* at 551–52.

207. *Id.* at 551.

208. *Id.*

209. *See* Will Herberg, PROTESTANT, CATHOLIC, JEW: AN ESSAY IN AMERICAN RELIGIOUS SOCIOLOGY (1960).

210. *In re* Mazzini Cultural Center, Inc., 58 N.Y.S.2d 529 (Sup. Ct. 1945). Justice Frank E. Johnson served on the New York State Supreme Court between 1939 and 1952. A native-born Protestant raised and educated in Brooklyn, he received a law degree from New York University Law School and served for two terms as a state senator before being appointed by Governor Herbert H. Lehman to fill a vacancy on the bench. *See F. E. Johnson Dies; Retired Justice*, N.Y. TIMES, Dec. 7, 1958, at 88 col. 5.

211. *Id.*

212. Joseph Mazzini (1805–1872) was a political theorist and republican revolutionary who fought for and wrote to promote Italian unification and independence. His views of nationalism and moral duty influenced political thought long after his death. *See* Stringfellow Barr, MAZZINI: PORTRAIT OF AN EXILE (1935); Charles F. Delzell, ed., THE UNIFICATION OF ITALY (1976).

213. *Id.*

214. *Id.* at 530. Compare this to discussion of the Elks case, *supra*.

215. *See In re* Voters Alliance for Americans of German Ancestry, Inc., 64 N.Y.S.2d 298 (Sup. Ct. 1946).

216. *Id.* at 299.

217. *See, e.g.,* Sidney E. Ahlstrom, A RELIGIOUS HISTORY OF THE AMERICAN PEOPLE (1975).

218. *Id.*

219. *See Deity's Commands Are Borne Up Peak*, N.Y. TIMES, Sept. 8, 1941, at 6 col. 3; *see also Church of God Head Opposed by Brother*, N.Y. TIMES, Nov. 27, 1943, at 14 col. 2; *Church of God Rift Widened by Election*, N.Y. TIMES, Dec. 9, 1943, at 13 col. 3.

220. As a religious church, it might have obtained most benefits that accrued under the Membership Corporation Laws under New York's Religious Corporation Law.

221. *Id.* at 545–46. Henry G. Wenzel was a member of the New York State Supreme Court between 1932 and 1959. He was appointed to the Appellate Division in 1944. He was renowned for supercilious remarks, particularly during matrimonial cases, such as stating that "the most expensive of all expensive hobbies is the collection of wives." On another occasion he made a plea for some social agency to "restrain the marriage of the gullible, foolish, and half-witted." During his years on the bench Justice Wenzel actively supported conventional social clubs, including the Elks and the Grand Street Boys Association. *See Henry G. Wenzel, Ex-Justice, Dies*, N.Y. TIMES, Aug. 31, 1960.

222. *See In re* Church of God World Headquarters, Inc., 46 N.Y.S.2d 545 (Sup. Ct. 1944).

223. *See, e.g.,* Jesse H. Chopper, *The Rise and Decline of the Constitutional Protection of Religious Liberty,* 70 NEB. L. REV. 651 (1991).

224. Regarding New York's law governing religious organizations, *see* N.Y. Religious Corporations Law and accompanying notes; *see In re* American Jewish Evangelization Soc'y, Inc., 50 N.Y.S.2d 236, 237 (Sup. Ct. 1944).

225. *See supra,* n. 227 and accompanying text.

226. *Id.*

227. *Id.* The groups were the American Jewish Evangelization Society and the American Jewish Missionary Society.

228. *Id.*

229. *Id.*; N.Y. CONST., art. 1 §3.

230. *See, e.g.,* Lovell v. Griffin, 303 U.S. 444, 58 S. Ct. 666, 82 L. Ed. 949 (1938); Cantwell v. Connecticut, 310 U.S. 296, 60 S. Ct. 900, 84 L. Ed. 1213 (1940); Cox v. New Hampshire, 312 U.S. 569, 61 S. Ct. 762, 85 L. Ed 1049 (1941); Martin v. Struthers, 319 U.S. 141, 63 S. Ct. 862, 87 L. Ed. 1313 (1943); Jones v. Opelika, 316 U.S. 584, 62 S. Ct. 1231, 86 L. Ed. 1691 (1942); Prince v. Massachusetts, 321 U.S. 158, 64 S. Ct. 438, 88 L. Ed. 645 (1944); Marsh v. Alabama, 326 U.S. 501, 66 S. Ct. 276, 90 L. Ed. 265 (1946); Niemotko v. Maryland, 340 U.S. 268, 71 S. Ct. 325, 95 L. Ed. 267 (1951).

231. *See In re* American Jewish Evangelization Soc'y, Inc., 50 N.Y.S.2d 236, 237 (Sup. Ct. 1944).

232. *Id.*

233. *Id.*

234. *Id.*

235. *Id.*

236. *Id.*

237. *Id.* at 238.

238. *Id.* at 237.

239. *See supra,* nn. 35–49 and accompanying text.

240. *See In re* Boy Explorers of America, 67 N.Y.S.2d 108, 109 (Sup. Ct. 1946).

241. *Id.* (emphasis added).

242. *Id.*

243. *See supra,* nn. 35–49 and accompanying text.

244. Boy Explorers of America, 67 N.Y.S.2d at 113.

245. *Id.*

246. *See* Application of United Winograder Medical Center in Israel, Inc., 125 N.Y.S.2d 279, 280 (Sup. Ct. 1953).

247. *Id; see also supra,* n. 253 and accompanying text. Justice Samuel M. Gold served on the New York State Supreme Court between 1950 and 1972. *See* Wolfgang Saxon, *Samuel M. Gold, 88, Retired New York Judge,* N.Y. TIMES, Feb. 13, 1985, at D27.

248. 125 N.Y.S.2d at 281.

249. *See* Matter of National Foundation for Diarrheal Diseases, 164 N.Y.S.2d 177 (Sup. Ct. 1957).

250. *Id.* at 178; *see also In re* Marine Corps Vets Foundation, Inc., 79 N.Y.S.2d 18 (Sup. Ct. N.Y. 1948) (rejecting an organization intended to support Marine Corps veterans, holding that "there are already a number of well-established, re-

spectable and representative veteran organizations performing all of the things that are proposed to be performed by this certificate of incorporation. By joining one of the already existing veteran organizations, the incorporators could more effectively and expediently accomplish their aims. Obviously, to attain some of the proposed ends on any reasonable scale, resort will be had to the public for funds. There are already too many fund-seeking organizations. There should be reasonable limits to all things"). *Id.*

251. *See In re* Waldemar Cancer Research Ass'n, Inc., 205 Misc. 560, 130 N.Y.S.2d 426 (Sup. Ct. 1954).

252. *Id.* at 426–27.

253. *See* Application of International Sports Foundation, Inc., 203 N.Y.S.2d 399, 400–401 (Sup. Ct. 1960).

254. *See also* Application of Knesseth Harabonim D'America, Inc., 131 N.Y.S. 2d 543 (Sup. Ct. 1954) (rejecting proposed orthodox rabbinical association because the court knew "of its own knowledge that there are already in existence rabbinic organizations comprised of orthodox rabbis," and "in view of that fact, the Court is not convinced of the need of any additional rabbinic organizations of orthodox rabbis"); Application of Council of Orthodox Rabbis, Inc., 171 N.Y.S.2d 664 (Sup. Ct. 1958) (withholding approval where justice was unconvinced that subscribers could accomplish creation of a new rabbinical academy, and justice was unconvinced of the necessity for one). Other states took different approaches on the question of suppressing rivals. *See, e.g., In re* Chain Yacht Club v. St. Louis Boating Ass'n, 225 S.W.2d 476 (Mo. 1949) (Missouri Court of Appeals refused to allow a rival yacht club to intervene in a proceeding held to consider the application for incorporation of a yacht club to set aside the decree of incorporation).

255. The standard of review on appeal from a trial court decision in this as in other cases was to test for "clear and convincing" error. *See In re* John A. Roosevelt, 3 A.D.2d 988, 163 N.Y.S.2d 403 (App. Div. 1957).

256. *See In re* John A. Roosevelt, 9 Misc.2d 205, 160 N.Y.S.2d 747, *aff'd,* 3 A.D.2d 988, 163 N.Y.S.2d 403 (App. Div. 1957), *aff'd,* 4 N.Y.2d, 171 N.Y.S.2d 841 (1958).

257. 171 N.Y.S.2d at 842.

258. *See* MEM. CORP. LAW, §10.

259. *Id.*

260. 171 N.Y.S.2d at 842.

261. *Id.*

262. *Id.* at 842–43.

263. *Id.* (*citing In re* Ross v. Wilson, 308 N.Y. 605, 617, 127 N.E.2d 697, 703 (Ct. of App. 1955).

264. *See* State v. Brown, 133 N.E.2d 333 (Ohio 1956).

265. *Id.* at 335.

266. OHIO REV. CODE ANN. §2905.31 (1956).

267. 133 N.E.2d at 335.

268. *Id.*

269. *See* Robert Post, LAW AND THE ORDER OF CULTURE viii (1991).

270. *Id.*

271. *See, e.g.,* Evan Haynes, THE SELECTION AND TENURE OF JUDGES 80–136 (1940) (1981, Rothman & Co. ed.); Philip L. Dubois, FROM BALLOT TO BENCH: JUDICIAL ELECTIONS AND THE QUEST FOR ACCOUNTABILITY 3–35 (1980).

272. *See, e.g.,* The Slaughterhouse Cases, 83 U.S. 36, 21 L. Ed. 394 (1873).

273. Although the court had determined that corporations were "persons" for other constitutional purposes, the protections of the bill of rights were extended to corporations unevenly. *See* Carl J. Meyer, *Personalizing the Impersonal: Corporations and the Bill of Rights,* 41 HASTINGS L.J. 577 (1990)

274. In this era the mainstream of thought favored the expansion of judicial review. Some political and intellectual opposition to the expansion of judicial review emerged during the Progressive Era and gained strength as the Supreme Court's "nine old men" invalidated many initiatives of the New Deal, but it focused chiefly on the power of courts to overturn legislative power. *See* Louis Boudin, GOVERNMENT BY JUDICIARY (1932).

275. *See, e.g.,* Edward F. Hennessey, JUDGES MAKING LAW 6–19 (1994) (discussing the normal judicial restraint exercised in and imposed by the imperatives of the common law system).

276. Joseph Raz, *The Relevance of Coherence,* 72 B.U. L. REV. 273, 310–22 (1992).

277. William H. Wood, *What Are Improper Corporate Purposes for Nonprofit Corporations,* 44 DICKINSON L. REV. 264, 272 (1940) (reviewing more than fifty Pennsylvania nonprofit incorporation cases).

278. *Id.*

279. Benjamin N. Cardozo, THE PARADOXES OF LEGAL SCIENCES 37 (1928).

# 4

## The Corrosion of the
## Discretionary Conception

*The judge must . . . find out the will of the government from words which are chosen from common speech and which had better not attempt to provide for every possible contingency. . . . Nobody does this exactly right; great judges do it better than the rest of us. . . . Let them be severely brought to book, when they go wrong, by those who will take the trouble to understand.*[1]

**Learned Hand (1935)**

*Law has reached its finest moments when it has freed man from the unlimited discretion of some ruler, some civil or military official, some bureaucrat.*[2]

**William O. Douglas (1951)**

The justifications for permitting close reviews of applications for the incorporation of nonprofit associations finally came into doubt. Why were commercial and nonprofit associations being treated differently? Why could only selected proponents of selected social and political ends use the corporate form to promote their own goals while avoiding taxes and other obligations? Were adequate principles of fairness being applied by state authorities? Fundamental questions that had seemed long settled and closed became unsettled and open.

Courts previously interpreted nonprofit incorporation statutes to contain an invitation to judges to apply personal standards to protect public values. The negative implications of chartering the "wrong" nonprofit corporations had appeared to justify discretionary elements in the process. Allowing the "wrong" groups to incorporate might undermine existing and traditionally defined charities. Exemptions might be given to unworthy groups. Available public revenues might be diminished and tax avoidance strategies promoted. Solicitations might be made by unworthy groups. The credibility associated with nonprofit status might be given to an undeserving organization. Judges and state officials had defended pre-incorporation scrutiny as an appropriate way to effectuate a public policy about incorporation that supported mainstream community values.

These objectives yielded to newer ones being erected in the postwar legal environment. To a new legal generation, the traditional scheme of supervision emerged as archaic, unjust, and completely inappropriate for a new age. The traditional scheme became objectionable from multiple perspectives, including antidiscretionary trends of jurisprudence in the legal academy, newer inclinations to treat many kinds of government benefits as entitlements, stronger ideological commitments to corporate free expression and "expressive pluralism," and generalized disapproval of discriminatory legal treatment for minorities. The supervision that judges and state agencies exercised in the area of nonprofit corporations seemed to work a disservice from each of these perspectives. It stuck out as an embarrassing throwback to an earlier era.

## Student Impudence and the Legitimacy of Judicial Authority

It is striking that the critique of the nonprofit incorporation process began as a matter of chiefly theoretical concern voiced by a few law students and recent law school graduates who expressed their views in law journals. These criticisms were taken quite seriously, however, and within a fairly brief period had been incorporated into judicial decision-making. Why did student criticisms have such force? An examination of certain facets of the culture of legal education at the time will help answer that question.

Students who attended major national law schools in the 1950s, like students in several other periods, often had an exaggerated view of their intellectual toughness, their problem-solving skills, and their common sense, based principally on their academic successes. The characteristic law school curriculum of the 1950s instilled an acute fear of failure as it encouraged students to measure their growth in terms of the formal grades and honorifics they received. "For first year law students . . . the danger of dismissal for failure to obtain the requisite grades is a constant spur, and for those with higher scholastic qualifications the law review represents a hope calculated to extend them to the limits of their abilities," wrote one dean.[3] Unlike students in other graduate and professional schools, furthermore, law students who mastered the system developed a high estimate of their ability to play a key role in lawmaking and social action, even at the earliest stages in their careers.[4] This nurtured a sense of empowerment that distinguished them, in the main, from previous generations of law students, who learned to wait until they had acquired maturity and experience.[5]

Especially among the better-performing students at the "elite" law schools, the atmosphere in which law students competed against one another for distinction, it was said, sometimes got "cocky" and "abrasive," but it nevertheless encouraged students to believe in the immediate value of their own ideas about the law.[6] The confidence that lawyers could "tackle any problem in any field," wrote David Riesman, a sociologist and 1954 graduate of Harvard Law School, percolated down from faculty to students, who imagined themselves lawyers and law professors in waiting. "If a law student does brilliantly on examinations, talks easily and crisply in classes, writes succinctly for the Law Review, faculty at his home institution may already see him as a prospective colleague, once he has served as a judge's clerk or assistant district attorney or had a year or so with Covington & Burling."[7] The appearance of an anointed elect, crowned through the process of objective law grading, created "one of the most remarkable self-confirming prophesies in vocational choice and selection."[8] A young man who earned high grades and made it to the law review was "ticketed for life as a first-class passenger on the talent escalator."[9]

The suggestion that a fine law student could revolutionize legal theory while still in school acquired greatest currency for those students who served on the premier law reviews or journals at the major national law schools. "It is a striking fact that once a person of superior intelligence learns to read the cases, acquires the vocabulary and becomes acquainted with legal materials, he is in a position to deal effectively with legal theory in almost any field, provided that he will devote to it the requisite amount of time," wrote Dean Havighurst of the Northwestern University Law School.[10] "Young men and women in this activity are not at a great disadvantage with their elders merely because they are young or because they are relatively new to this way of thinking and writing."[11]

For those who made it to the law reviews, there was little hesitation to call a judicial opinion bad, a statute poorly drafted, or a politician's or a judge's or a law professor's analysis flatly wrong. After only a year at school, students could become law review editors and as such review the casebooks of their professors and even prevent the publication of their articles.[12] It was not pleasant, one professor wrote, "for a mature scholar to be subjected to the supreme and irrevocable judgment of incompletely trained students."[13]

There was nothing comparable to these student-run law reviews in the other graduate schools:

> Nothing in any other professional group . . . remotely resembles the law re-
> view, this guild of students, who, working even harder than their fellows,
> manage to cooperate sufficiently to meet the chronic emergency of a period-
> ical. . . . The resulting standards often become so high that the contributed
> articles by law teachers and practitioners are markedly inferior to the stu-
> dent work both in learning and in style and, in fact, often have to be rewrit-
> ten by the brashly serious-minded student editors.[14]

A former editor of the *Columbia Law Review* actually proposed that since
the law reviews did a better job at teaching skills and values, law schools
should *become* law reviews. "There is general agreement among practic-
ing lawyers that the Review man is much better prepared than the non-
Review man for the practice of law—or rather, for the beginning of the
practice of law."[15]

The competitive educational process, the professorate, and the experience on the law journals reinforced student understanding that student
legal scholarship, especially first-rate law notes, could redirect legal doctrine and even rearrange the social order.[16] In combination with the substantive education they were receiving about the nature of judicial behavior and judicial authority, their acculturation led them to seek to
address what was perhaps the most important problem being discussed
in the law schools of that day—the problem of justifying judicial authority to uphold the rule of law.

The students who challenged nonprofit chartering in the postwar period were responding to lessons they were receiving in school about the
evenhanded application of law, the design of the legal process, and the
nature of legitimate and illegitimate judicial authority. They were being
schooled in the realist's critique of judging and also in the response that
legal realism was drawing from "process" theorists, who argued that the
interwar generation of legal theorists improvidently and excessively emphasized the interdependence of law and its social context. The students'
doubts about the wisdom of permitting judges to exercise discretion to
withhold nonprofit charters, in other words, found expression as part of
the chorus of concern by scholars of the 1950s about diminished respect
for judicial authority and the need to reconstruct a new basis for public
support for the judicial power.

Collectively, the realists and their forerunners had developed theories
to explain the outcome of legal disputes which devastated the conceit
that judges mechanistically deduced holdings from precedents and
statutes. They applied psychological and sociological and economic and
anthropological insights to the study of judicial behavior and for the
most part treated judges as only too frail and only too human and only
too susceptible to their environment. As Justice Cardozo wrote in his ef-

fort to disabuse readers of heroic illusions about judging in *The Nature of the Judicial Process,*

> I do not doubt the grandeur of the conception which lifts [judges] into the realm of pure reason, above and beyond the sweep of perturbing and deflecting forces. Nonetheless, if there is anything of reality in my analysis of the judicial process, they do not stand aloof on these chill and distant heights; and we shall not help the cause of truth by acting and speaking as if they do.[17]

As Alexander Bickel recalled this lesson in his 1961 book *The Least Dangerous Branch,*[18] it was the work entirely of the realists, who had learned from Justice Holmes that logical inference and deduction, either from statutes or from the lessons of personal experience, did not determine legal decisionmaking:

> The realists taught . . . that "the vivid fictions and metaphors of traditional jurisprudence" are no more than "poetical and mnemonic devices for formulating decisions reached on other grounds." Or, to quote another famous passage of Felix Cohen: "Rules of logic [or of constitutional construction] can no more produce legal or moral doctrines than they can produce kittens. On the whole, it is safe to assume that those legal doctrines that claim to be the offspring of logic are either not proud or not aware of their real parents."[19]

Without rejecting the legitimacy of judging, the realist generation redefined its essential character: rather than respond to the imperative commands of statutes and constitutions, they claimed that routine judicial behavior involved the exercise by judges of subjective interpretation and pragmatic good sense to decide cases according to their best personal judgment.[20] The realist viewpoint encouraged judges to conform "static" laws to the "felt needs of the time" by validating conduct of judges that incorporated a broad range of sociological, psychological, economic, and political considerations into their decisionmaking.[21] It invited the public to treat judicial decisions as products of economic and political relations rather than legal deductions.

If any of those scholars who had a realist orientation had bothered to study the approach taken by the judges in the nonprofit chartering cases, they would not have been surprised by their doctrinal foundation.[22] Instead—had they noticed—they might have used the chartering cases to illustrate their claims about the social construction of the judicial system and the role it played in supporting existing social and economic relations.

Believing that nontraditional explanations accounted for court decisions undermined the conventional basis for accepting the legitimacy of
judicial opinions. If statutes or constitutions did not direct judges to
reach the proper outcome, then the exercise of judicial discretion resembled law *making* rather than law *interpreting*—especially, the argument
went, since judges were generally unelected and lacked effective democratic checks on their postappointment conduct.[23] This proposition stung
because it devalued the currency of judicial authority.[24]

Some judges and scholars did not seem to care about the problem of
the legitimacy of judicial decisions. Professor Bickel, who taught at Yale,
criticized the Supreme Court's exercise of judicial review during recent
years as "the final fruit of neo-realism." The Court, he stated, had taken a
"genial, nihilistic attitude" and shown "a complete lack of interest in the
process by which the work is achieved, or in the proper role of that
process in a democratic society."[25] As Professor Michael Wells has recently described Bickel's lament, "if judges weren't bound by precedents
and statutes, then the fear arose that they might decide cases according to
their personal preferences without the constraints imposed by accountability to the electorate."[26] Of course, intentionally encouraging judges to
express their "naked personal preferences" put the lie to the democratic
goal of a government by laws.

The problem of reconstructing a coherent and widely supported justification for judicial authority at the level of both constitutional and common law surfaced well before suggestions that nonprofit chartering had
been too strongly affected by naked preferences. It occupied many of the
most talented legal scholars at leading law schools in postwar America.
"Anyone who accepted the Realist critique of nineteenth century formalism either had to agree that judicial lawmaking was a form of legislation,
or else had to develop a new justification for judicial intervention," Wells
has written.[27] For Professor Bickel—who had been a law clerk to Justice
Felix Frankfurter—the best approach was a doctrine of judicial restraint
that would not "concede unchanneled, undirected, uncharted discretion"
or "concede decision preceding from impulse, hunch, sentiment,
predilection, inarticulable and unreasoned."[28]

The reconstructed foundation for the legitimacy of the exercise of judicial power did not emerge directly from Bickel's "judicial restraint" viewpoint but from the work of scholars who were more concerned with making judicial activism philosophically reasonable and socially palatable.
These scholars of the 1950s, prominently including Lon Fuller, Henry Hart,
Albert Sacks, and Herbert Wechsler,[29] accepted the realist teaching that
judges received many kinds of guidance apart from precedents and statutory texts, but they insisted that judicial authority was not necessarily im-
pugned as a result. By their theories, the refinement of many different ad-

judicatory techniques and forms, of many different methods for inquiring into facts and law, with differing legal standards and burdens—the "pluralism of legal process"—permitted the development of appropriate methods for using "reasoned elaboration" by "competent" judicial institutions. Attention to fair legal processes, they claimed, permitted courts to manage and at least provisionally resolve controversial issues of public policy and to legitimately employ judicial discretion within the context of appropriate procedural deliberation, articulation, and review.[30]

It was concern about the absence of consistency and fair legal procedure in judicial decisionmaking that led the author of the student note published in the 1955 *Columbia Law Review*, titled *Judicial Approval As a Prerequisite to Incorporation of Non-profit Organizations in New York and Pennsylvania* ("the Columbia Note")[31] to the firm opinion that pre-incorporation screening of nonprofit corporate purposes presented problems of elemental fairness without significant compensating benefits.[32] In all likelihood the note writer studied criminal law or took federal courts with Professor Herbert Wechsler or administrative law with Professor Walter Gellhorn.[33] In the course of preparing his note for the *Law Review,* he discovered that virtually every state granted charters for *commercial* purposes "automatically." But many states vested administrative officials, or the governor or the secretary of state or the courts, with the power to exercise discretionary control over the formation of nonprofit corporations.[34]

Although the idea that incorporation was a privilege rather than a right dated back to "the era when charters were regarded as unusual favors granted by the Crown,"[35] the Columbia Note did not find any good reason to perpetuate it. In fact the author expressed strong reservations about discretionary approvals in general and about systems that involved approval by courts in particular.[36] The paternalism inherent in the idea of qualifying for a "privilege," the absence of methodical investigation to make determinations, and the use of the judiciary for what seemed more like administrative functions, provided adequate reasons for doubting the continuing validity of the older ways.

Legislatures in both New York and Pennsylvania authorized their courts in broad statutory language and in so doing failed to provide standards for examining applications that might form the basis for an appeal upon denial.[37] The generality of the legislative guidance allowed glaring inconsistencies "in . . . areas of disagreement even as to the nature of the inquiries being made."[38] Some judges approved charters as long as they were "not objectionable";[39] others required an affirmative showing of some quid pro quo to the community in return for the grant of corporate privileges.[40] Some judges required a showing that incorporation was necessary for the applicants to carry on their work.[41]

Judges gave their personal opinions too much weight in the process of investigating beyond the face of a proposed charter, the student forcefully argued.[42] The student did not quarrel with judges who disapproved groups that tried to practice medicine without a license or evade the liquor laws.[43] But the denial of a charter to a proposed home for unwed mothers because the home would "benefit immoral women" and permit "frauds on prospective husbands" reflected simply the subjective personal opinion of the judge.[44]

And where did these subjective beliefs originate? The law allowed them to, and they did conduct many of their inquiries ex parte ("on one side only").[45] When they wished, they privately consulted sources whom they knew opposed an applicant's certification. They consulted with rival organizations, civic groups, and public officials; they relied on their colleagues; they drew on their own personal knowledge of other groups, as well as literature, history, "statistics," previous litigations, recent events, and "common knowledge."[46] Although Pennsylvania judges provided an opportunity to respond to derogatory information, never had any challenge to the ex parte proceeding arisen in New York.[47]

The record revealed a blatant lack of equal treatment; for example, a Pennsylvania case in which Company D of the Irish Volunteers was denied incorporation although Company B, with an identical charter, was approved by a different court.[48] Or the case of the grand jurors' association that was denied incorporation in the Bronx on the ground that it "might subvert the necessary freedom of thought and expression among the grand jurors," while an identical association was approved in Brooklyn.[49] It might be appropriate for legislatures to limit the privileges of nonprofit incorporation to certain categories of groups, the student argued, but it was "doubtful that permitting value judgments to be made by individual judges on an *ad hoc* basis is in keeping with a tradition of equal treatment before the law."[50]

And how much abuse of donated funds and the public's trust did all this activity prevent? Was pre-incorporation investigation, either by judges or agencies, saving the public more than could be saved by permitting corporations to function as nonprofits until one of the administrative agencies discovered they engaged in abusive behavior? "Advance denial might avert some misuse of privilege, but only where the applicants were law-abiding citizens ignorant of the fact that their purposes were actually illicit, although lawful as accidentally misstated," the student author asserted.[51] Incorporators who intentionally misstated their purposes would continue to mislead the public, since "subscribers who are not above prevarication are not above fraudulently claiming to be chartered."[52]

Without canvassing all of the many reasons that judges had provided for denying charters, the Note assailed one of the most common grounds for disapproval: the denial of charters for reasons related to duplicating the effort of existing groups that were already inadequately supported. Denial because of unnecessary duplication was likely to be an ineffective cure for the defect it complained of, the note indicated, since unincorporated groups might continue to solicit funds and other support too. This was not to accept the position of later "law and economics" proponents that competition among all nonprofits was necessarily a good idea, however.[53] Coordination of the efforts of similar nonprofits might better be prevented by a central administrative agency "to regulate all groups who intend to engage in fund-raising campaigns."[54] Permitting judges to withhold charters from associations with legal purposes only because they might, for example, be "unnecessary" was undesirable "because of the risk that the judge's personal convictions [are] the controlling factor."[55] At least, the note declared, the system of judicial approvals must be subjected to new procedures designed to ensure fairness, including the reasoned elaboration of basis for decisions in opinions that were subject to readily available appellate review.[56] Better yet, pre-incorporation judicial determinations needed to cease entirely. They needed to be replaced by "centralized specialized agencies with control of all groups in the field regardless of their formal structure."[57] Substituting an administrative process of adjudication for a judicial one would produce more evenhanded results.

No disapproval should occur on the grounds of public policy, in any event, the note concluded, unless the applicants proposed truly unlawful conduct. If legislatures were unwilling to permit nonprofit incorporation for every lawful purpose, then they "should spell out in detail those activities which, though legal if performed by individuals or unincorporated associations, [they do] not wish to encourage by the grant of a corporate charter."[58] Judges had demonstrated that without firm guidance they were inadequate to the task of drawing a bright and evenhanded line.

The best solution of all would be to handle nonprofit and commercial incorporation identically: those applications that were proper on their face ought to be filed automatically, subject to revocation for any subsequent illegal activities. Supervision of all business activity by administrative agencies ought to be strengthened and should apply to all nonprofit groups, whether incorporated or not.[59]

Adopting the perspective of a mistreated practitioner in a much briefer but equally pointed criticism entitled *"Objections to Judicial Approval of Charters of Non-profit Corporations,"* George H.P. Dwight in the 1957 *Business Lawyer* agreed with the position taken by the student in the

*Columbia Law Review*.[60] He voiced impatience with the practical mechanics of the nonprofit incorporation law: the judicial approval device was decidedly "unmodern." Current examples of arbitrariness in the law ought to "spur on lawyers and legislators in New York and elsewhere in their efforts to rid the statute books of this and similar outmoded devices."[61] Dwight by this time had practiced for five years, after graduating from Columbia Law School in 1952. He had been a student of Professors Wechsler and Gellhorn, and he had served as articles editor on the *Columbia Law Review*.[62] From Dwight's perspective, all judicial determinations that were made about the merit of a proposed not-for-profit corporation inherently suffered from speculativeness—because judges could base their decisions only on statements of purpose made before corporations actually engaged in their proposed activity. In such amorphous situations the "eccentric standards" and personal convictions of particular decisionmakers would always threaten to control a decision to approve or disapprove.[63]

Several recent cases of the 1950s made the point.[64] Was it appropriate for the court in *Council for Small Business, Inc.*,[65] to reject the group's certificate because its proposed activities included "inspir[ing] and support[ing] legislation beneficial to independent business," Dwight wanted to know.[66] The justice deciding the case believed that such language was so vague that it sanctioned "pernicious lobbying activities."[67] This hardly warranted disapproving a charter, Dwight wrote. After all, the charters for typical small family charitable corporations prudently, as a matter of good lawyering, contained provisions that were far more general than the one in *Council for Small Business*. Generality of language was necessary "to avoid *ultra vires* problems and the necessity for subsequent amendment of the certificate . . . to include additional purposes."[68] In any event, "pernicious" activities that the council engaged in while it was incorporated would be punishable by sound administration of the New York criminal and tax laws.[69] In actual practice, Dwight wrote, the statements of purpose in nonprofit corporate charters frequently—and for good reasons—expressed general aims instead of specific goals.

The regime of unprincipled discretion simply placed too heavy a burden of persuasion on applicants. In *Howard Memorial Fund*,[70] for example, a corporation tried to change its corporate purposes to allow it to solicit contributions and distribute funds "to needy persons . . . for the purpose of furthering the education of such persons, and to civic or community organizations serving children."[71] The court rejected the application because nothing in the papers demonstrated that the purposes could be achieved and "because the corporation would in all likelihood duplicate the work of other organizations of similar character in New York City."[72] Wasn't it pointless to require proof of the ability to help the needy,

Dwight asked? Wasn't it impossible for an applicant to demonstrate persuasively that an as yet nonexistent association would not duplicate the work of one that was already operating?[73]

Dwight hypothesized, without substantiation, that the legislature could not have intended to allow discretion to extend so broadly; he argued, therefore, that the court inappropriately substituted its judgment for that of the legislature by withholding its approval based only on "the possibility of wrongful practices . . . which the legislature has indicated call for [administrative] regulation but not denial of the privilege to incorporate."[74] The judge held "virtually free rein" to indulge his own views, without elaboration, in a way that would permit practitioners to understand the basis for the rejection of current and future applications on other than personal terms.[75]

The problem of fraudulent conduct by nonprofit groups soliciting funds made oversight of such groups necessary. But was exercising such a broad judicial discretion at the pre-incorporation stage better than permitting administrative discretion afterward? Dwight made clear his disdain for the entire judicial approval process—without stopping to ask whether, at any point, "free rein" could or should be modulated into the reasonable exercise of bounded discretion. New administrative agencies, such as the State Department of Social Welfare, recently had been assigned the authority to regulate fund-raising activities of charitable organizations,—whether or not the organizations were incorporated. Administrative apparatus like this enabled nonprofit law to sidestep the difficulties that were attached to the judicial approval approach.[76] They rendered unnecessary the judicial oversight of charters at the pre-incorporation stage.[77]

New York, he said, should follow the approach taken in Illinois, Missouri, Virginia, and the recently promulgated Non-Profit Corporation Act.[78] These states had already done away with the discretionary power of judges or departments of state to "veto" the organization of nonprofit corporations.[79]

## Broadening Corporate Expression in an Interest Group State

The discretionary conception for chartering groups also conflicted with broadly held views about steps that were needed to advance democracy in modern America. Political theories popular during the 1950s significantly elevated the importance of interest group participation in civic affairs. The inability of various noncorporate interest groups to articulate their views had been a matter of concern earlier, during the Progressive Era.[80] Again, in the middle 1950s, the need to ensure a diversity of viewpoints—an "expressive pluralism"—amid growing concentrations of power and more costly outlets for disseminating ideas, became a pressing matter.

By 1955, business corporations sponsored almost all television, radio, and newspaper communications.[81] The spread of "corporatism" and corporate "mentality," along with well-publicized social trends including the rapid growth of the suburbs, the broadening of the middle class, and the "decline of the individual," became new verities in political and intellectual discourse.[82] "America has paid much attention to the economic and political consequences of big organization—the concentration of power in large corporations, for example,— . . . but no less important is the principal impact that organization life has had on the individuals within it,"[83] wrote William H. Whyte. The sociologist C. Wright Mills provided a pessimistic description of the results of this corporatization: diminished political freedom and economic security. "The cradle-condition of classic democracy," he wrote, "no longer exists in America. This is no society of small entrepreneurs—now they are one stratum among others: above them is the big money; below them, the alienated employee; before them, the fate of politically dependent relics; behind them, their world."[84]The ways in which Congress reconciled the clash of corporate interests with each other and with other organized group interests in society through the political process became a matter of careful study. In structural descriptions of the American political process, distinguished professors, including Arthur Bentley, David Truman, Robert Dahl, and Seymour Martin Lipset, formulated a version of American democracy that placed organized interest groups, rather than individuals, at the core of representative politics. The pluralist conception of the democratic state posited that the views of ordinary individuals no longer accounted for very much in the political process, except as they were expressed by groups.[85] It was a continuous state of interest group advocacy and accommodation that produced social equilibrium.[86]

The rapid proliferation of associations in the 1950s was "largely responsible for focusing the attention of both layman and specialist upon the role of groups in government."[87] The newer interest group and pressure group theories presupposed that groups of similarly affected individuals—not merely business corporations but voluntary associations including PTAs, church groups, labor unions, and consumer groups—were, as they should be in the American tradition, inclined and equally situated under the laws to organize on their own behalf, to articulate their views, and otherwise to advance their own interests.[88] "The process of government cannot be adequately understood apart from the groups, especially the organized and potential interest groups, which are operative at any point in time," Professor Truman wrote.[89]

What counted was the influence of organized interest groups—corporate and otherwise—who were equipped to protect their own interests.[90] In the pluralist state, competing interest groups would accept defeats in institutional politics because their individual members held many other interests at the same time, and because they believed that the rules of the reform process allowed them to continue to work for change on an equal footing with those in power, without legal restrictions that might ensure their failure. Quiescent or "potential" interest groups—including even fraternal orders, religious groups, and trade associations—remained so because they assumed that they could organize and do so effectively if their interests were adversely being affected. "Multiple memberships in potential groups based on widely held and accepted interests . . . serve as a balance wheel in a going political system like that of the United States," Professor Truman wrote.[91] Professor John Kenneth Galbraith, an economist at Harvard, emphasized that the capitalist economy also depended on the development of "countervailing power." Faith in capitalism's ability to regenerate itself required establishing "a certain minimum opportunity and a capacity for organization, corporate or otherwise."[92]

The legal process school discussed earlier in many respects furthered and drew strength from the propositions about corporatism and pluralism that the interest group theorists were advancing.[93] Much of the school's emphasis on what Lon Fuller called "the morality of law,"[94] for example, consisted of providing evenhanded access to legal remedies and adequate opportunities for aggrieved parties to be heard in court. This sustained an understanding of the government as a "referee" or an "umpire"—metaphors that were integral to the pluralist vision of American democracy.[95] Many process school propositions about federalism sustained doctrines of judicial review by treating individual states as, essentially, mobilized regional interest groups.[96] Deliberative and methodical administrative processes ensured that organized interest groups would have opportunities to participate and to bring lawful pressure to bear in proportion to their strength.

Both the legal process school and the interest group theorists tended to agree that evenhandedly providing all interest groups with theoretically equal and adequate opportunities to be heard and to influence public policy would satisfy the constraints on decisionmaking imposed by democratic imperatives of fairness and constitutional right. Treating interest groups in these evenhanded ways would provide decisionmakers with balanced information and also subject them to appropriately proportional pressure from constituents. It would help them depersonalize and de-escalate domestic conflict; it would help the inevitable losers in adversarial political and legal proceedings to accept defeat and play "within the rules." Evenhandedness also appeared to meet another postwar and

Cold War imperative—the need to achieve a working consensus about social and political values in the face of real and imagined communist attempts to exploit the wide diversity of ethnic, racial, and cultural divisions in American life.

The embrace by the legal process school of interest group theories also served to rationalize the continuing growth of judicial procedures—such as adversarial proceedings and hearings of many kinds—in the administrative state.

But as pluralist theory enhanced respect for administrative procedures, it undermined the traditional discretion exercised by common law judges.[97] Administrative processes professedly produced consistent results that were arrived at deliberately—after the application of any necessary specialized expertise—and after a fair hearing at which all sides had a chance to present their views. The problem with conventional judicial review thereby illuminated was not merely that individual judges and courts occasionally strayed from the responsibility of "reasoned elaboration." Where statutory authority permitted broad discretion to be exercised ex parte by judges, as with the nonprofit incorporation process, the problem was that judicial processes were inherently less adequate than administrative decisionmaking.[98] They tolerated too much institutional protection for individual judges to privilege some interest groups at the expense of others.[99]

### Governmental Largesse As an Entitlement

A growing tendency to characterize many kinds of governmental awards as entitlements rather than dispensations of privilege clashed with the discretionary approach to granting nonprofit charters. The laws affecting the incorporation of nonprofit corporations in New York had not changed in essential respects since 1895, but the laws governing the granting and retention of other kinds of government licenses and benefits apart from corporation charters evolved dramatically during the 1950s.[100]

Traditionally, "due process" in its Fourteenth Amendment meaning was constitutionally required only when the government sought to deprive someone of "life, liberty or property."[101] This view relaxed substantially as the administrative state grew, however, and by 1951 Justice Frankfurter could assert that the right to "life, liberty or property" meant the right "to be heard before being condemned to suffer grievous loss of any kind."[102]

What had been treated unambiguously as the affirmative dispensation by government of many different kinds of privileges now appeared to resemble the indiscriminate recognition of rights that were not to be deprived without due process. Courts began to hold that occupational or professional licenses could not be denied or revoked without affording applicants notice and hearing.[103] Doctors, lawyers, real estate brokers, and taxi drivers, for example, were given increasing rights not to be denied their livelihood without some minimum procedure.[104] The New York Court of Appeals in 1952 declared that individual driver's licenses were "of tremendous value to the individual" and could not be taken away, except by due process.[105] The logic which maintained that since government might completely withhold some benefit or privilege it could grant a benefit on any terms whatsoever was being challenged.[106] Appellate courts were reviewing some licensing determinations for the sufficiency of the evidence for making the determination, to see if a basis for official action existed in fact.[107] The U.S. Court of Appeals for the First Circuit held that it was "unimportant, [whether] for one purpose or another, a license to operate motor vehicles may properly be described as a mere personal privilege rather than as a property right" because, irrespective of the distinction, a Fourteenth Amendment liberty interest in driving existed that could not be abridged without observing due process of law.[108] For reasons related to the vesting of due process rights in the retention of "privileges" conferred by government, it was becoming much more difficult than ever before to terminate government licenses and grants once they had been given.

On the other hand, the ability of government to act with broad discretion in the *initial* conferral of undisputed privileges continued, fundamentally unaltered. Determinations of entitlement to such personal benefits as social security payments and unemployment insurance were virtually unreviewable. The grant of a valuable federal savings and loan association charter, for example, was said to rest in the virtually unreviewable discretion of the Federal Home Loan Bank Board.[109]

Writing in 1964 about events of the previous decade, Professor Charles Allan Reich recognized and gave a name to these massive new distributions and deprivations of government wealth in his perceptive article *The New Property*.[110] The Great Society spending and welfare programs proposed by Lyndon B. Johnson only manifested part of the larger trend—the "transformation of society as it bears on the economic basis of individualism."[111] In the decade of the 1950s, he wrote, the government had drawn in revenue and "pour[ed] forth wealth." Enormously increased revenues, increased government deficit spending, and greater government control over people's lives led government to dispense "money, benefits, services, contracts, franchises and licenses" as a matter of routine.[112]

One class of the new property, Reich observed, was the "largesse" of government occupational licenses and franchises. Licenses were required before it was possible to do many kinds of work. Franchises were partial monopolies created and parceled out by government. Regulating access to franchises and licenses, he wrote, had given rise to certain essential legal distinctions, particularly the distinction between *rights*, which could only be deprived after various protections had been observed, and *privileges*, which might be revoked without notice or hearing.[113]

In all of the cases concerning individual rights in largesse, Reich wrote, the exact nature of the government action that precipitated the controversy made a great difference. A controversy over government largesse might arise from such diverse situations as denial of the right to apply for a benefit, the denial of an application for one, the attachment of conditions to one, the modification of a benefit already granted, the suspension or revocation of one, or some other sanction. "An applicant for largesse is thought to have less at stake, and is therefore entitled to less protection."[114] When government handed out something of value, it automatically gained the power necessary "to supervise its largesse," including the power to control the "moral character" of the recipients.[115] Reich referred for support to cases including the deprivation of Sonny Liston's boxing license by the state of New York because of his "bad character"[116] and a case in which a doctor's medical license was suspended because he refused to cooperate with the House Committee on Un-American Activities.[117] Objections to regulation faded, Reich complained, before the argument that government needed to make sure that its bounty was used in the public interest.[118]

Procedural safeguards were essential to preserve civil liberty in the face of dependence on governmental largesse, Reich argued. New standards were necessary to shield individuals from the arbitrary exercise of governmental authority. The New Dealers' disrespect for conservative encomiums of private property needed to be reappraised because property, including government largesse, was indeed the bedrock of liberty:

> Property performs the function of maintaining independence, dignity and pluralism in society by creating zones within which the majority has to yield to the owner. Whim, caprice, irrationality and "anti-social" activities are given the protection of law; the owner may do what all or most of his neighbors decry. The Bill of Rights also services this function, but while the Bill of Rights comes into play only at extraordinary moments of conflict or crisis, property affords day-to-day protection in the ordinary affairs of life.[119]

Reich asserted that government's arbitrary control over the new property was potentially as great a threat to individual liberty as that of private employers. Government, as a dispenser of wealth, had been exploiting the theory that it was handing out "gratuities" to claim a managerial power as great as that which "earlier generations of capitalists" claimed.

Government determinations of professional status were critical to individual rights. "Today it is the combined power of government and the corporations that presses against the individual," Reich warned.[120] He urged that the law should convert forms of largesse that protected professional and associational status into rights. Status, he wrote, "must . . . be surrounded with the kinds of safeguards once reserved for personality."[121] Benefits such as unemployment compensation, public assistance, and old age insurance should be treated as entitlements rather than privileges.

Reich would later reflect on the prescience of his earlier article and remind a new generation of readers that the magnitude of the problems in distributing government largesse was apparent earlier than the appearance of *The New Property* (1964).[122] He himself had been confronted with the issue of liberty and the new property as early as the 1953–1954 term of the U.S. Supreme Court, while clerking for Justice Hugo Black, he wrote.[123] By the late 1950s, it had become evident that the matter of providing greater procedural protections for those who sought licenses and benefits from the state was an emerging issue requiring a considerable reordering of legal rules.

It also was becoming apparent that the grant of access to nonprofit status shared characteristics common to other government grants that Reich had argued were really "largesse." As such, the decisionmaking procedure for conferring nonprofit status could be subjected to the same sort of procedural protections that Reich urged the government to adopt when it parceled out other benefits.

### A Roadblock in the Struggle for African-American Civil Rights

The problems with the discretionary model were nowhere as apparent to the public, and especially to college and law students, as in the civil rights movement. Many of the perceived difficulties with both common law judicial adjudication and with the arbitrary dispensation of status by government emerged plainly in the course of litigation over black civil rights, as the struggle of black Americans' to obtain social justice and achieve racial equality accelerated during the 1950s.[124] The success of the black civil rights movement depended largely on the organizational skills, moral vision, and legal strategies of major not-for-profit associations that were challenging existing laws and practices;[125] it depended on the churches, political parties, and especially on several dedicated civil rights organizations, particularly the National Association for the Advancement of Colored People (NAACP).

The NAACP was incorporated in 1909 as a nonprofit membership corporation organized under the law of New York "to promote equality of rights and eradicate caste or race prejudice among the citizens of the United States."[126] It operated through chartered affiliates that were independent unincorporated associations, with membership in the affiliates being equivalent to membership in the corporation. Together with the NAACP Legal Defense Fund, a related but separate organization that had been chartered in 1940, the NAACP worked at the state and federal levels to challenge segregation in the courts. Demonstrations and marches, employment disputes and consumer boycotts, public accommodations controversies and voting contests often ended in NAACP and Legal Defense Fund court challenges that tested the capacity and inclination of the law and legal institutions to accommodate the impulse for reform.

Confining the social struggle to lawful channels, however, depended on the ability of courts to accept and direct their own transformation into institutions impartial in matters of race. Nowhere did the clash between abstract theories about the equal rights of interest groups and the reality of malleable laws become as apparent as in the southern state courts, where such rules as parade laws, voting rights laws, antitrust laws, and education laws were employed by government officers in discriminatory ways in an attempt to prevent racial integration and deter further legal reform.[127]

Not least important, the laws governing nonprofit corporations were prevailed upon to deter efforts of civil rights organizations to promote their interests.[128] In pursuance of their power to exclude foreign corporations, Texas, acting through its attorney general, permanently enjoined all activities of the NAACP. Louisiana banned local unincorporated chapters of the NAACP as well, for failing to file membership lists pursuant to corporation laws, which the NAACP feared for its members to do.[129]

In 1956, the attorney general of Alabama sued in equity to prevent both the New York–chartered NAACP and its unincorporated but related local affiliates from operating in the state. The attorney general alleged that the NAACP unlawfully opened up offices in the state, gave financial support and furnished assistance to Negro students seeking admission to segregated schools, and recruited members and solicited contributions within the state. He also alleged that the NAACP supported the Negro boycott of the bus lines in Montgomery to compel the integrated seating of passengers.[130]

Alabama had a statute, similar to that of many other states, that required a foreign corporation to qualify before doing business by filing its corporate charter with the secretary of state and designating a place of business and an agent to receive service of process.[131] The state attorney general claimed that the NAACP caused an irreparable harm "by continuing to do business in Alabama without complying with the qualification statute."[132] The state further moved for the production of a large number of the association's records and papers, including the names and addresses of all Alabama "members" and "agents" of the NAACP. The NAACP admitted that it had not qualified to do business in the state but refused to comply with the production order.[133]

After the NAACP was held in contempt, the organization complied with the request and produced all the data called for by the production order except copies of its membership lists. The NAACP contended that Alabama could not constitutionally compel their disclosure. The state Supreme Court twice dismissed petitions to review the final contempt judgment. The U.S. Supreme Court granted *certiorari* to consider the issues involved in 1957.[134] The pending case attracted the attention of law students and law journals to the relation between free expression and corporate governance.

While the NAACP's challenge to the Alabama incorporation laws proceeded, a law student at Yale published *State Control over Political Organizations: First Amendment Checks on Powers of Regulation* in the 1957 *Yale Law Journal* (the "Comment" or "Yale Comment").[135] The Yale Comment reflected exceptional social perspective and creativity; it revealed awareness that corporations had emerged during the short period of time since World War II as the most influential actors in the economic and political life of the nation;[136] it demonstrated a desire to support the struggle for black civil rights that occupied the center of national political debate, legal argumentation, and social controversy;[137] it displayed familiarity with blazing discussion at law schools around the country about the legitimacy of judicial review;[138] and it conveyed a recognition of the importance of nonprofit organizations to meaningful free expression and to theories of interest group pluralism and legal process then dominant in the academy.[139] Because the Yale Comment reflected emerging demands for greater constitutional protection for the nonprofit sector, it is worth examining it in some detail.

Denials of nonprofit incorporation constituted restraint on the right to promote a cause "by joint action," the Comment claimed.[140] The significant role that interest groups played in disseminating ideas demanded that the powers of states to place restrictions on dissemination had to be curtailed.[141] The imperatives of American pluralism required that interest group politics be insulated from state favoritism. Courts—particularly federal courts deciding constitutional questions—should use the First Amendment, as included in the Fourteenth, to nullify "state-imposed curtailments upon the rights of associations to communicate."[142]

Referring to the influential book *The Modern Corporation,* which had been written two decades earlier by Adolf Berle and Gardiner Means,[143] the Comment presented corporate form as not only critical to economic growth and prosperity but also fundamental to the expression of political and social views. It was common knowledge that, beginning in approximately 1850, commercial enterprises demanded an easily accessible form of organization that would limit the liability of investors and facilitate the conduct of business.[144] As everybody knew, commercial corporations had come to dominate American economic life and to influence the political process as well.

Less well-known was the use of the corporation laws by associations that engaged in "influencing public opinion." Opinion-molding associations followed the same route as commercial ones by incorporating themselves to protect individual members and promote their views more effectively. Pressure groups such as the American Legion, the Veterans of Foreign Wars, the American Civil Liberties Union, and the NAACP were now incorporated.[145]

Although the barriers to commercial incorporation had been eliminated, they still existed for political associations. Many states continued to vest administrative officials or judges with discretion to deny incorporation, without clear standards for exercising this power.[146] Beyond denying corporate charters to associations, state authorities employed other parts of the nonprofit laws to inhibit corporate activities. The NAACP, as a foreign corporation, had been excluded from doing business in several states. Unincorporated chapters as well as parent corporations had been banned because groups failed to comply with demands to publish their membership lists.[147] State control over political organizations that operated in nonprofit forms allowed state authorities to privilege some expressions of opinion and to suppress others by licensing and regulating them.[148] Recent displays of antipathy toward civil rights groups by southern authorities using the corporation laws manifestly demonstrated that these controls required fundamental reform. But on what legal grounds might state barriers to nonprofit activities be challenged?

Ironically, the new liberal argument for restraining government intrusion on nonprofit corporations depended on arguments about the soundness of protecting corporate autonomy, personhood, and capacity—which a century of liberal reformers *opposed* as a cornerstone of excessive corporate power.[149] Corporations, the Comment argued, were entitled to the "liberty" interest of all persons, whom the Fourteenth Amendment protected. Notwithstanding powerful case law to the contrary,[150] the Comment insisted that intrusions by government corporation laws upon the activities of nonprofit "political organizations" (which were never defined or distinguished from "nonpolitical" ones) should be considered abridgments of free speech and equal protection rights guaranteed through the use of the word "liberty" in the language of the Fourteenth Amendment. The Fourteenth Amendment, it asserted, should be used to restrict state corporation law restrictions.[151]

The court's distinction between a corporation (without bill of rights protections) and its personal agents (who held such protections) was said to be unprincipled and "obscure."[152] With a boldness that student authors share and the professoriate sometimes lacks, the Comment boldly declared that the agent/group distinction would ultimately fail:

> Courts must interpret the Fourteenth Amendment in one of two ways: either an association or corporation is not a person entitled to free speech and its agents acting in an official capacity cannot claim protection; or such organizations are persons entitled to free speech protection and the organizations as well as their individual agents have standing to enforce this right. From the standpoint of constitutional interpretation and public policy, the construction that organizations have a right of free speech is preferable.[153]

It followed from the Yale Comment's analysis of the free speech rights of associations and corporations that there existed a First Amendment right of associational expression which limited the ability of states to use as criteria for incorporation the "vague," content-sensitive standards that had developed under current state laws.[154]

The Comment addressed two criteria that were being used by state officials to prevent incorporation or the doing of business by a foreign corporation that appeared to spuriously inhibit free expression—the frequently employed test that the principles of associations accord with public policy, and the test that they must not conduct activities that are adequately performed by other organizations.[155] To condition a certificate of incorporation upon public approval of principles advanced by an association would discourage the advocacy of ideas deemed offensive to the community. The First Amendment only permitted states to discourage the advocacy of ideas that were "libelous, obscene, seditious or imminently provocative of serious violation of law,"[156] and states were forbidden from disapproving of ideas that fell outside the permissible zone.[157] Under such a standard the author of the Yale Comment might have permitted a Nazi Bund to get a charter as the price of First Amendment protection for all political perspectives.

The second spurious basis for rejecting charters appeared to be on the ground that they duplicated the functions of other, existing nonprofit corporations. Although the restriction of economic competitors could be a basis for limiting commercial incorporation where monopolies were necessary as inducements to enter a market, the author expounded that using such a rationale to exclude nonprofit political organizations from forming could "never be sustained," since it was "inconsistent with the First Amendment's goal of a free marketplace of ideas."[158] To deny incorporation to political associations merely because others with identical principles were in existence was an unconstitutional abridgment of the guarantee of free speech, and in addition a denial of equal protection of the law.[159]

Constitutionally, the Yale Comment suggested, equal protection claims should prevail against applications of both these tests whenever particular nonprofit groups were chartered while other groups were denied corporate status on a discriminatory basis, without a reasonable foundation.[160] Allowing some political organizations to incorporate "must" preclude a state from arbitrarily denying that privilege to others.[161]

There was a powerful, traditional objection to the Comment's constitutional arguments, however, which the Comment did not fully address. The traditional objection stated that although the Constitution prevented states from abridging or denying certain rights, it did not demand that states *facilitate and encourage* the exercise of rights by all persons equally.

There was no constitutional impediment to discretionary awards by the government that allowed some groups to exercise their constitutional rights more forcefully than others. Justice Holmes captured this view in his famous opinion upholding the termination of a government employee for engaging in politics, where he wrote that "there is nothing in the constitution or the statute to prevent the city from attaching obedience to this rule [banning the solicitation of funds for political causes] as a condition to the office. . . . The petitioner may have a constitutional right to talk politics, but he has no constitutional right to be a policeman."[162] The state's grant of incorporation status arguably did not prevent unincorporated groups from expressing themselves or from seeking to incorporate as for-profit incorporations or from accomplishing their purposes in other corporate forms. Nor did the approval of the charters of other groups guarantee that incorporated entities would receive public subsidies, direct subsidies, tax deductible contributions, or other kinds of support from governments. In this view the presence or absence of support was not guaranteed by the First Amendment and was not an index of the extent to which the right to free speech was being honored. The denial of corporate status did not deprive corporations of their rights to free expression; it only denied them certain privileges—or diminished the likelihood of obtaining privileges such as tax exemptions and tax deductible contributions—that might amplify those rights to free expression. Why should government be restrained from creating tests by which basic rights to free speech and association were *augmented*?

The trouble with applying this "Holmesian" position to the NAACP facts rested with the distinction between the government's power to withhold or grant certain privileges within its legislative power, on the one hand, and its responsibility to ensure equal rights of free expression and association, on the other. The "privilege" analysis did not apply at all, moreover, to unincorporated associations such as the NAACP local chapters. Unless they advocated certain kinds of violence or revolution, unincorporated associations of individuals surely were sheltered by a First Amendment right—not at all resembling a privilege—equally to express themselves and to associate free from government interference.

And though a grant of incorporation might be regarded as mere "facilitation" and not a grant of substantial rights to expression, this was not necessarily the case. If arbitrary disapprovals resulted in a sort of diminished constitutional right to free expression that attached to unincorporated individuals and associations, then more than mere facilitation of the "privileged" groups was involved. If speech by unincorporated groups were somehow "second-class," then the denial of incorporation might be an abridgment of free speech contrary to the First Amendment, unless the discrimination could be justified by a "substantial public purpose."[163] If incorporation as a nonprofit was crucial to protected expression and association, then its withholding was therefore not appropriately the target of the Holmesian "policeman" reply.[164]

The logic of treating incorporation as a right to be obtained upon demand instead of a privilege to be granted upon discretionary review depended for its force on the centrality of incorporation to associational expression. For that reason, perhaps, the Yale Comment offered a brief historical and theoretical discussion of nonprofit incorporation that emphasized the hardships worked upon nonprofit groups that operated in an unincorporated form.[165] Unincorporated groups could not hold or convey property or sue in their own name without recognition as legal entities.[166] Lacking incorporation, members of unincorporated associations had been held personally liable for the debts of the association on an agency theory.[167] Nonprofit groups without incorporated status operated without the permanency and fund-raising ability of incorporated groups. Denial of incorporation placed rejected applicants "at a serious competitive disadvantage with incorporated associations."[168]

If it was an impermissible violation of constitutional rights for states to prevent the incorporation of nonprofit political organizations, it followed that it also violated the rights of nonprofit corporations to exclude them from conducting business in another state. A group that was denied incorporation in one state might continue to operate in that state in unincorporated form, but excluding a foreign corporation from doing business had always been interpreted to mean that the group could not operate at all once it was excluded. This assertedly constituted a prior restraint, "the most extreme form of First Amendment abridgment," because a state that excluded a nonprofit corporation from doing business was effectively punishing the organization for conduct that the group had not yet committed.[169]

Although the Supreme Court had upheld the power of states to exclude foreign commercial corporations to maintain the integrity of its incorporation laws, its interest seemed attenuated in the context of nonprofit political organizations, where maintaining a local incorporation policy designed to monitor corporate activity appeared "too insubstantial to justify a prior restraint of free speech."[170] In the NAACP cases, "any agent of the NAACP who addressed a meeting in Alabama or Texas, the states from which the association was ousted by court injunction, would be subject to criminal contempt."[171] By any reasonable test, the student author believed, the power of the states to control expression and association was impermissibly great.[172] The student author actually discussed his ideas with NAACP attorneys Thurgood Marshall and Robert Carter, who then were appealing the Alabama decision. References to the Comment found their way into the appellant's brief.[173]

The opinion of the U.S. Supreme Court in *NAACP v. Alabama* ex rel. *Patterson* moved constitutional law in the general direction advocated by the *Yale Law Journal* student author. In a unanimous opinion delivered by Justice Harlan, the Court imposed new restrictions on the capacity of states to control the activities of unincorporated and incorporated nonprofit associations. It declared that the relationship between the freedoms of speech and assembly was a close one and that "effective advocacy of both public and private points of view, particularly controversial ones," was enhanced by group association.[174] The order requiring the NAACP to produce records, including the names and addresses of all members and agents, was held to be a denial of due process because it was likely to impose a substantial restraint upon the exercise by its members of their right to freedom of association.[175]

Of great import for nonprofit associations generally, the Court determined that under the Due Process clause, the type of association that would be protected under the Fourteenth Amendment was to be broadly construed. It was immaterial whether the beliefs sought to be advanced by an association pertained to political, economic, religious, or cultural matters.[176] Unincorporated and incorporated groups alike were protected. The Court observed that "beyond debate," the freedom to engage in association for the advancement of beliefs and ideas was an inseparable aspect of the "liberty" assured by the Due Process clause and that this liberty interest embraced the freedom of speech.[177]

Abridgment of indispensable liberties of speech, press, or association, though unintended, might inevitably follow from varied forms of governmental action. The intimidation of members could occur by the unrelated regulation of the organization to which they belonged.[178] Actions under the corporation laws and other laws that might curtail the freedom to associate therefore would be subject to the closest scrutiny under the Due Process clause.[179]

Although the decision in *Patterson* eventually would be used to support the protection of nonprofit associational activities from arbitrary state actions,[180] the Supreme Court confined its ruling to the effect of Alabama's order to produce records; it declined at that time to go so far as to decide whether the restraining order excluding the NAACP from soliciting support in Alabama was an unconstitutional abridgement of First Amendment or due process rights.[181] Thus, although *Patterson* imposed a direct free expression constraint on the ability to control unincorporated associations and incorporated ones, it did not make any determination of the permissible procedures through which nonprofit incorporation might be denied or limited or constrained, or the grounds on which state nonprofit incorporation laws might lawfully encourage some purposes while prohibiting others.

## The End of Judicial Oversight As a Significant Means for Supervising Nonprofit Corporations

The constitutional constraints imposed by *NAACP v. Patterson* did not settle the question of whether denials of incorporation or exclusions from doing business would be considered arbitrary if they denied charters for any reason other than the unlawfulness of corporate purposes. In an ironic twist, the landmark case that did change the landscape of judicial discretion and discretionary review of nonprofit incorporation charters more generally was a civil rights case of a different sort, *Association for the Preservation of Freedom of Choice v. Shapiro.*[182] It was a case in which a New York Supreme Court justice acted out of a liberal regard for civil rights causes rather than in opposition to them.

The Association for the Preservation of Freedom of Choice, Inc., formed in 1958 "to promote the right to individual freedom of choice and freedom of association."[183] At the time, federal and state civil rights laws forbidding discrimination in public accommodations, housing, and other areas were being enacted at the state and local levels. The title and purposes of the Association suggested to Shapiro, in the context of that period, that the organization's members aimed to foster resistance to the civil rights laws.[184] The certificate came for approval to Justice J. Irwin

Shapiro, then a fifty-five-year-old justice who recently had been appointed to the state supreme court. Justice Shapiro had graduated from New York University Law School in 1925. He served as an assistant district attorney, a New York City magistrate, a state commissioner of investigation, and a well-respected county court judge before joining the court.[185]

Citing *General Von Steuben Bund*,[186] *Daughters of Israel Orphan Aid Society*,[187] *Stillwell Political Club*,[188] and *Deutsch-Amerikanischer Volksfest-Verein*,[189] Justice Shapiro portrayed the duty of the court as seeing to it that the objects and purposes of the proposed corporation were lawful, in accord with public policy, and not injurious to the community.[190] Beneath the appealing language in the purposes clause of the charter, Justice Shapiro stated, was "the negation of a whole series of fundamental and basic rights which are the warp and woof of the way of life vouchsafed to *everyone* by the United States Constitution and that of the State of New York."[191] Individuals might indulge in prejudices and bigotries, but "their purposes and practices should not be sanctioned by receiving the imprimatur of this court."[192] Justice Shapiro then cited the Japanese exclusion case *Hirabayashi*[193] for the proposition that distinctions based on ancestry were odious to a free people.[194] He referred to the New York state constitution, which provided that no person "because of race, color, creed or religion," would be subjected to discrimination in civil rights by any other person or by the state.[195]

The New York legislature had passed laws prohibiting discrimination in places of public accommodation, in employment, in education, and in publicly assisted housing.[196] Justice Shapiro referred to these laws and to the decision in *Catalonian Nationalist Club*[197] for the proposition that organizations that perpetuated the division of people into racial groups should not receive state sanction.[198] He concluded that the association's proposed purpose, "to promote the right to individual freedom of choice and freedom of association," was a cloak for its real purpose:

> To say to certain segments of our population:
>> You can't enter here.
>> You can't ride here.
>> You can't work here.
>> You can't play here.
>> You can't study here.
>> You can't eat here.
>> You can't drive here.
>> You can't walk here.
>> You can't worship here.[199]

If the court were to approve the charter, it would enable the corporation to engage in "indiscriminate impositions of inequalities."[200] "No matter how grandiose the language, when the malevolent purpose is apparent, the law should not permit itself to be used to further such ends," he wrote.[201] Justice Shapiro denied the organization's application for approval of the certificate with a final quotation from Balzac: "Hatred is the vice of narrow souls; they feed it with all their littleness, and make it the pretext of base tyranny."[202]

The Appellate Division unanimously dismissed the association's petition to order Justice Shapiro to revoke or annul his opinions. It affirmed Justice Shapiro's opinion squarely on the permissibility of the substantive determination by a judge that "the objects and purposes of the proposed corporation are lawful, in accord with public policy and not injurious to the community."[203] Preservation of Choice told the trial court that it intended to carry out its purposes through lawful means, such as by putting out educational material, filing amicus curiae briefs, and appearing before legislative committees. Supreme Court Justice Shapiro believed that the innocuous purposes were a "cloak for the real purpose for which the corporation is sought to be organized."[204]

Failing in New York, Preservation of Choice obtained a charter as a nonprofit corporation in the District of Columbia without difficulty. The justice, however, retaliated by signing orders denying Preservation of Choice approval as a New York membership corporation under section 10 of the Membership Corporations Law. He also prohibited the District of Columbia corporation from doing business in New York.[205] Preservation of Choice litigated numerous appeals through the trial and appellate courts and ultimately to the New York Court of Appeals.[206]

During the three-year procedural history of Association for the Preservation of Freedom of Choice, and before the court of appeals delivered its final decision in the case, two other law review comments appeared.[207] Anthony Charles Vance, a newly minted lawyer, published an article titled *Freedom of Association and Freedom of Choice in New York State* in the *Cornell Law Quarterly*.[208] In it he argued that the New York Membership Corporations Law imposed improper restraints on the right to organize for purposes that were "not only protected by the first and fourteenth amendments but which are clearly necessary if intelligent representative government is to flourish." Never, Vance exclaimed, was the problem so clearly illuminated by any case.

The function of courts was not to make substantive policy judgments but to act in a ministerial fashion, Vance argued. He reminded his readers of dicta in the *Matter of Lithuanian Workers' Literature Society*,[209] which might have produced a much more limited understanding of judicial discretion to disapprove of nonprofit incorporations. There the Second Department had nodded to the importance of objectivity:

> It is not the province of this court in any of its departments to set itself up as a censor of the tastes, social or political, of the people. However repugnant to our minds and consciences the Socialist program may be, we are not to stand in the way of organizations to promote its accomplishment, provided only it is clear that the purpose and intent of those organizations is to seek the accomplishment of that program by lawful methods.[210]

The true role of the court, the Cornell article asserted, was not to determine whether the cause or the purpose of a proposed corporation was normatively good or bad. Approval should be withheld only in cases where the proposed activity would be unlawful even if conducted by individuals or unincorporated groups.

Vance engaged in some wishful thinking that was contradicted by the long tradition of judicial discretion. He suggested that *Daughters of Israel Orphan Aid Soc'y*[211] had actually misread the intent of the New York legislature to let judges decide what was "unlawful" and thus laid the groundwork for subsequent unfairness. *Daughters of Israel* held that courts were responsible for coming to a conclusion about whether the objects and purposes of proposed corporations were in accord with public policy, "a determination that is more than ministerial and not a mere duplication of the function of the Secretary of State." It was this holding, he asserted, that distorted the statutory scheme and "spawned hideous judicial progeny."[212] His feeling was that *Daughters of Israel* promoted unbridled discretion, which had led one nonprofit charter to be withheld because the equity of the method of taxation it advocated was "a matter of speculation"[213] and another "because the Justice thought the corporation ought to be named after an American."[214]

With undisguised contempt, Vance offered up the nonprofit approval process as a paradigm of arbitrariness and subjectivity:

> A careful lawyer advising a group of incorporators as to the law could in truth suggest only that they study the political, economic, social, religious and other background of all of the justices of the supreme court in the county, select the one most likely to be in personal agreement with the corporation's purposes, watch until he is sitting in special term, and then present the certificate for approval, keeping their fingers crossed that by reason of illness, press of judicial business, etc., he is not transferred to another part. Such a game of judicial "Russian roulette" mocks the concept that we have of a government of laws and not of men.

This approval process represented the epitome of injustice; neutral principles were nowhere to be discovered. Moral argumentation found its way into almost every opinion. The outcome of cases appeared to have more to do with what the judges read and believed and aspired to than with any predictable legal rules.

The second article that appeared was a comment in the *Howard Law Journal, In re Application of the Association for the Preservation of Freedom of Choice*.[215] Lloyd McAulay and Carroll Brewster, the authors, were 1960 graduates of Yale Law School, with some reason to be aware of the Comment that appeared earlier in the *Yale Law Journal*. The thesis of their article was that the right of nonprofit corporations to incorporate was central to free speech rights, to pluralism, and to the amelioration of social conflict in America.

McAulay and Brewster began their article by emphasizing the importance of group rights. "If we are individualists now, we are corporate individualists. Our 'individuals' are becoming groups," they wrote, quoting the statement made by Ernest Barker in 1915.[216] Turning to the political scientist V.O. Key, they postulated that a primary function of government was to adjust the relation between associations: "labor unions, professional associations, NAACP, each [association] demanding and receiving loyalty from its members." Many if not most of these organizations had incorporated as nonprofit corporations.[217]

They emphasized that although the "privileges" of incorporation were not essential to free association, they were significant. A certificate conveyed a great deal that was generally unavailable to the unincorporated: the ability to hold property in common, the ability to take a devise or a bequest as an entity, relief from the fear of unlimited personal liability, and the right to sue in a common name.[218] Much more stood to be gained in terms of consumer acceptance and public reputability:

> The imprimatur of incorporation gives the organization a badge of legality which, though trivial to such organizations as the American Legion, may be of extreme importance to organizations whose programs are offensive to a large part of the community. Other privileges such as relief from the usually groundless fear of unlimited personal liability, or the right to sue or be sued, may be less important.[219]

Nonprofit incorporation was not really a privilege; it was (or rather should be) treated as a right.

The *Howard Law Journal* authors echoed the Yale Comment. They pointed out that under recent decisions of the court,[220] the speech and association "for which the APFC is attempting to incorporate" were constitutionally protected.[221] They equated the denial of the certificate of incorporation with a prior restraint of speech in violation of the First Amendment protection of freedom of speech[222] and with a state abridgment of the First Amendment protection of the right to associate.[223] They further compared the denial of a certificate on grounds of offensive purposes to the denial of a tax exemption for offensive speech.[224]

In the case of the Association for the Preservation of Freedom of Choice, McAulay and Brewster pointed out that the application for a charter was ex parte and that because the application was unopposed, the judge was required to "draw freely on his own knowledge and experience as well as whatever other sources of information might be available."[225] The Association for the Preservation of Freedom of Choice was unable to confront or even to know the judge's sources of information against it. No record had been built. The appellate court had only the general statement of purpose contained in the group's application and the judge's opinion, including his characterization of the association as a "hate group."[226]

Denying incorporation to the association would be a severe blow to it, the authors claimed, if only because of the damaging publicity and the "imprimatur of illegality" that Preservation of Freedom of Choice had received as a consequence of the court's disapproval. "Charter Denied to 'Hate Group'" led an article in the *New York Times*. The *New York Post* had run an article entitled "Court Refuses to Charter Hate Group." Similar stories were printed in other papers. "To allow incorporation to the NAACP and not to the APFC," the *Howard Law Journal* article stated, was "to deprive the members of the APFC of free association, and to violate the First and Fourteenth Amendments," since all protected speech and association must be equally protected.[227]

Should groups ill disposed to public discourse receive the full protections of the First Amendment?[228] The authors assured readers who believed that reactionary or racist organizations deserved not to receive state charters that a wiser perspective about the marketplace of ideas would lead them to understand that it would be wrong to privilege the new orthodoxy of integration any more than it was to privilege the old orthodoxy of segregation:

> Many there are who demand equality and the liberty to proclaim that demand. But of these many fall short of demanding liberty for reasons more fundamental than their own equality. They identify their outlook with that of the majority to show the dominant group that they deserve equal treatment as brothers in thought and deed. But their mettle is shown in victory. Victorious, they may stamp out the former orthodoxy, or they may preserve an open society as did the founding fathers with a Bill of Rights.[229]

They concluded with a reference to Professor Herbert Wechsler's newly published oration in the *Harvard Law Review* about the importance to judicial review of subscribing to "neutral principles."[230] However reactionary, government-chartered nonprofit "hate groups" were preferable to government intervention in the "marketplace of ideas":[231]

> Victory over one more ugly inequality before the law is in the process of being realized (the social victory will come much more slowly). By this decision New York would hammer home so just an orthodoxy by quelling all atavistic opposition. But the First and Fourteenth Amendments protect the freedom of those who wish to stand their ground or travel back as well as those who would go forward to close a gap between ideal and practice. . . . Because the world is so far from a workable solution [to the problems engendered by segregation and prejudice] a state should not only say "I defend to the death your right to say it" but should provide an atmosphere for men of all opinions to speak as clearly and effectively as possible. While there are significant elements in society who disagree with the aims and practice of racial integration, they should be encouraged to speak, for only then will a better position emerge with some accord.[232]

Establishing a right to nonprofit incorporation through a court decision in *Association for the Preservation of Freedom of Choice* or by legislative reform would erase an unpleasant and dangerous tolerance for discretion in the law. It would prove that the civil rights movement had nothing to fear from groups with opposing agendas and ideas.

When it was delivered, the 1961 opinion of the Court of Appeals made it clear that New York's highest court had indeed bridled discretion. The *Association* majority opinion declared that the common law enlargement of the authority to review certificates had "engrafted erroneous" views about legislative intent for judicial review, which was "to ascertain whether the proposed incorporation was for a lawful purpose . . . but only that and nothing more."[233] The court stated that the meaning of an "unlawful purpose" had been misunderstood through a long line of cases and the significance of judicial "approval" had been exaggerated:

> It is perfectly lawful for an individual or group of individuals to agitate for the repeal or modification of any law on the statute books of the State, or even for a change in the form of the State government itself, provided such agitation is not coupled with the advocacy of force and violence . . . Of course approval of a corporate charter devoted to such a purpose does not imply approval of the views of its sponsors. It simply means that their expression is lawful, and their sponsors *entitled to a vehicle for such expression.*[234]

The court observed that dissenting organizations, as well as organizations that supported existing laws, had "equal rights, so far as freedom of expression is concerned" and deserved "an equal and objective application of the statute."[235]

In dissent, Judge Burke framed the issue in traditional terms. This was not a matter of freedom of speech, he claimed, but of deciding whether the state must bestow privileges on all groups that wanted them equally. When the court approved of a not-for-profit charter, it was placing the "imprimatur of incorporation, bearing the blessing of the Supreme Court, the benediction of the Secretary of State, and the right to affix the characterization 'Incorporated under the Laws of the State of New York' to public matter so as to enable the organizers to assure themselves the prestige which accompanies the privilege."[236]

In Pennsylvania, another jurisdiction in which discretionary judicial approvals had been the norm, the discretionary conception was also overthrown.[237] There the state's highest court reversed a ruling that denied incorporation to a group whose object was the "militant and belligerent" conversion of Catholics to Protestantism.[238] "Whether the court because of personal predilection on the subject, does not wish it to appear that it approves of the purposes of the corporation, is beside the point," the court stated. The point, it declared, was that the First Amendment and the Fourteenth Amendment guaranteed the free exercise of religion, and that the privilege of incorporation as a nonprofit was "wholly statutory." In a long and emphatic dissent, another justice insisted that incorporation conferred a badge of state approval on a nonprofit group.[239]

*            *            *

Within five years, between 1957 and 1962, court rulings at state and federal levels reordered thinking about the formation of nonprofit corporations. Following these decisions, state legislatures dismissed the old justifications and reformulated the law of nonprofit incorporation according to new ones. New state court rules and newly imposed federal constitutional constraints abruptly curtailed the permissible basis for refusing to allow nonprofit associations to incorporate and also restricted the permissible ways in which they might be regulated.

The transformation that occurred was part of the larger reconception of the importance of nonprofit endeavor—but it was immediately influenced in no small measure by a generation of law students and recent law school graduates writing in academic law journals. The court of appeals in *Association for the Preservation of Freedom of Choice* in fact cited all of the five academic comments discussed above: The Columbia Note, Dwight's Observation, the Yale Comment, the Cornell Note, and the

Howard Article were all cited.[240] It is little short of astonishing that *no case law* was cited as precedent for the majority view: these were the *only* sources cited by the court of appeals in support of its final opinion.[241]

The theory about nonprofit incorporation that had now emerged subordinated traditional concerns—about such matters as the misuse of public subsidies, the diversion of scarce charitable funds, the confusion of the public, and the contravention of public policy—to newly heightened concerns about creating legal rules that would not disenfranchise unpopular causes, inhibit movements for law reform, or burden the expression of underprivileged groups. It emphasized the importance of nonprofit corporations to First Amendment values and pluralist democracy, in addition to stressing the public face of "charity" and the potential for public gain through nonprofit enterprise.[242] It elevated their role—their "rightful" role in political and social life. It strengthened the public estimation of nonprofit contributions to political discourse and to meeting social needs.

By the mid-1960s, the approval of a nonprofit charter had become in all states an entitlement—for virtually any group asserting that it would operate in a legal manner and according to the formal rules for governance and distribution of revenues that were laid out either in special nonprofit laws or general incorporation laws. As part of a broader reformulation of the role of nonprofit associations, corporations, according to the newer concept, deserved to be chartered as long as they fell into broad categories of activity and met minimal formal requirements for the distribution of profits and assets.

### Notes

1. Learned Hand, *Is a Judge Free in Rendering a Decision? in* THE SPIRIT OF LIBERTY: Papers AND ADDRESSES OF LEARNED HAND 82–85 (1935) (ed. Irving Dillard 1959).

2. U.S. v. Wunderlich, 342 U.S. 98, 101 (1951) (Douglas, J., dissenting).

3. *See* Dean Harold C. Havighurst, *Law Reviews and Legal Education*, 51 JL. LEG. ED. 22, 23 (1956).

4. David Riesman, *Toward an Anthropological Science of Law and the Legal Profession*, 57 AM. J. SOC. 121 (1951), *reprinted* in David Riesman, INDIVIDUALISM RECONSIDERED 27 (1954); Riesman, *Law and Sociology: Recruitment, Training, and Colleagueship*, 9 STANFORD L. REV. 643 (1957); S. Warkov, LAWYERS IN THE MAKING (1965); Philip C. Kissam, *The Decline of Law School Professionalism*, 134 U. PA. L. REV. 251 (1986).

5. The distinctiveness of law students among other graduate students in these years could be understood by analyzing the decisions that college students made to become lawyers. Surveys of college seniors found that those who were headed for law schools were, "next to premeds, the most well-to-do and metropolitan,

disproportionally Jewish and Catholic, somewhat more inclined to want money than the chance to be original and creative." David Riesman, *Some Observations on Legal Education*, 68 WIS. L. REV. 63, 63–64 (1968). Even more than prospective physicians, students were likely to be male, and the environment that they entered was a "hard" one, reported David Riesman, who was both a sociologist and a 1934 graduate of Harvard Law School. For "maleness" and "hardness," Riesman wrote, the pursuit of law education appeared "for the higher status groups [to have an] appeal similar to that of engineering."(*Id.* A few women did attend the elite law schools during the 1950s, including Justice Ruth Bader Ginsberg) Entering law students might view themselves as prospective social reengineers, even though few law.teachers would have identified themselves this way.

6. Riesman, *Law and Sociology* at 652 (referring to colleagueship).

7. Riesman, *Observations on Legal Education* at 69, 71.

8. *Id.*

9. Riesman, *Law and Sociology* at 648.

10. Harold C. Havighurst, *Law Reviews and Legal Education*, 51 JL. LEG. ED. 22, 22 (1956).

11. *Id.*

12. *Id.*

13. Arthur Nussbaum, *Some Remarks About the Position of the Student-Editors of the Law Review*, 7 JL. LEG. ED. 381, 381 (1955).

14. David Riesman, *Toward an Anthropological Science of Law and the Legal Profession*, 19 U. CHI. L. REV. 1 (1951), *reprinted* in David Riesman, INDIVIDUALISM RECONSIDERED 452 (1954).

15. Howard C. Westwood, *The Law Review Should Become the Law School*, 31 VA. L. REV. 913, 914 (1945).

16. "The atmosphere of such [elite law] schools . . . may help narrow the range of curiosity for some of the more humanistically oriented, but, unlike what often happens in graduate school to social scientists, law students do not become stupider and more cowed than they were as undergraduates. . . . People *do* get through law school in three years; there is very little of the protracted uncertainty of much graduate study, or of the umbilical clinging to one's teachers which failure to finish a thesis permits. . . . The validity of their profession is only marginally in question: its success is historically solid and daily attested in the marketplace of American careers. While to be sure sensitive lawyers and law professors suffer because of some popular disesteem for lawyers (though Supreme Court justices stand at the very top, even above physicians and physicists) . . . it seldom shakes their belief in the legal career as such, but rather reinforces their belief in a variant model of it, such as the Brandeis-at-the-bar model, or the small-town independent lawyer model, or that of the crusading government lawyer." *See* Riesman, *Law and Sociology* at 646–47.

17. Benjamin N. Cardozo, THE NATURE OF THE JUDICIAL PROCESS 168 (1922).

18. *See* Alexander M. Bickel, THE LEAST DANGEROUS BRANCH: THE SUPREME COURT AT THE BAR OF POLITICS (1962). *See also* David Cole, *Beyond Unconstitutional Conditions: Charting Spheres of Neutrality in Government-Funded Speech*, 67 N.Y.U. L. REV. 675 (1992).

19. *Id.* at 79–80.

20. *See* Michael Wells, *Behind the Parity Debate: The Decline of the Legal Process Tradition in the Law of Federal Courts*, 71 B.U. L. REV. 609 (1991).

21. *See* Edward A. Purcell, THE CRISIS OF DEMOCRATIC THEORY; SCIENTIFIC NATURALISM AND THE PROBLEM OF VALUE (1973); Kalman, *infra* n.22.

22. *See* Morton J. Horwitz, THE TRANSFORMATION OF AMERICAN LAW, 1780–1860 vol. 2 (1992); *see also* Norman Silber and Geoffrey Miller, *Toward "Neutral Principles" in the Law: Selections from the Oral History of Herbert Wechsler*, 93 COLUM. L. REV. 854 (1993); Laura Kalman, LEGAL REALISM AT YALE (1986). Among them were Roscoe Pound, Karl Llewellyn, Jerome Frank, Arthur Corbin, William O. Douglas, and others.

23. Regarding the process of appointment of New York Supreme Court justices, the modern structure of the New York State Supreme Court evolved from the 1846 Constitution, which abolished the New York Court of Chancery and established a supreme court having general jurisdiction in law and equity. For most of the court's history, the justices of the state supreme court were formally elected to fourteen-year terms. Their nomination and reappointment, however, was generally within the hands of the political parties. The governor, furthermore, exercised significant appointment power, especially to appellate positions. Appointments to vacancies on the court have been made by the governor without legislative or elective ratification. *See* 28 NY Jur 2d, Courts & Judges §§3, 4, 67 (1983); *See also* Office of Judicial Administration, A GUIDE TO COURT SYSTEMS 44–49 (1971, 5th ed.); note, *Judicial Selection in New York: A Need for Change*, 3 FORDHAM URB. L.J. 605 (1975).

24. This became apparent as early as the 1937 Court-packing plan presented by the Roosevelt administration, when few appeared to doubt that changing the composite age or political allegiance of the justices would dramatically change constitutional law. *See* William Leuchtenburg, THE SUPREME COURT REBORN: THE CONSTITUTIONAL REVOLUTION IN THE AGE OF ROOSEVELT (1995); Leuchtenburg, *The Origins of Franklin D. Roosevelt's "Court Packing" Plan*, 1966 SUP. CT. REV. 347 (1966); *see also* Michael Arens, *A Thrice-Told Tale, or Felix the Cat*, 107 HARV. L. REV. 620 (1994).

25. Bickel, *supra* n. 18 at 81.

26. *See* Wells, *supra* n. 20 at 618.

27. *Id.*

28. Bickel, *supra* n. 18 at 132–33.

29. Their students, among them Paul Bator, Alexander Bickel, Ronald Dworkin, John Hart Ely, Henry Monaghan, and Philip Kurland, continued the tradition into the 1960s and beyond, elaborating on the work of their predecessors and diverging philosophically among themselves.

30. *See* Gary Peller, *Neutral Principles in the 1950s*, 21 U. MICH. J. L. REFORM 561, 595 (1988). *See also* Gary Minda, *The Jurisprudential Movements of the 1980s*, 50 OHIO ST. L.J. 599 (1988).

31. Note, *Judicial Approval As a Prerequisite to Incorporation of Non-Profit Organizations in New York and Pennsylvania*, 55 COLUM. L. REV. 380 (1955).

32. *Id.*

33. For many of those working on the *Columbia Law Review* during those years, Gellhorn was an inspiring teacher and "Wechsler was something of a guru." Tele-

phone interview with Yale Kamisar, Columbia '55, October 21, 1994. Many students on the *Review* were employed by Wechsler on American Law Institute and on other legislative drafting projects, and some were moved to consider teaching as a result. *Id.* The *Columbia Law Review* editorial boards of 1954 and 1955 included an exceptional number of students—at least eleven persons—who went on to careers in legal education. Among them were Barbara A. Black, Lino Graglia, Robert Haft, Geoffrey C. Hazard, Mark Hughes, William K. Jones, Yale Kamisar, Harold L. Korn, Robert Pitofsky, Warren Schwartz, and Michael I. Sovern.

34. Note *supra,* n. 31 at 380.

35. *Id.* at 381.

36. *Id.* at 394.

37. *Id.* (*citing* N.Y. MEM. CORP. LAW §10; PA. STAT ANN. tit. 15, §2851–207 [1938]).

38. *Id.* at 383.

39. *Id.* at 383–84 n. 20 (*citing, e.g.,* Lake Ynola Ass'n, 3 Pa C.C.626 [C.P. 1 887] [purpose approved unless injurious]; *In re* Wynnefield Jewish Center, 50 Pa. D.& C. 257 [C.P. 1944] [same]).

40. *Id.* at 383 n. 23 (*citing, e.g.,* Deutsch-Amerikanischer Volkfest-Verein, 200 Pa. 143, 145, 49 Atl. 949 [1901], *reversing* 24 Pa. C.C. 489, 9 Pa. Dist. 753 [C.P. 1900]).

41. *Id.* at 383 n. 22 (*citing, e.g., In re* Grand Jurors Ass'n, Bronx County, 25 N.Y.S. 2d 154 [Sup. Ct. 1942], 54 HARV. L. REV. 1235 [1941]).

42. *Id.* at 388.

43. *Id.*

44. *Id.* at 388.

45. *Id.*

46. *Id.* at 390–91 (footnotes omitted).

47. *Id.*

48. *Id.* at 388 (*citing* Company D Irish Volunteers, 21 Pa. Dist. 913 [C.P. 1912]).

49. *Id.* (*citing* cases).

50. *Id.* at 389.

51. *Id.* at 392.

52. *Id.*

53. *See* Susan Rose Ackerman, *Charitable Giving and "Excessive" Fund Raising,* 97 Q. J. ECON. 195–212 (1982).

54. *Id.*

55. *Id.* at 395.

56. *Id.* at 393. The authority of the New York Supreme Court justices allowed no statutory basis for declaring that the trial judge's power was ever "wrong," since it provided no standard for "unlawfulness" short of corruption or bad faith. Professor Rosenberg later classified this kind of authority, in which judges are never wrong, as a situation of "primary" discretion. *See* Maurice Rosenberg, APPELLATE REVIEW OF TRIAL COURT DISCRETION (1977). This is distinguishable from "secondary" discretion—judges might be found in error because their discretion was bounded, but the rules nevertheless gave the trial judge the "right to be wrong without incurring reversal." *Id.* New York justices possessed discretion that embraced both kinds of immunity from appellate criticism: they had the power to approve or disapprove charters without standards for ap-

proval and, because of the absence of legislative standards, they had a right to promulgate opinions, even legally erroneous ones, that were functionally incapable of review.

57. *See supra,* n. 31 at 395.

58. *Id.* In a footnote the author expressed reservations about the proposal in which a Bund might be concerned. Individuals who otherwise had a right to study the language and culture of a foreign government had no necessary right to secure the "privilege of a corporation." *Id.* at 394 n. 95 (*citing In re* General Von Steuben Bund, 159 Misc. 231, 234, 287 N.Y.S. 527, 530 (N.Y. Sup. Ct. 1936). On the other hand, the author said in defense, "if the activities of such person are sufficiently detrimental to the interests of society, there is no apparent reason why they should be permitted to operate as an unincorporated association." The advantages of incorporation, which are relatively minor, at least in this area, would not seem to make them significantly more dangerous, and it is submitted that denial of a charter is merely an empty gesture." *Id.*

59. *Id.*

60. *See* George H.P. Dwight, *Objections to Judicial Approval of Charters of Nonprofit Corporations,* 12 Bus. Law. 454 (1957).

61. *Id.* at 454.

62. Dwight went on to become a partner with the firm of Emmet, Marvin & Martin in New York City.

63. Dwight, *supra* n. 60 at 457.

64. *Id.* at 454.

65. *See In re* Council for Small Business, Inc., 155 N.Y.S.2d 530 (Sup. Ct. 1956).

66. Dwight, *supra* n. 60 at 456.

67. *Id.*

68. *Id.*

69. *Id.*

70. 155 N.Y.S.2d 126 (Sup. Ct. 1956).

71. *Id.* at 127.

72. Dwight, *supra* n. 60 at 455 (*citing* Howard Memorial Fund, 155 N.Y.S.2d 126 [Sup. Ct. 1956]).

73. *Id.*

74. *Id.* at 456.

75. *Id.*

76. *Id.* In succeeding decades, confidence in the ability of administrative law procedures to adhere to appropriate legal standards under delegated authority would wane considerably. Concern about "bureaucratic drift" and "judicialization" later became widespread. *See, e.g.,* Lauren A. Smith, *Judicialization: The Twilight of Administrative Law,* 85 Duke L.J. 427 (1985).

77. *Id.*

78. Model Nonprofit Corp. Act §68 (ABA, 1964 rev.); *see also Id.* at 2; *see infra* (concerning the Model Act).

79. Dwight, *supra* n. 60 at 457 (*citing* Ill. Stat. Ann., c. 32, §163a1-a100 [1954]; Mo. Stat. Ann., §355.010–520; Va. Code §13.1–13.1–201–292 [1956]; Model Nonprofit Corp. Act, §30 [1952]) (requiring a nondiscretionary finding by the secretary of state that "the articles of incorporation conform to law").

80. *See* John Morton Blum, V WAS FOR VICTORY: POLITICS AND AMERICAN CULTURE DURING WORLD WAR II (1976).

81. *See generally* Otis A. Pease, THE RESPONSIBILITIES OF AMERICAN ADVERTISING: PRIVATE CONTROL AND PUBLIC INFLUENCE, 1920–1940 (1958).

82. *See* William Hollingsworth Whyte, THE ORGANIZATION MAN (1956); Hans Gerth and C. Wright Mills, CHARACTER AND SOCIAL STRUCTURE (1953); C. Wright Mills, THE POWER ELITE (1956); C. Wright Mills, WHITE COLLAR: THE AMERICAN MIDDLE CLASSES (1951).

83. Whyte, *supra* n. 82 at 4.

84. Mills, *supra* n. 82 at 59.

85. *See generally* Mills, *supra* n. 82.

86. *See* Arthur Bentley, THE PROCESS OF GOVERNMENT (1949); David B. Truman, THE GOVERNMENTAL PROCESS (1951); Robert Alan Dahl, A PREFACE TO DEMOCRATIC THEORY (1956); Robert Alan Dahl, WHO GOVERNS? DEMOCRACY AND POWER IN AN AMERICAN CITY (1961); Seymour Martin Lipset, POLITICAL MAN (1960); W. W. Crosskey, POLITICS AND THE CONSTITUTION IN THE HISTORY OF THE UNITED STATES vol. 2 (1953); Talcott Parsons, THE STRUCTURE OF SOCIAL ACTION (1949); Talcott Parsons, THE SOCIAL SYSTEM (1951); L. Harmon Zeigler, INTEREST GROUPS IN AMERICAN SOCIETY (1964); Betty H. Zisk, AMERICAN POLITICAL INTEREST GROUPS: READINGS IN THEORY AND RESEARCH (1969). *See also* Gordon Wood, THE RADICALISM OF THE AMERICAN REVOLUTION (1992) (suggesting that interest group theory was at the heart of the American revolution).

87. Truman, *supra* n. 86 at 66.

88. *See* Robert A. Dahl, DILEMMAS OF PLURALIST DEMOCRACY (1982); *but see* Mancur Ohlson Jr., THE LOGIC OF COLLECTIVE ACTION (1965) (offering explanations for the underrepresentation of certain interest groups).

89. Truman, *supra* n. 86 at 502.

90. *Id.*

91. *Id.* at 514.

92. John Kenneth Galbraith, AMERICAN CAPITALISM: THE CONCEPT OF COUNTERVAILING POWER 131–32 (1952).

93. On the legal process school, *see, e.g.,* Gary Peller, *Neutral Principles in the 1950s,* 21 U. MICH. J. L. REFORM 561 (1988); Morton Horwitz, THE TRANSFORMATION OF AMERICAN LAW vol. 2 (1992).

94. *See* Lon L. Fuller, THE MORALITY OF LAW (1979).

95. *See* Dahl, *supra* n. 88; *see also* Daniel Bell, THE END OF IDEOLOGY: ON THE EXHAUSTION OF POLITICAL IDEAS IN THE FIFTIES (1962).

96. *See* Herbert Wechsler, *The Political Safeguards of Federalism: The Role of the States in the Composition and Selection of the National Government,* 54 COLUM. L. REV. 543 (1954).

97. *See* John Hart Ely, DEMOCRACY AND DISTRUST: JUDICIAL REVIEW AND REPRESENTATIVE GOVERNMENT (1980).

98. *Id.; but see* Charles Reich, *The New Property,* 73 YALE L.J. 733 (1964).

99. Ironically, the legitimacy of the administrative state permitted government to take upon itself—especially during the late Eisenhower, Kennedy, and Johnson years—the direct performance of many social welfare activities previously confined to the voluntary, private, nonprofit world. Arguably, the government's in-

volvement in social welfare activities diminished the necessity for nonprofit groups to receive government subsidies.

100. *Id.; see also* William E. Nelson, *The Growth of Distrust: The Emergence of Hostility Toward Government Regulation of the Economy*, 25 HOFSTRA L. REV. 1 (1996).

101. U.S. CONST. amends. V, XIV.

102. *See* David P. Currie, THE CONSTITUTION IN THE SUPREME COURT: THE SECOND CENTURY, 1888–1986, *quoting* Joint Anti-Fascist Committee v. McGrath, 341 U.S. 123, 168 (1951) (Frankfurter, J., concurring) (arguing that the attorney general's list of subversive activities offended the Due Process Clause of the Fifth Amendment).

103. *See, e.g.*, Willner v. Committee on Character and Fitness, 373 U.S. 96, 83 S. Ct. 1175, 10 L. Ed. 2d 224 (1963).

104. *See* note, *Licensing by Local Governments in Illinois*, 1957 U. ILL. L. REV. 1 (1957).

105. *See* Wignall v. Fletcher, 303 N.Y. 435, 441 (1952).

106. *See* note, *Unconstitutional Conditions*, 73 HARV. L. REV. 1595, 1609 (1960) (indicating that the imposition of conditions on government benefits is "a distinct exercise of power which must find its own justification"). More recent discussions of the problem of unconstitutional conditions include Van Alstyne, *The Demise of the Rights-Privileges Distinction*; Richard Epstein, BARGAINING WITH THE STATE (1993).

107. *See* Schware v. Board of Bar Examiners, 353 U.S. 232, 77 S. Ct. 752, 1 L. Ed. 2d 796 (1957); Konigsberg v. State Bar, 353 U.S. 252, 77 S. Ct. 722, 1 L. Ed. 2d 810 (1957).

108. Wall v. King, 206 F.2d 878, 882 (1st Cir. 1953).

109. Federal Home Loan Bank Bd. v. Rowe, 284 F.2d 274 (D.C. Cir. 1960).

110. Charles A. Reich, *The New Property*, 73 YALE L.J. 733 (1964).

111. *Id.* at 786.

112. *Id.*

113. *Id.* at 740.

114. *Id.* at 744.

115. *Id.* at 746–47.

116. *Id.* at 747.

117. *Id.* at 757 (*citing* Barsky v. Board of Regents, 347 U.S. 442, 74 S. Ct. 650, 98 L. Ed. 829 [1954]).

118. *Id.* at 749.

119. *Id.* at 771.

120. *Id.* at 773.

121. *Id.* at 785.

122. Charles A. Reich, *The Liberty Impact of the New Property*, 31 WM. & MARY L. REV. 295, 305–6 (1990).

123. *Id.*

124. *See* Taylor Branch, PARTING THE WATERS: AMERICA IN THE KING YEARS, 1954–1963 (1988).

125. *See* Richard Kluger, SIMPLE JUSTICE: THE HISTORY OF BROWN V. BOARD OF EDUCATION AND BLACK AMERICA'S STRUGGLE FOR EQUALITY (1976).

126. *See* Jack Greenberg, CRUSADERS IN THE COURTS 14–25 (1994); NAACP v. Patterson, 357 U.S. 449, 451–52, 78 S. Ct. 1163, 1166, 2 L. Ed. 2d 1488, 1491 (1958).

127. *See generally* Kluger, *supra* n. 125.

128. *See* Taylor Branch, PARTING THE WATERS: AMERICA IN THE KING YEARS, 1954–1963 at 143–205 (1988).

129. *See* Petition for Writ of Certiorari at 28–29, NAACP v. Patterson, 353 U.S. 972, 77 S. Ct. 1056, 1 L. Ed. 2d 1135 (No. 91) (1957); Motion and Brief of *Amici Curiae* at 22, NAACP v. Patterson, 353 U.S. 972, 77 S. Ct. 1056, 1 L. Ed. 2d 1135 (No. 91) (1957).

130. NAACP, 357 U.S. at 452. The first Alabama affiliates were chartered in 1918. In 1951, the association opened a regional office in Alabama but never complied with the qualification statute. *Id.; see also* Branch, PARTING THE WATERS at 186–87.

131. ALA. CODE, tit. 10 §§192–198 (1940).

132. NAACP, 357 U.S. at 453.

133. *Id.*

134. *See* NAACP v. Patterson, 353 U.S. 972, 77 S. Ct. 1056 (1957), *cert. granted,* mem. 1 L. Ed. 2d 1135 (U.S. Ala., May 27, 1957) (No. 846).

135. Comment, *State Control over Political Organizations; First Amendment Checks on Powers of Regulation,* 66 YALE L.J. 545, 545 (1957). The author of the article was David Klingsberg. After graduating from Yale in 1957, Klingsberg clerked for Judge Dimock in the U.S. District Court for the Southern District of New York, then worked in the office of the U.S. Attorney for the Southern District of New York, and became a partner in the law firm of Kaye, Scholer, Fierman, Hays, and Handler.

136. *See, e.g.,* Whyte, *supra* n. 82 (corporate power).

137. *See* Richard Kluger, SIMPLE JUSTICE (1976) (regarding the civil rights movement's impact on American Life). *See also* Branch, *supra* n. 124.

138. *See* Alexander M. Bickel, THE SUPREME COURT AND THE IDEA OF PROGRESS (1970).

139. *See* comment, *State Control over Political Organizations, supra* n. 135.

140. *Id.*

141. *Id.*

142. *Id.*

143. Adolf Augustus Berle and Gardiner Means, THE MODERN CORPORATION AND PRIVATE PROPERTY 10–17 (1932).

144. Comment, *State Control over Political Organizations; at* 454, 550 (1957).

145. *Id.* at 551 n.37.

146. *Id.* at 551.

147. *See NAACP, supra* n. 132 at 453–54 and accompanying text.

148. *See* comment, *State Control over Political Organizations, supra* n. 135.

149. *See, e.g.,* Carl J. Mayer, *Personalizing the Impersonal: Corporations and the Bill of Rights,* 41 HASTINGS L.J. 577, 579–601 (1990).

150. Comment, *supra* n. 135 at 547 (*citing* Pierce v. Society of Sisters, 263 U.S. 510, 535, 44 S. Ct. 177, 202, 68 L. Ed. 414, 439 (1925) (educational corporation possessed no right to "liberty"); Western Turf Ass'n v. Greenberg, 204 U.S. 359, 363, 27 S. Ct. 384, 388, 51 L. Ed. 520, 524 (1907) (business corporation not entitled to "liberty"); *Northwestern* Nat'l Life Ins. Co. v. Riggs, 203 U.S. 243, 255, 27 S. Ct. 126, 138, 51 L. Ed. 168, 180 [1906]).

151. *Id.;* U.S. Const. amend. XIV, §1. The Fourteenth Amendment states that no state may deprive any person of "life, liberty, or property, without due process of law."

152. Comment, *State Control over Political Organizations; First Amendment Checks on Powers of Regulation, supra* n. 135.

153. *Id.* at 548–49.

154. Hague v. Committee for Industrial Organizations, 307 U.S. 496, 59 S. Ct. 954, 83 L. Ed. 1423 (1939).

155. *Id.* at 551–52.

156. *Id.* (*citing, e.g.,* Chaplinsky v. New Hampshire, 315 U.S. 568, 571, 62 S. Ct. 766, 769, 86 L. Ed. 1031, 1034 (1942); Near v. Minnesota, 283 U.S. 697, 51 S. Ct. 625, 75 L. Ed. 1357 (1931)).

157. *Id.*

158. *Id.* at 555.

159. *Id.*

160. *Id.* at 552 (*citing* Fowler v. Rhode Island, 345 U.S. 67, 73 S. Ct. 526, 97 L. Ed. 828 (1953) (denial of use of public park held unconstitutional); Niemotko v. Maryland, 340 U.S. 268, 71 S. Ct. 325, 95 L. Ed. 267 (1951).

161. *Id.*

162. McAuliffe v. New Bedford, 155 Mass. 216, 29 N.E. 517 (1892) (Holmes, J.). *See Adler v. Board of Education,* 342 U.S. 485, 72 S. Ct. 380, 96 L. Ed. 517 (1952) (relating to the ineligibility for employment).

163. Comment, *State Control over Political Organizations; First Amendment Checks on Powers of Regulation, supra* n. 135 (*citing* American Communications Ass'n v. Douds, 339 U.S. 382, 70 S. Ct. 674, 94 L. Ed. 925 [1950], where the court denied the privilege of using the NLRB to unions whose officers refused to sign non-Communist affidavits. The *Yale Law Journal* author observed that the court, *Id.* at 390, stated that some denials of privileges could constitute abridgements of First Amendment rights).

164. *See* Steven Shiffrin and Jesse H. Choper, The First Amendment 509 (1991); David Fellman, The Constitutional Right of Association 34–38 (1963); M. Glenn Abernathy, The Right of Assembly and Association 197–234 (1981); James E. Leahy, The First Amendment, 1791–1991 at 223–42 (1991).

165. Comment, *supra* n. 135.

166. *Id.*

167. *Id.*

168. *Id.* at 553.

169. *Id.* at 556.

170. *Id.* at 559.

171. *Id.* at 556–57.

172. *Id.*

173. Telephone interview with David Klingsberg, Oct. 14, 1994. *See* Petition for Writ of Certiorari at 28–29, NAACP v. Patterson, 353 U.S. 972 (No. 91) (1957); Motion and Brief of *Amici Curiae* at 22, NAACP v. Patterson, 353 U.S. 972 (No. 91) (1957). Both court documents cite the *Yale Law Journal* Comment.

174. NAACP v. Patterson, 357 U.S. 449, 460, 78 S. Ct. 1163, 1171, 2 L. Ed. 2d 1488 (1958).

175. *Id.* at 465. The court distinguished the case of New York ex rel. Bryant v. Zimmerman, 278 U.S. 63, 49 S. Ct. 61, where it upheld a New York anti-Ku Klux Klan law requiring all unincorporated associations that demanded oaths as a condition to membership to file copies of their governing documents and the oath, as well as a membership roster of their membership, with state officials. The court distinguished that case on the basis of the record of Klan violence before the New York legislature at the time, which provided a basis for legitimating the membership list request requirement.

176. *Id.*

177. *Id.* at 460.

178. *Id.*

179. *Id.* at 460–61.

180. In 1963, for example, in NAACP v. Button, 371 U.S. 415, 83 S. Ct. 328, 9 L. Ed. 2d 405, the court permitted the nonprofit corporation to assert a due process liberty right, namely, the right to solicit legal representation from school children's parents in desegregation suits.

181. *Id.* at 466.

182. 17 Misc.2d 1012, 187 N.Y.S.2d 706 (Sup. Ct. 1959); *aff'd on rehearing*, 18 Misc.2d 534, 188 N.Y.S.2d 885 (Sup. Ct. 1959); *application denied*, 10 A.D.2d 604, 199 N.Y.S.2d 435 (App. Div. 1959); *appeal denied*, 10 A.D.2d 711, 199 N.Y.S.2d 439 (App. Div.); *petition to revoke opinions denied*, 10 A.D.2d 873, 202 N.Y.S.2d 218 (App. Div.); *motion to clarify order and decision denied*, 8 N.Y.2d 910, 204 N.Y.S.2d 151 (1960); *reversed*, 9 N.Y.2d 376, 214 N.Y.S.2d 388 (1961).

183. 17 Misc.2d at 1014.

184. *Id.*

185. *See* Application of Ass'n for Preservation of Freedom of Choice, Inc., 187 N.Y.S.2d 706 (Sup. Ct. 1959); *see also J. Irwin Shapiro Dies: A Retired State Judge*, N.Y. TIMES, Oct. 3, 1985 at 23 col. 1.

186. *See supra*, ch. 3.

187. *See supra*, ch. 3.

188. *See supra*, ch. 3.

189. *See supra*, ch. 3.

190. Ass'n for Preservation for Freedom of Choice, Inc., 187 N.Y.S.2d 706, 707 (Sup. Ct. 1959).

191. *Id.* at 707 (emphasis added).

192. *Id.*

193. *See* Hirabayashi v. United States, 320 U.S. 81, 100, 63 S. Ct. 1375, 1385, 87 L. Ed. 1774, 1784 (1943).

194. 187 N.Y.S.2d at 708.

195. *Id.* at 708 (*citing* N.Y. CONST. art. 1, §11).

196. *Id.* (*citing* CIV. RIGHTS LAW §§40, 41; State Law Against Discrimination, EXEC. LAW §291; EDUC. LAW §313).

197. *See supra*, ch. 2, nn. 54–63 and accompanying text.

198. 187 N.Y.S.2d at 708.

199. *Id.*

200. *Id.* at 709 (*citing* Shelley v. Kraemer, 334 U.S. 1, 21, 68 S. Ct. 836, 846, 92 L. Ed. 1161, 1171 (1948).

201. *Id.* at 709.

202. *Id.* at 709 (*quoting* Balzac, *Le Cure du Tours* [The priest of Tours]).

203. *Id.* at 706.

204. *Id.* at 708.

205. *Id.* The Supreme Court's ruling in NAACP v. Alabama ex rel. Patterson had not forbidden the exclusion of corporations whose purposes were unlawful. *See supra.* Justice Shapiro did not refer to the ruling in the NAACP case in his opinion. *Id.*

206. Association for the Preservation for the Freedom of Choice, Inc. v. Shapiro, 214 N.Y.S.2d 388 (1961).

207. *See* Anthony Charles Vance, *Freedom of Association and Freedom of Choice in New York State*, 46 CORNELL L.Q. 290 (1961); Lloyd McAulay and Carroll Brewster, *In re Application of the Association for the Preservation of Freedom of Choice*, 6 HOWARD L.J. 169 (1960).

208. *Id.* at, 211. Vance graduated from George Washington University Law School in 1960.

209. 196 A.D. 262, 265, 187 N.Y.S. 612, 614 (App. Div. 1921).

210. Vance, *supra* n. 207 at 292.

211. 125 Misc. 217, 219, 210 N.Y.S. 541, 543 (Sup. Ct. 1925).

212. Vance, *supra* n. 207 at 292–93.

213. Vance, *supra* n. 207 at 293 (*citing* Matter of Council for Small Business, Inc., 155 N.Y.S.2d 530 (Sup. Ct. Kings Co. 1956).

214. Vance, *supra* n. 207 at 293 (*citing* Matter of Mazzini Cultural Center, Inc., 185 Misc. 1031, 58 N.Y.S.2d 529 [N.Y. Sup. Ct. 1945]).

215. Lloyd McAulay and Carroll Brewster, *In re Application of the Association for the Preservation of Freedom of Choice*, 6 HOWARD L.J. 169 (1960).

216. *Id.* at 169 (*quoting* Sir Ernest Barker, POLITICAL THOUGHT IN ENGLAND, 1848 TO 1914 at 158 [1954]).

217. *Id.*

218. *Id.*

219. *Id.* at 169–70 (footnotes omitted).

220. *Id.* at 172 (*citing* Beauharnais v. Illinois, 343 U.S. 250, 72 S. Ct. 725, 96 L. Ed. 919 (1951); NAACP v. Alabama, 357 U.S. 449, 78 S. Ct. 1163, 2 L. Ed. 2d 1488 [1957]).

221. *Id.* at 172.

222. *Id.* at 173.

223. *Id.* at 173 (*citing* NAACP v. Alabama, 357 U.S. 449, 78 S. Ct. 1163, 2 L. Ed. 2d 1488 [1959]).

224. *Id.* at 173–74 (*citing* Speiser v. Randall, 357 U.S. 513, 78 S. Ct. 1332, 2 L. Ed. 2d 1460 [1957]; objectionable oath required by veterans' group inadequate justification for withholding tax exemption). *See infra*, ch. 6.

225. *Id.* at 171 (*quoting In re* Boy Explorers of America, Inc., 67 N.Y.S.2d 108 [Sup. Ct. 1946]).

226. *Id.* at 171.

227. *Id.*

228. *See* Robert C. Post, *The Constitutional Concept of Public Discourse: Outrageous Opinion, Democratic Deliberation, and Hustler Magazine v. Falwell*, 103 HARV.

L. REV. 603 (1990); Robert C. Post, *Recuperating First Amendment Doctrine*, 47 STAN. L. REV. 1249 (1995).

229. McAulay & Brewster, 6 How. L.J. at 177 (footnotes omitted).

230. *Id.* at 177–78 (*citing and quoting* Herbert Wechsler, *Toward Neutral Principles of Constitutional Law*, 73 HARV. L. REV. 1 [1959]).

231. *See* John Stuart Mill, ON LIBERTY (1859) (ed. Stefan Collini 1989).

232. McAulay & Brewster, 6 How L.J. at 178.

233. Association for the Preservation of Freedom of Choice v. Shapiro, 214 N.Y.S.2d 388, 390–91 (1961). Examining the language and history of the relevant portion of the Membership Corporation Law, the majority opinion stated that "no standards are set up to guide the exercise of judicial power. It would seem logical, therefore, to assume that the function of judicial scrutiny as intended by the Legislature was to ascertain whether the proposed incorporation was for a lawful purpose." *Id.* at 390.

234. *Id.* at 391–92 (emphasis added).

235. *Id.* at 392.

236. *Id.* (*Citing In re* Stillwell Political Club, 26 Misc.2d 931, 109 N.Y.S.2d 331 (Sup. Ct. 1951); *In re* Patriotic Citizenship Ass'n, 26 Misc.2d 995, 53 N.Y.S.2d 595 (Sup. Ct. 1945).

Judge Froessel, who had written the opinion disapproving the *Patriotic Citizenship Association* in 1945 (*In re* Patriotic Citizenship Ass'n, Inc., 53 N.Y.S.2d 595 [N.Y. Sup. Ct. 1945]), and who since had been elevated to the state's highest court, concurred with the dissent. He understood the statutory prohibition on "unlawful purposes" to embrace the rejection of more than simply illegal ones. Unlawful purposes, he said, meant illegal objects "necessarily inconsistent with public policy as declared by public law." Judge Froessel concluded that it was inconceivable that the legislature would itself specially charter a corporation whose avowed purposes were inconsistent with public policy. This organization continued to oppose public policy. How, he asked, could the majority of the court conclude that the legislature would intend that justices should tolerate the incorporation of groups that the legislature itself would not charter? *Id.* at 394–95.

237. Conversion Center Charter Case, 388 Pa. 239, 243, 130 A.2d 107 (Sup. Ct. Pa. 1957).

238. *Id.*

239. *Id.* (Musmanno, dissenting).

240. *See* 55 COLUM. L. REV. 380 (1955); 66 YALE L.J. 545 (1957); 6 HOWARD L.J. 169 (1960); 46 CORNELL L.Q. 290 (1961); 12 BUS. LAWYER 454 (1956).

241. *See* Ass'n for the Preservation of Freedom of Choice v. Shapiro, 214 N.Y.S.2d 388 391 (1961).

242. *See* Robert Dahl, DILEMMAS OF PLURALIST DEMOCRACY 138–66 (1982).

# 5

## Transition to a New Regime

Many organizations and institutions contributed to changing the place of voluntary groups in American life during the 1950s and 1960s, but courts played the central role in reforming the way nonprofit corporations were created and supervised by the states.[1] As a result of the court rulings discussed in previous chapters, a nonprofit corporation could be chartered by any group of incorporators as long as it asserted some public benefit and met minimal, formal requirements for the distribution of its profits and assets. The traditional privileges of incorporation became available to a much broader set of nonprofit associations than ever before. Relying on their new legal status, a much larger set of organizations, pursuing a much broader variety of purposes, now could obtain benefits and solicit others—including exemptions, subsidies, grants, and donations—from governmental units and the public.[2]

Student notes and other commentaries had suggested that judicial screening probably made little difference in preventing inappropriate nonprofit activities from being created. Even if such screening did make a difference, they had argued, liberalizing the ability to create nonprofit incorporations made sense based on two inconsistent lines of reasoning.

The first line of reasoning minimized the importance of denying groups incorporation based on the modest, even trivial nature of the benefit involved, which rendered efforts involved in screening a waste of judicial and administrative resources. Exemptions from taxes, it was claimed, and not incorporation were the main benefit that accrued to nonprofit groups (incorporated or otherwise) and for these exemptions it was necessary to satisfy additional requirements in order to qualify. Incorporation meant nothing in and of itself.

The second line of reasoning proceeded along an opposite line. It maintained that the benefits conferred by incorporation were essential to nonprofit groups, rendering denial, when it occurred, a serious barrier to free expression. Incorporation, it was claimed, was central to the opera-

tion of most nonprofit organizations because of the particular reputational and more tangible advantages that attached to the nonprofit legal
personality. Either way—because the benefits of incorporation were insignificant or because they were highly significant—the end of the discretionary model could be justified.

Whichever path one took to the new view about liberalizing access to
nonprofit incorporation led away from the historic purposes that justified state screening of nonprofit corporation charters. Preventing nonprofit corporations from overstating their ability to accomplish their purposes, or from wasting resources, was no longer an appropriate goal at
the formation stage. Instead, there were newly heightened concerns that
motivated the drive for a permissive incorporation theory, including concerns about legal rules that disenfranchised unpopular causes, inhibited
law reform, stifled charitable impulses, chilled free expression, and otherwise burdened unincorporated groups.[3]

The mechanical operation of the new conception supposed that states
would cease trying to screen out unworthy nonprofit groups when they
applied for a charter or, in the parlance of some states, "registered to do
business as a nonprofit corporation." The fact that an applicant opposed
prevailing moral, social, or economic policies now presented inadequate
grounds for courts or bureaucrats to disapprove charters. From the new
perspective, in fact, groups advocating the repeal of existing laws operated in the public benefit, *by definition*, since they strengthened the
process of democratic government—and for that reason they *furthered*
public policy. Unless a legislature directed otherwise, only "illegal" purposes—those that on their face violated existing laws—warranted disapproval by state authorities as being "unlawful." To the extent that judges
and administrators continued to review applications for incorporation,
they would, in the future, need to behave within narrowly prescribed
rules that set ministerial boundaries on their discretion.

### The Judges Adjust to Their Subordinated Status

The doctrinal transformation took hold with some difficulty. At first,
judges resisted the deprivation of their authority. When it became clear
that meaningful supervision by courts had ended, the office of the secretary of state tried to compensate for the diminished judicial discretion
by manifesting greater discretion on its own part. Finally, the secretary
of state's authority diminished and the implementation of the new doctrine became fairly routinized. By the end of the 1960s, nonprofit corporations of all kinds were incorporated under statutory and common law
rules that differed in only minor respects from commercial incorporation doctrines.

Some New York Supreme Court justices chafed at the criticism of their jurisprudence and the loss of discretion they had suffered. At first, their resistance bordered on insubordination. When in 1963 the *Fraternidad Hispana Americana* (Spanish-American Brotherhood) proposed to develop "a program to meet the cultural, physical, mental and community needs of the individual,"[4] Justice Benjamin Brenner withheld his approval. He acknowledged that *Association for the Preservation of Freedom of Choice* enjoined him from evaluating the objects and purposes of the proposed corporation to find whether they were lawful and in accordance with public policy. He also conceded that disapproving of a corporate charter because it was "injurious to the community" was now too vague a standard to apply.[5]

The justice resentfully described the way his wings had been clipped by the Court of Appeals in *Association for the Preservation of Freedom of Choice* and belittled his "sole remaining function," that of applying judicial scrutiny to "ascertain whether the proposed incorporation was for a lawful purpose."[6] How could a lawful purpose be determined solely on the basis of a facial examination? Justice Brenner complained that it was impossible to exercise his judicial role only "on the basis of the explicit language of the objectives as they are set out in the proposed certificate."[7] Only naive revolutionaries or stupid charlatans would broadcast the unlawful nature of their objectives on the face of their certificate.[8]

> To be sure, the State could not lend its prestige and its franchise of incorporation for the very purpose of promoting its self-destruction through unlawful means. Yet it should be obvious that no group seeking such an objective would plainly state so in its proposed certificate and would naturally dissemble and hide its illegal purpose in language which is innocuous and otherwise acceptable. Thus it is difficult to conceive of any proposed certificate containing plain language descriptive of an unlawful organizational purpose.[9]

Brenner withheld his approval until the incorporators identified their assets and gave some indication that they would suffer significant liability if it later developed that the stated objectives of the corporation were false.[10]

In the next case that came along Justice Brenner tried to deflect criticism of his judgment by holding fact-finding hearings—to cure any suggestion that his opinions were framed without sufficient evidence. Unfortunately, even an evidentiary hearing could not eliminate the necessity to render a subjective, qualitative judgment about whether a corporation might have ulterior motives notwithstanding its explicitly stated purposes. When the attorney general opposed the certificate of the

Wholesale Milk Distributors Association because it seemed like a price-fixing group, Justice Brenner complained about having been enjoined from indulging in "personal predilections."[11] "Though I have taken evidence I am, nevertheless, restrained from speculating as to the economics of the situation," he stated. "It follows, too, that I cannot prejudge guilt or exercise 'judicial objectivity' on pure doubt however much I may share that doubt or suspicion with the Attorney General."[12] Under the circumstances the justice believed he could do nothing but approve the proposed certificate—although with a formal modification of the language of purposes to prohibit anticompetitive activities.[13] The new limits set by *Association for the Preservation of Free Choice* and by the federal constitutional jurisprudence of the First Amendment had effectively curbed the ability even to make an educated guess.

Judicial power to review the purposes of nonprofit corporations lingered in one area of law, notwithstanding the legal sea change. It proved especially hard for judges to disassociate personal interests from professional tasks when it came to reviewing the creation of legal entities that wanted to become nonprofit corporations. Legal defense funds to advance the interests of certain minority groups received special consideration, notwithstanding the newly imposed court rules.

When the Thom Lambda Legal Defense and Education Fund applied for approval in 1972 as a legal assistance corporation to provide "without charge legal services in those situations which give rise to legal issues having a substantial effect on the rights of homosexuals; [and] to promote the availability of legal services to homosexuals by encouraging and attracting homosexuals into the legal profession,"[14] a supreme court justice withheld his approval. On appeal, the appellate court agreed that Thom Lambda's purposes as stated were neither benevolent nor charitable nor of primary use to the poor, as was required of a fund for legal defense:

> It is not shown that the private sector of the profession is not available to serve this clientele, nor that, as to indigents, the existing legal assistance corporations are not available. A supplemental affidavit does indicate a lack of desire on the part of some attorneys who work *pro bono publico* to take the cases of homosexuals, but this appears to be no more than a matter of taste.[15]

The same court earlier had approved the application of the Puerto Rican Legal Defense and Education Fund, Inc. Nonetheless, the court distinguished the Puerto Rican group based on its demonstration that "indigence is rife amongst the intended clientele"[16] and because the court, disputing the group's statement of purposes, believed that homosexuals were not deprived of legal representation on that account.[17] The recent expansion of funds to support legal assistance corporations and their "proliferation" led the court to announce that demonstrations of "real need" would henceforth be more carefully reviewed. The court would not any longer put its "imprimatur" on a legal practice corporation "for no more reason than that it claims to represent a minority."[18] The court denied the not-for-profit legal assistance corporation its approval. Legal assistance corporations seeking to advance black rights also faced difficulties obtaining approval for their certificates.[19]

Nonprofit groups with charters whose purposes intimated some involvement with dispute resolution faced rejection of their certificates on the ground that they proposed unlawfully to offer legal services. When the Queens Lay Advocate Service tried to incorporate in 1972 to help "protect and expand the rights of pupils, parents and general public in their relation with the school system, including assisting persons involved in school grievances or disciplinary, suspension and other proceedings," and to arrange legal representation "where appropriate,"[20] it met with disapproval.

Justice William C. Brennan interpreted the corporate name as suggestive of legal advocacy.[21] Notwithstanding the language of the certificate, he believed that the statement of purposes in the proposed charter indicated that the corporation would perform duties "generally reserved for lawyers who have the education, training and responsibility that better qualifies them for such tasks."[22] Approving the certificate would "constitute a giant step in the wrong direction, encouraging swift erosion of the safeguards [provided by professional bar standards] so carefully promulgated."[23] The purposes contained in the Lay Advocate Service certificate transgressed "far beyond the borderline so established for the protection of the public."[24] Justice Brennan withheld his approval without prejudice to resubmitting an application under a different name and with nothing in it that intimated lawyering.[25]

Notwithstanding rearguard judicial resistance to relinquishing discretion, the old edifice crumbled. It is doubtful that judges refrained entirely from exercising a veto over charters by using their powers of dissuasion; but after 1963, the reported New York cases in which judicial approval of charters was withheld disappeared.[26] By the end of the 1960s, the law appeared resettled: It was reversible error for courts to withhold incorporation for reasons other than illegality or formal irregularities presented in the application for incorporation.[27]

\*     \*     \*

Developments in the drafting of a model nonprofit corporation act reflected some of the same problems New York was experiencing. In New York, incorporation as a nonprofit might be had for "any lawful purpose" but nonetheless involved judicial screening to determine whether such a purpose was indeed permissible. The laws of the other states took different forms but faced similar difficulties. During the post–World War II period nonprofit statues were, as they are now, generally considered a hodgepodge.[28] In states where legislatures had enumerated different categories of nonprofit organization, debates from time to time centered on whether to add or subtract in a piecemeal fashion from their lists of permissible purposes, and departments within state government spent time determining whether a corporate mission fell within the boundaries of a defined category. Uncertainty about the duties of officers and directors, vague record keeping and reporting requirements, and incomplete rules for the dissolution of corporations, furthermore, presented troublesome problems for the lawyers who counseled nonprofit groups. They were more troublesome because these matters were addressed quite differently in different states.

The desirability of bringing greater uniformity to nonprofit laws appeared evident to many of those familiar with corporate nonprofit law soon after the war. The American Bar Association and the American Law Institute, the bar's leading professional organization and leading learned society, respectively, responded by undertaking to develop a model law designed to govern nonprofit corporations. The ABA adopted several versions of a model nonprofit corporation act (MNPCA) during the 1950s and 1960s, believing that the result would eventually be "a highly desirable degree of uniformity."[29]

The rather small community of lawyers who were professionally involved in nonprofit law during that period disagreed about whether to limit or expand the types of purposes for which nonprofits could be formed. There were proponents for the New York approach, which did not enumerate the permissible purposes for which nonprofits could be formed but left judges to screen applications for charters. Other states (e.g., Illinois) specified in detail particular charitable purposes for which nonprofit corporations could be formed and left it up to state officials to determine whether applications for charters fell within the defined categories.[30] Attempts to arrive at one model for all states generated fundamental questions about the qualities any nonprofit corporation needed to possess.

The 1952 version of the MNPCA did not follow the New York method of screening charters by judges. Instead, it established various types of permissible nonprofit activity that administrative officials would need to match against the proposed purposes of a new corporation.[31] The 1952 version met criticism, however, because its rules made qualification for nonprofit incorporation more difficult than, and different from, the for-profit incorporation laws.[32] Aspects of the 1952 model act became law in a few states, but it was not generally adopted. Work started again.

By 1957, a revised version of the law emerged. Hoping to accentuate the revision's greater similarity to general incorporation laws, the drafters advertised their opinion that "the Nonprofit Act as now revised does not, in our opinion, depart seriously from this general parallel with the Business Corporation Act except to the extent that in the nature of things an act relating to clubs, colleges and charities should properly depart from an act relating to business institutions."[33] The members of the committee were divided among themselves about acceptable purposes of nonprofit groups and whether access to nonprofit incorporation was an entitlement or a privilege—whether, that is, it should be no more difficult than for-profit incorporation to obtain.[34] They also did not offer a model that provided much assistance to states concerned about abuse of the form. By the end of 1963, only nine states had adopted some version of the MNPCA,[35] although four others listed the model act as a basis of the state enactment. The ABA committee tried again with a new promulgation.

The 1964 model tracked the model business corporation laws closely and attempted to strengthen the enforcement power of attorney generals of the states. This time the drafters frankly acknowledged irreconcilable differences among themselves about the problem of establishing a unitary rule to define those groups eligible for corporate formation. Some favored limited access to the benefits of nonprofit status while others did not:

> The most difficult decision of policy in drafting the Model Non-Profit Corporation Act is the determination of the purposes for which corporations may be organized under it. A majority of the Committee are of the opinion that the purposes should be limited to those which are not for pecuniary profit. . . . [but] A substantial minority of the Committee favors broadening the permitted purposes to any purpose not forbidden by law."[36]

Because of differences on the committee, the 1964 revision offered states that might choose to adopt it two radically different options. The first "purposes" option established a traditionally restrictive set of permissible activities. The alternative provision declared that "Corporations may be organized under this Act for any lawful purpose or purposes except . . . [list, if any]."[37]

The prospect of debating major changes over these questions must have daunted legislators and policymakers. The first option, a list of activities, invited a battle over what purposes were permissible, while the second option required those who were accustomed to exercising discretion—principally state court judges and officials working with the secretary of state—to relinquish their screening functions almost entirely. New York and California were working on their own approaches, which they hoped would provide for greater accountability than the model act. Avoiding conflict about what was a legitimate basis for conferring nonprofit status and whether even groups with "pecuniary motives" could be nonprofits, few leading jurisdictions moved the act toward adoption.[38] The states continued their nonuniform practices with respect to procedures and justifiable purposes for the establishment of nonprofit corporations.

After nearly a decade of hearings and debate, the New York legislature in 1970 repealed its membership corporation law and replaced it with a new not-for-profit corporation law (NPCL).[39] Although in many matters of substance the NPCL resembled the membership corporation law, its structure mirrored the state's business corporation law, which had been enacted in 1961.[40] The NPCL and the BCL contained substantially similar provisions concerning many routine matters of governance and powers.[41]

The NPCL varied from the BCL in important respects, however. At the heart of New York's new nonprofit law was an innovative new provision, § 201, which established categories or "types" of nonprofit corporations.[42] Each "type" reflected a category of nonprofit endeavor that federal tax law and prior experience suggested was distinguishable. Typing presumably would assist those who subsequently would supervise and award benefits to determine the qualifications of different sorts of nonprofit groups.

Once typed, the corporation was to be subjected to a different kind of supervision and different kinds of tax and other benefits, according to other rules established in the course of legislative and administrative processes. "If the New York Not-for-Profit Corporation Law is destined for primacy in its field," one of its authors wishfully conjectured, much of the credit would be due to the "careful and imaginative drafting" of section 201:

> For the first time, it provides the state with a rational and well-balanced system of laws expressing a legislative philosophy which cannot fairly be labeled too permissive or too onerous. It bridges frustrating gaps that could not be spanned under the old law, codifies and clarifies the rights and duties of members and their managers, polishes and sharpens the state's tools designed to protect the public interest, gives elbow room to the imaginative social planner, and provides for greater financial flexibility while maximizing fiscal responsibility.[43]

The NPCL typologies adopted "functional" and "economic" tests to determine into which classification a proposed nonprofit corporation would be placed. They even allowed a profit-making venture to qualify as a nonprofit corporation, so long as it engaged in a "lawful business purpose to achieve a lawful public or quasi-public objective."[44]

In connection with other provisions of the NPCL, § 201 of the law also scaled back the types of nonprofit organizations that would require the "consent" of a court to incorporate. For several classes of nonprofits, even ministerial judicial approval would no longer generally be necessary. Civic, patriotic, political, social, fraternal, athletic, agricultural, horticultural, animal husbandry, and commercial nonprofit organizations were now classified as "Type A" corporations, whose certificates received minimal review and whose incorporators would not be required to obtain the approval of justices of the supreme court.[45] As had been required by the membership corporation law, however, the NPCL continued to demand that other prospective corporations, including charitable, educational, religious, scientific, literary, and cultural organizations, seek the approval of justices of the state's supreme court in most cases. Depending on the purposes of the organization being created, it also would be necessary for some groups to obtain the consent of assorted administrative bodies.[46]

Although one prominent authority commented that the NPCL's consent and typology mechanisms "continued New York's position as the most restrictive of the minority of states that deny, in the nonprofit area, automatic incorporation upon compliance with the formalities of a general law and the payment of prescribed fees," the realities were otherwise.[47] This statement exaggerated the exceptionalism of New York's jurisprudence, since the judicial approval process in New York had been interpreted as "ministerial" in nature—eliminating substantial pre-incorporation review by the judiciary or, for most nonprofits, anyone else.[48] Although the NPCL retained portions of the structure of a "review jurisdiction," furthermore, the modified consent process in New York and in other "review" states was actually limited in its reach by design.

The various requirements of the new law for administrative consents required incorporating groups to "introduce themselves" to the agencies that would be likely to regulate them after their incorporation and in that way were important to the new scheme.[49] Consents were not designed to encourage substantive evaluation of the qualifications and suitability of a group for incorporation. Their chief purpose was to trigger administrative awareness of the existence of new corporations and allow them to be categorized and typed according to the kinds of legal and regulatory treatment they would receive in the future.

Frequently, however, the greatest impact of the consent requirements was only to lead incorporators and their lawyers to search for artful ways of stating purposes language to avert the need for consents, thus removing corporations—often permanently—from regulatory oversight. By redrafting the purposes provisions, many nonprofit organizations were created without the need to obtain consents. Many that did obtain consents were not subjected to meaningful regulation. When the consent process imposed substantive hurdles to formation, it ran the risk of common law and constitutional objections similar to those that judicial discretion had encountered.

## The Emergence of Administrative
## Surrogates for Judges

After judicial authority to reject applications declined in New York, aspects of the screening role migrated to offices where consents were granted and certificates were filed. Administrative consents soon became more problematic than judicial ones to obtain, and the standards for withholding consents allowed broad administrative discretion. This discretion was narrowed by judicial interpretation, however, and discretion migrated once more. The secretary of state was soon asserting discretion to refuse to file certificates that had passed through all the other required ministerial hoops. Thus the case law reveals that the secretary of state refused to accept for filing proposed certificates that had already been approved by courts and consented to by other agencies.

The power to regulate corporations—like most other kinds of power—abhors a vacuum. The deprivation of the judicial power to review charters created something of a void waiting to be filled. It became apparent, once the authority of judges had diminished, that applicants for administrative consents were vulnerable to the expression of subjective preferences by officials who claimed that their discretion was statutorily authorized. The administrative officers claimed to find authority for their exercise of discretion in the intrinsic logic of the enacted law—just as the New York justices claimed to have uncovered a morality built into the law when they were directed to apply preexisting law with very general standards.[50] Skirmishes occurred about whether consents to file (or waivers of consents) should be necessary for the incorporation of particular types of organizations; and if so, whether the granting of a consent should be subject to restraints on discretion. Finally, the secretary's power to reject certificates that had received all necessary endorsements from the court and other agencies became a matter of controversy.

Failing to obtain a required administrative consent doomed certain corporate applications but not other ones. In 1964, a group called the Association for Psychoanalysis presented a certificate that proposed to advance theories of psychoanalytic psychology and to "promote and develop facilities for training and study for its members" to the secretary of state for filing.[51] The certificate was approved by a justice of the supreme court, but the secretary of state refused to file it because the association did not try to obtain the consent of the commissioner of education, even though "training and study" educational language appeared in its proposed charter. The association may have been concerned that the necessity for an organization of psychoanalytic psychologists would be denied a consent because of opposition waged or anticipated from traditional psychoanalysts. The association brought a *mandamus* action against the secretary of state after its certificate was rejected.

The association initially prevailed at the trial level based on an equal protection argument. Requiring a consent was unlawful, the trial court stated, because the secretary of state had accepted the certificate of an earlier group, *devoid* of administrative consent, which contained identical "training and study" language.[52] The appellate court, however, reversed. According to the court disparate treatment did not violate federal or state equal protection standards because the commissioner of education of the board of regents had been empowered by the legislature to withhold consent from membership associations according to its own rules.[53] For a short time at least, it appeared that the secretary held a broad power to control access to the sector by interpreting whether particular groups needed particular consents.

But the court soon made it clear that the secretary of state could not behave in ways that judges had been prohibited from behaving. As when the discretionary power of judges was challenged in *Association for the Preservation of Freedom of Choice*, the court of appeals a few years later would curb the authority of the secretary of state in the *Gay Activists Alliance* case. In 1973 the Gay Activists Alliance attempted to organize "as a homosexual civil rights organization, working within the framework of the laws of the United States and the several States, but vigilant and vigorous in fighting any discrimination based on sexual orientation of the individual" and "to work for the repeal of all laws regulating sexual conduct and practices between consenting adults."[54] Notwithstanding judicial approval of the certificate, the secretary of state refused to accept it for filing.

In the secretary's opinion, the word "gay" was inappropriately obscene and vulgar. The veiled purpose of the organization appeared to be to promote conduct that contravened laws prohibiting homosexual acts.[55] The appellate court refused to compel the secretary to accept the Gay Activists' certificate, but the court of appeals reversed.[56] As in its earlier ruling in *Preservation of Choice*, the court interpreted the law as limiting the secretary of state to testing proposed certificates against the formal requirements of the statute.[57] It declared that the secretary had no discretion to determine what words, other than those proscribed by the legislature, were inappropriate as names for a corporation.[58] Nor did the trial court have the authority to label the Gay Activists Alliance potentially injurious to public policy:

It has been clearly established by *Matter of Association for Preservation of Freedom of Choice* . . . that the public policy of the State is not violated unless the expressed purposes contained in the proposed certificate are unlawful. Were it otherwise it would, in effect, permit the Secretary of State to impose his personal opinion on what he considers improper conduct.[59]

Because the Gay Activists Alliance complied with all formal requirements and because the purposes for which the corporation formed were lawful, the court ruled that "the Secretary of State lacked the authority to label those purposes violative of 'public policy.'"[60] The court of appeals announced its decision without dissent.[61]

Administrative and judicial discretion to police the formation of incorporations now had been diminished sharply by New York's court of appeals.[62] What had been wide-ranging discretion to supervise had been reduced to a limited opportunity to "review." In other states too courts circumscribed the discretion afforded to the secretary of state and other administrative bodies as a matter of law.[63] Substantive pre-incorporation review, whether by judges or other state officials, had practically disappeared.

## Notes

1. State and federal legislatures and federal tax authorities played their own part in the reconception of the nonprofit sector, of course. *See supra*, ch. 1 (discussing scope of this study).

2. *See* note, *Permissible Purposes for Nonprofit Corporations*, 51 COLUM. L. REV. 889, 889–90 nn. 6–7 (1951) (indicating that in California, Colorado, and New Jersey, for example, incorporation under a nonprofit law resulted by statute in a complete or partial exemption from the state franchise tax and carried substantial weight in determining federal income tax exemption).

3. *Id.*

4. *See In re* Fraternidad Hispana Americana, 39 Misc.2d 106, 240 N.Y.S.2d 110, 111 (Sup. Ct. 1963).

5. *Id.*

6. *Id.*

7. *Id.*

8. *Id.*

9. *Id.*

10. *Id.* at 112.

11. *See In re* Wholesale Milk Distribs. Ass'n, Inc., 241 N.Y.S.2d 944, 945 (Sup. Ct. 1963).

12. *Id.*

13. *Id.* at 946.

14. *See In re* Thom Lambda Legal Defense & Educ. Fund, Inc., 337 N.Y.S.2d 588, 589 (App. Div. 1972).

15. *Id.*

16. *Id.*

17. *Id.*

18. *Id.* at 590.

19. *See In re* Community Action for Legal Services., Inc., 274 N.Y.S.2d 779, 26 A.D.2d 354 (App. Div. 1966) (proceeding for approval of incorporation certificate on three applications on behalf of proposed corporations wishing to practice law). The supreme court, Appellate Division, Breitel, J., held that an organization that had built-in incentives to compete with existing antipoverty law offices operating in same area and that subjected lawyer operations to lay control would not be approved. *See also* ex rel. Green et al. v. Brown, Secretary of State, 176 Ohio St. 155, 198 N.E. 2d 447 (1964) (denying a writ of mandamus ordering the secretary of state to file the application of a legal defense group, finding that "some of the purposes set forth in that purpose clause describe activities which would amount to the practice of law." (*citing* State ex rel. Green v. Brown, Secy. of State, 173 Ohio St., 114, 180 N.E.2d 157 [nudist case]).

20. *See In re* Application of Queens Lay Advocate Service, Inc., 71 Misc.2d 33, 335 N.Y.S.2d 583, 584 (Sup. Ct. 1972).

21. It is possible that the Queens Advocate Group might have had better luck if it approached him personally and in private, since Justice Brennan accepted bribes while he was on the bench. Justice Brennan worked first as a Transit Authority police officer, obtained a law degree from New York University in 1948, and then represented the Borough of Queens in the state assembly and then the senate before being appointed justice in 1969. In 1985, Justice Brennan was convicted of taking $45,000 from organized crime figures to fix cases in Queens. He was found guilty of twenty-six counts, including racketeering, conspiracy, attempted extortion, and fraud by telephone. *See* Michael Reskes, *A Year-Long Look at Government's Underside,* N.Y. TIMES, Jan. 4, 1987, at 6 col. 7.

22. *In re* Application of Queens Lay Advocate Service, Inc., 71 Misc.2d 33, 335 N.Y.S.2d 583, 584 (Sup. Ct. 1972).

23. *Id.* at 586.

24. *Id.*

25. *Id.* at 586; *see In re* Howard Beach Appeal Fund, Inc., 534 N.Y.S.2d 341 (Sup. Ct. 1988) (holding that the organization which proposed to pay for legal expenses incurred by three named defendants of racial attack were "lawful but not charitable" and therefore not entitled to Type A status under the Not-for-Profit Corporations Law).

26. But *see infra,* n. 50–59 and accompanying text, concerning disapproval of nonprofit legal corporations in the later period. Some judges continued to ask probing questions of groups when reviewing applications and continued to take an interventionist role.

27. Lueken v. Our Lady of the Roses, 97 Misc.2d 201, 410 N.Y.S.2d 793, 794 (Sup. Ct. 1978) ("[S]ole basis for review and approval of a certificate of incorporation" of a not-for-profit corporation by the court "is to determine whether the purposes of the corporation are in conformity with the law; [t]he court may not interject its own opinion as to the social desirability of those purposes," pursuant to Not-For-Profit Corporations Law §404(a) [petition denied on other grounds]).

28. Some states employed general nonprofit laws to govern all nonprofit corporations. *See* COLO. REV. STAT. §§7–20 to –29 (1986); CONN. GEN. STAT. ANN. §§33–416 to –526 (1987); MISS. CODE ANN. §§79–11–1 to –33 (1973) (repealed 1987); TEX. REV. CIV. STAT. ANN. Art §§1396–1.01 to –11.01 (1980); WASH. REV. CODE ANN. §§24.03.005 –935 (1969); other states used special rules within general business incorporation statutes to govern nonprofits, *e.g.,* DEL. CODE ANN. TIT. 8 §§201–298, while others divided nonprofit organizations into "religious," "public benefit," or "mutual benefit" types. *See* Michael Hone, *Aristotle and Lyndon Baines Johnson: Thirteen Ways of looking at Blackbirds and Nonprofit Corporations: The American Bar Association's Revised Model Nonprofit Corporation Act,* 39 CASE W. RES. L. REV. 751, 758 (1988–89).

29. MODEL NONPROFIT CORP. ACT (1957).

30. *See supra,* ch. 2 (notes quoting the New York Membership Corp. Law and the Illinois statute).

31. MODEL NONPROFIT CORP. ACT (1952).

32. *See* Lizabeth Moody, *The Who, What, and How of the Revised Model Non-Profit Corporation Act,* 16 N. KY. L. REV. 251 (1988).

33. *Forward to the 1957 Edition,* MODEL NONPROFIT CORP. ACT at vii (ABA, 1957 rev.).

34. *Id.*

35. See Lizabeth Moody, *The Who, What, and How of the Revised Model Non-Profit Corporation Act,* 16 N. KY. L. REV. 251 (1988).

36. *Preface to 1964 Edition,* MODEL NONPROFIT CORPORATION ACT at viii (ABA, 1964 rev.); Moody, *The Who, What, and How of the Revised Model Non-Profit Act* at 262 n. 57; Harry G. Henn and Jeffrey H. Byrd, *Statutory Trends in the Law of Nonprofit Organizations: California Here We Come!,* 66 CORNELL L. REV. 1103, 1110 (1981).

37. Moody at 259–70; *see also* 1964 Act at 2, sec. 4.

38. Moody, *Id.*

39. L. 1969, ch. 1066 §2 (repealer); L. 1969, ch. 1066 §3 (effective date). The process of creating a separate New York Not-for-Profit Corporations Law began in earnest in 1961 when a joint legislative committee began to explore the need for a new law. *See* White, NEW YORK CORPORATIONS, VI, par. 100.01 (1994).

40. L. 1961, ch. 855 (effective Sept. 1, 1963).

41. *See, e.g.,* BCL §104, NPCL §104 ("Certificates, requirements, signing, filing, effectiveness"); BCL §104-A, NPCL §104-A ("Fees"); BCL §202, NPCL §202 (Powers); BCL §301, NPCL §301 ("Corporate Name"); BCL §401, NPCL §401 ("Incorporators"); BCL §601, NPCL §602 ("By-laws")

42. NPCL §201.

43. *See* White, *supra* at 201.01.

44. NPCL §201 (Type C corporations). The comments suggested that it was contemplated that urban development corporations, for instance, would incorporate under the provision.

45. Although trade associations were categorized as Type A, they continued to be subject to consent and approval requirements. *See* NPCL §404.

46. NPCL §201(b). In New York the parties from whom consent might be required included the regents of the state of New York, the superintendent of insur-

ance, the commissioner of health, the commissioner of education, the cemetery board, fire districts, the Society for the Prevention of Cruelty to Children or for Prevention of Cruelty to Animals, the chairman of the national board of the Young Men's Christian Associations (YMCAs), the chief of staff of the armed forces (armed forces support), the Industrial Board of Appeals (labor matters), the superintendent of banks, the heads of political parties, the American Legion, the Public Health Council, the commissioner of mental hygiene, the director of the Division of Substance Abuse Services, the director of the Division of Alcoholism and Alcohol Abuse, as well as state attorneys general and federal tax authorities. *See* NPCL §404. The "Type B" classification facilitated obtaining status as an organization exempt under §501 (c)(3) of the federal Internal Revenue Code, whose language it approximately tracked.

47. *See* White, NEW YORK CORPORATIONS, VI, par. 100.01 (1994).

48. *See supra*, text at ch. 4 nn. 185–239.

49. *See* Council of New York Law Ass'n, GETTING ORGANIZED 36–42 (ed. Alan R. Bromberger 1989).

50. Raz observes: "Anyone who is tempted to deny that courts have discretion when they are directed to apply a preexisting law with very general standards of application, on the ground that morality has been made into law by the directive to the courts to apply moral standards, will have a hard time to avoid denying that delegated legislators and administrative agencies ever have rulemaking powers. What appears to be the making of a new law will, on this view, be no more than a declaration of the discovery of a preexisting law." Joseph Raz, *Dworkin: A New Link in the Chain*, 74 CAL. L. REV. 1103, 1115–16 (1986).

51. *See* Ass'n for Psychoanalysis, Inc., 21 A.D.2d 209, 250 N.Y.S.2d 253, 254 (App. Div. 1964).

52. *Id.* at 254–55.

53. *Id.*

54. *See* Owles v. Lomenzo, 38 A.D.2d 981, 329 N.Y.S.2d 181, 182 (App. Div. 1972).

55. *See* Gay Activists Alliance v. Lomenzo, 66 Misc.2d 456, 320 N.Y.S.2d 994 (1971).

56. *Id.* at 997.

57. *See In re* Gay Activists Alliance, 31 N.Y.2d 965 (1973).

58. *See Owles*, 329 N.Y.S.2d at 183 (*citing* NPCL §§301[a][5], 404).

59. *Id.*

60. *In re* Gay Activists Alliance, 31 N.Y.2d 965, 966 (1973) (*citing* Matter of Association for Preservation of Freedom of Choice v. Shapiro, 9 N.Y.2d 376 [1961]).

61. *Id.* at 966; *but see* State ex rel. Grant v. Brown, 39 Ohio St. 2d 112, 313 N.E.2d 847 (1974) (Ohio's secretary of state rejected articles of incorporation for a nonprofit corporation that had as its purpose the promotion of homosexuality because it deemed homosexuality a lifestyle lawful but nonetheless contrary to the public policy of Ohio; the state's highest court ruled that although R.C. 1702.03 stated that "a corporation may be formed for any purpose or purposes for which natural persons lawfully may associate themselves," that language should be interpreted to give the secretary of state discretion in determining which articles of incorporation he will accept [Stern, J., dissenting]).

62. *See also* Owles v. Lomenzo, 329 N.Y.S.2d 181 (1972), *aff'd*, 341 N.Y.S.2d 108, *aff'd*, 31 N.Y.2d 965 (1973).

63. The states that adopted the Model Nonprofit Corporation Act in whole or in part included Wisconsin, Alabama, North Carolina, Virginia, Nebraska, North Dakota, Oregon, Texas and the District of Columbia. The states that listed the Model Act as the basis of the state enactment include Arizona, Alaska, Iowa, Hawaii, and Montana. *See* Lizabeth Moody, *The Who, What, and How of the Revised Model Nonprofit Corporation Act*, 16 N. Ky. L. Rev. 251 (1988).

# 6

# The New World of
# Nonprofit Activity

## Explosive Growth After the Change

The nonprofit sector diversified dramatically during the thirty-five years following *NAACP ex rel. Patterson v. Alabama* and *Association for the Preservation of Choice*. The variety of activities conducted by the sector's corporations and other entities came to defy meaningful characterization. One professor, despairing of ever finding a precise definition of groups eligible for inclusion in the sector, settled on any group consisting of "at least two people engaged in some activity other than cohabitation not for the primary purpose of making money for themselves."[1]

For more than a century, labor unions, churches, foundations, hospitals, museums, universities, opera companies, orphanages, sports organizations, fraternities, temperance societies, and political parties were organizable as nonprofit trusts or corporations.[2] After 1960, however, the sector expanded to include catering businesses, vacation resorts, dance foundations, jazz festivals, covens of witches, mobile home associations, real estate ventures, ceramic tile manufacturers, teleministries, nudist camps, employment agencies, laundries, legal defense funds, feminist publications, homosexual rights organizations, disposers of environmental waste, child care centers, bar review courses, beauty pageants, housing projects, industrial enterprise zones, computer networks, and the "Mikes of America, which wants only to get anyone named Mike elected president of the United States."[3] There were no practical legal restraints on the permissible ends of endeavor within the nonprofit form, and as this legal reality became apparent, the comparative advantages became great enough to generate a boom.

Measured in economic terms, the growth of the nonprofit sector in the decades after 1960 was astonishing. The nonprofit workforce increased as a proportion of the overall work force from less than 4 to at least 7 percent.[4] By one estimate, by 1994 there were at least 1,243,000 nonprofit organizations employing nearly 8 million workers and attracting the volunteer work of 80 million more.[5] Nonprofits came to employ more civilians than the federal government and the fifty state governments combined.[6] The income produced by the nonprofit sector, adjusted for inflation, grew geometrically as a proportion of the whole.[7] Studies indicated an 83 percent growth in the total revenues of the nonprofit sector between 1975 and 1982, with a reported total in revenues of $196.3 billion by the end of 1982.[8] Donations exploded, absolutely and relatively. In 1993, average Americans were estimated to be giving five times as much as the average French citizen and three times as much as average British and Spanish citizens to charitable groups.[9] By 1998, according to a Gallup poll, seven in ten American households were contributing to charitable organizations, and 55.5 percent of adults were doing significant volunteer work every week.[10]

Not surprisingly, laws related to nonprofits also burgeoned after 1960. The laws governing the supervision, taxation, and dissolution of nonprofit groups multiplied geometrically in their complexity. Until about 1955, articles addressed to lawyers on the subject of tax exemption or the formation of nonprofit corporations specializing in the nonprofit sector were limited in number;[11] thereafter, the appearance of such literature in larger volume suggests that tax-exempt law and nonprofit legal representation began to expand and to thrive as a specialty.[12] Partnerships with for-profit ventures proliferated, as did concern by for-profits about unfair competition from nonprofit business activities.[13] Interpretations of foundation laws, nonprofit taxation laws, laws, and not-for-profit corporation laws became more heavily litigated.[14] Media and prosecutorial allegations of abuses of the nonprofit form increased as well, including suits alleging fraudulent solicitations of funds, improper evasion of tax liabilities, and the improper use of nonprofit corporate forms to engage in unlawful business activities.[15] The definition of what qualified as legitimate and illegitimate tax exempt nonprofit activity came into doubt. Newsletters and loose-leaf services on the subject of the law of nonprofit and tax-exempt organizations proliferated.[16] New treatises on the specialized subjects of nonprofit corporations and tax-exempt entities appeared.[17] Academic and practitioner curiosity, as reflected by publications in the area, flourished.[18]

The number of chartered nonprofit corporations increased dramatically—from a few thousand to more than 100 thousand in New York state, for example—during the years between 1960 and 1993.[19] Out of approximately 900,000 domestic corporations in New York state in 1993, approximately 200,000 were chartered under the state's not-for-profit corporation law; this compared to a much smaller number of federally tax-exempt organizations in the state.[20] Evidently the benefits to structuring these ventures as nonprofit corporations (or registered charitable trusts) outweighed the disadvantages of the legal form with greater frequency.

The number of nonprofit groups with state charters always exceeded the number of those that held federal income tax exemptions, but the number of federally tax-exempt organizations also grew substantially after 1960. The number of categories of federally exempt activities grew from 90 to 260 between 1965 and 1987.[21] For the ten years prior to 1965 the Internal Revenue Service received 5,000 to 7,000 applications per year for tax-exempt status. The number of completed applications in 1985 was more than 45,000.[22] Between 1968 and 1988, the number of federally tax-exempt entities doubled, to 866,000.[23] Federal and state tax revenue foregone by reason of nonprofit tax-exempt status increased markedly and has amounted to billions of dollars since 1960.[24]

Changes in other benefits received by nonprofit organizations over this period are harder to track. For example, since tax assessors generally did not bother to value exempt property precisely, local property-tax exemption patterns were hard to measure.[25] It would appear, however, that the value of exempt real property has grown faster than the tax base in the past few decades.[26] One study in 1977 estimated that 9 percent of all private property in this nation was exempt;[27] taking into account government property, an advisory commission on intergovernmental relations estimated that fully one-third of America's real estate was tax-exempt by 1980.[28] Various states and municipalities attempted to tax formerly exempt property or to capture "service fees" from nonprofits in an attempt to expand their revenue base.[29]

Like the stars in our galaxy, the groups in the U.S. nonprofit sector grew inexorably and without apparent containment. As they did, critics argued that some of this growth was socially undesirable and that the nonprofit sector was not intrinsically uncontrollable—just out of control. The Milky Way galaxy was never presumed to be within the jurisdiction of the government of the United States or the states and its political and judicial officers. Corporation and tax laws *could* limit the nonprofit sector, if that was their purpose.

The Internal Revenue Service, for example, was approving approximately 24,000 new publicly supported organizations each year in the mid–1970s, while revoking the exempt status of only twenty-five or thirty.[30] Much criticism focused on the ease with which charities could receive and maintain tax exemptions, and donors could keep their charitable deductions. During the 1990s, only twenty to thirty organizations per year actually lost their tax-exempt status.[31] Critics proposed conditional tax exemptions, more frequent revocations of status, and greater scrutiny of charitable contributions. That a person engaged in substantial charita-

ble giving no longer appeared to convey to others a preponderantly altruistic motive—it bespoke as much clever strategic financial planning.
"Charity used to be a good word," Representative Hancock of Missouri
stated in 1994. "It's getting so that it isn't a good word anymore."[32]

Federal, state, and local campaigns were launched to reduce government subsidies, to control fraudulent and deceptive conduct on the part
of nonprofit organizations, to limit the compensation of officers and directors of nonprofits, and to place for-profit businesses on a more even
footing with their nonprofit competitors.[33] Efforts were made to prevent
nonprofits that did business with the government from lobbying.[34] Campaigns to change dramatically the tax-exemption eligibility rules and disclosure rules did not gain widespread support, nor did they sharply
dampen enthusiasm for supporting nonprofit corporations. They did,
however, lead to deliberate efforts to tighten administrative supervision
and to conceptualize and defend the advantages that flowed to the sector
as a result of the tax laws.[35]

### Anemic Disclosure and Administrative Remedies

In retrospect, the problems that developed as a consequence of the reconception of nonprofit corporate activity were just as predictable as the
swift growth in the number, size, and activities of nonprofit organizations. The collapse of limitations on permissible purposes expanded the
sector, but in doing so made its supervision much more problematic than
before. Expectations that the move from a paradigm of subsidy to a paradigm of entitlement would not present formidable problems for effective
supervision were mistaken.

The substitute that the student law review commentators offered to diminish scrutiny of nonprofit purposes was a more aggressive and ongoing scrutiny of the corporate nonprofit sector *after* nonprofit associations
became corporate. Achieving social policy objectives and exerting control
over the purposes of groups in the corporate nonprofit sector might have
been worthwhile in some abstract sense, but these tasks now would have
to be performed, if at all, subsequent to incorporation. Improved performance by nonprofits would henceforth be achieved, first, through improved disclosure by them of their actual conduct—by reforms requiring
them to make compulsory disclosures, at regular intervals, to appropriate authorities and to the public about their governance, operation, and
finances. Second, those who had dismantled the incorporation privilege
paradigm contemplated that diminished supervision at that stage would
be compensated for by strengthened enforcement efforts designed to police and discourage particular types of misconduct. Third, they presumed that tax authorities would take up any necessary slack. None of
these turned out to be sufficiently effective.

The supposed effectiveness of disclosure rules as a way for either consumers or the government to spot fraud, inefficiency, or an absence of social value in nonprofits was vastly overrated.[36] The reconception supposed that strengthened reporting and disclosure requirements would
promote greater accountability of nonprofit corporations to the public.
But the disclosure rules were not significantly strengthened with respect
either to their substantive content or their timing or availability. Nonprofit corporations were not required to report directly to the constituen-
cies or clienteles they served. In few cases were nonprofit corporations
required to do more than circulate annual reports to the officers and
members of their organizations.[37]

Congress did not begin to address the absence of uniform disclosure
practices for nonprofits until 1973, when it established the Commission
on Private Philanthropy and Public Needs, known as the Filer Commission.[38] Addressing the problem of disclosure as at bottom an accounting
problem, the commission recommended that all tax-exempt organizations with annual budgets above $100,000 file annual reports available to
the public.[39] Reform did not move quickly, however, and the filing of annual reports was not required of even the larger federally tax-exempt
nonprofits until 1981.[40] Even then, disclosure of information in the annual reports of nonprofit groups proved too obscure to be genuinely in-
formative to the public. So limited was general awareness of the state role
in the enforcement of the nonprofit laws that the public and even most
board members of nonprofit corporations—up to the present day—
nearly universally confused state nonprofit corporation reporting requirements with federal reporting requirements related to the mainte-
nance of tax-exempt status.[41]

Even the best of disclosure rules would not have ensured the improved
performance of nonprofits, however, because of the special characteristics of many nonprofit transactions. In many cases, inherent imperfec-
tions of the marketplace prevented those who learned about defects in
the provision of nonprofit services from communicating with those who
supported or supervised the nonprofits.[42] The assumption that more
stringent rules compelling nonprofits to disclose their record of performance would generate appropriate marketplace responses, as Professor
Hansmann and others later pointed out, was misplaced in many nonprofit transactions. Where third party beneficiaries of a contract (flood
victims, for example) did not communicate directly or indirectly with the
parties who arranged for their relief (donors or grantors), a classical case
of inherent market imperfection existed—and the inferior performance of
the vendor might never be detected and cured.[43] Disclosure remedies in
these cases were extremely limited in their effect.

Of course, corrective responses to the information contained in disclosures about income and expenditures would not have sufficed to

prevent nonprofits from abusing donors or defrauding consumers. These approaches alone, measured in terms of public confidence and support, would not establish that a group's purpose warranted operation pursuant to a nonprofit charter. Establishing the popularity and efficiency of groups did not prove that they provided a public benefit, that is, unless no distinction was to be drawn between *worthy* and merely *successful* organizations.[44]

Reliance on the expectation that there would be heightened, conduct-oriented enforcement activities by state regulators also proved to be misplaced. The substitutes recommended by the student authors and the Model Act supposed that state officials would devote increased attention to tasks such as interim certifications to operate particular kinds of enterprises, or else on inspections, waivers, penalties, revocations, and dissolutions. These recommendations presumed that administrative bodies and enforcement agencies possessed or would come to possess sufficient power and resources with which to work effectively.

The questionable premise behind confidence in conduct-oriented supervision was that agencies would do better if they were no longer preoccupied with formal legal categories and governance distinctions—for example, "trusts," or "corporations," or "associations." Administrative bodies would presumably do better to conserve their resources and capitalize on specialized expertise by devoting their attention to functional categories of economic activity—laws against fraud, misrepresentation, or price-fixing, for example.

As a general matter, it is true that the conduct-oriented efforts to supervise nonprofits that were undertaken in most states at all levels throughout the 1960s and thereafter were intentionally insensitive to the legal form of the entities being monitored. Laws intended to prevent abuse in most cases ignored the *structure* of the entity and focused instead on the *activity* of the charity.[45] State fund-raising and lobbying restrictions were applied wholesale to tax-exempt entities irrespective of their nonprofit corporate form.[46] Despite the smaller likelihood that a nonprofit corporation's wrongdoing would be spotted or pursued by its members or constituents, enforcement agencies usually satisfied themselves with reacting to complaints, for example, about tax evasion or fraud or monopolistic behavior—instead of directing efforts to finding wrongdoing among nonprofit corporations per se.

This approach was flawed because it ignored the reality that differences among corporate forms produced different incentives and sent signals of different intensity for regulators to take action. For example, the creation of a trust relationship usually involved the appointment of a beneficiary with a stake in monitoring and enforcing the performance of a trustee. Or, where there were shareholders and a profit-making corporate form, internal monitoring could lead quickly and naturally to external, regulatory inquiries. With respect to nonprofit corporations, however, the absence of owners with a stake in the profits and growth in all probability made the exposure to regulators and courts of misconduct and poor performance less frequent than otherwise. While the balance sheet of a commercial corporation, or complaints from its customers or shareholders, provided clues to the need for disciplinary action by licensors or government regulators, these alarms would not sound as loudly or at all in the not-for-profit context. The inadequacy of nonprofit supervision according to topical categories was further attributable to the fact that nonprofits were receiving more favorable treatment from states, in comparison to for-profit entities, in deference to their reconsidered role in the political process.[47] Rulings that limited the standing to sue of nonprofits made enforcement by private parties far less likely.[48]

Reliance on "topical" approaches to regulate particular types of conduct by nonprofit corporations reflected a hit-or-miss approach that acquiesced in a post hoc regulatory response as a by-product of notorious instances of abuse. To a considerable degree, such approaches were mounted with insufficient resources or follow-up to be effective. Although some state and federal agencies performed at high levels of efficiency, others proved ill equipped, ill disposed, and ill timed to serve the substantive policy roles that the reconception envisioned.

A particular kind of topical regulation, dealing with nonprofit fundraising, appeared to present an alternate solution to the problem of supervision of nonprofits that would be both constitutional and effective.[49] The inadequate supervision of charitable and other fund-raising efforts received much attention during the Eisenhower administration and subsequently. In the mail, at the doorstep, and over the radio and television, solicitations for charitable crusades and political causes became ubiquitous.

In 1958, committees of the House of Representatives looked into high-pressure salesmanship and fraudulent fund-raising practices on the part of several charities. A group of citizens, supported by the Rockefeller Foundation, formed another private committee at the same time to study potential improvements in the operation of charities—especially in the light of adverse public relations they were receiving.[50] The Rockefeller committee warned that if the public continued to fall victim to unscrupulous and unsound fund-raising initiatives, and if responsible charities employed questionable fund-raising tactics, then much of government's favorable treatment of charities might be lost, and the well of public and private charitable support poisoned for the entire nonprofit sector. The committee urged that stiffer reporting requirements, including disclosure of fund-raising practices, could improve the reputation of charitable and philanthropic activities.

Rather than investigate whether nonprofit organizations, including charities, were breaching their corporate obligations and their contractual duties to members and clients, the focus of state and local efforts to improve charities shifted during the late 1950s to an emphasis on proper financial accounting and fund-raising methods.[51] Twenty-one states had some sort of law regulating charities by the end of 1959, mostly aimed at improving accounting rules, strengthening reporting requirements, and tightening fraud statutes.[52] Between 1960 and 1980, twenty-eight states and many municipalities imposed fund-raising limits.[53] Most of these laws and regulations placed ceilings on fund-raising costs to protect donors and to make charitable fund-raising more efficient.[54]

Within a decade of their enactment, effective fund-raising limits were invalidated by the U.S. Supreme Court because of the threat they posed to the existence of advocacy groups and charities that promoted unpopular or fringe causes—and because nonprofit solicitations mixed protected communication about their causes along with their requests for donations.[55] First Amendment issues that had been of concern in the matter of chartering were of concern at the level of the Supreme Court with respect to permissible limits on fund-raising. In the view of a majority on the Supreme Court,[56] nonprofit political organizations engaged in noncommercial activities were entitled to express themselves and to solicit funds under the protection of the First Amendment. Limits on the sums organizations could spend on fund-raising discriminated, the Court announced, against young, small, unpopular charities that retained professional fund-raisers only by paying higher commissions.

Along the lines of the reasoning employed in *NAACP v. Alabama*,[57] the Court's 1980 decision in *Village of Schaumburg v. Citizens for a Better Environment*[58] and later decisions extended free expression analysis to fund-raising efforts, making constitutional regulation of solicitation ever more difficult. At first the Court attempted to protect "political organizations" differently from "social welfare" ones, but this scheme fell apart four years later.[59] The Court's doctrine imposed a rule that generally made fund-raising costs "unknowable" to consumers and government.[60]

Even if the solicitation rules had not faced constitutional impediments, however, it became apparent that these limits were inadequate to achieve larger objectives of supervision. Once considered pivotal, the regulation of fund-raising by such means as controlling the percentage that professional solicitors could retain, or by discretionary systems of licensing groups to make public appeals for funds, did not live up to its billing as a "panacea" for the problem of fraud, abuse, inefficiency, and waste in the nonprofit sector.[61] The fund-raising limits were merely a palliative; they mainly "supported public confidence in charity, . . . limited marginal fund-raising and tended to maximize the overall portion of contribution used for charitable purposes."[62] The limits would not serve, nor had they been designed to serve, as surrogates for more direct state supervision to determine whether nonprofit groups were observing their responsibilities toward donors, grantors, and clients.

The spotty behavior of states in regulating post-incorporation conduct through disclosure rules or rules directed at general misconduct or topical rules became increasingly apparent.[63] Although theory presumed that inappropriate conduct could be detected as easily in one form of organization as another, complaints about inadequate supervision multiplied.

### Misreliance on the Tax Scheme

Hopes for effective post-incorporation supervision chiefly came to rest at another line of defense—with preexemption determinations of eligibility by taxing authorities.[64] A federal income tax classification under IRC §501 (c)(3) and IRC §170, for example, would allow income tax charitable contribution deductions for donors to nonprofit corporations and better income tax treatment for themselves. Or a real property tax exemption might allow a nonprofit corporation to dramatically reduce its operating costs. At this point, vigorous scrutiny of associations and organizations was possible.

Those who had dismantled the previous conception of nonprofit supervision dismissed a fairly basic point. The revenue officials who supervised and made determinations of tax exemption were, after all, principally concerned with watching over government revenue. They were (and still are) not generally charged with evaluating the myriad of social and political issues that might bear on government support for nonprofit organizations, nor equipped in any special ways to evaluate them. The history of the federal tax-exemption statutes indicated that tax-exemption determinations were not intended for broader purposes of general nonprofit supervision nor to provide opportunities for the federal government to modify the determinations of states as to the merit of allowing groups to have nonprofit status.

The history of the treatment of nonprofit organizations by the Internal Revenue Service validated the expectation that the IRS could, if it wanted to, control the quantity and quality of nonprofit activities by administering the Internal Revenue Code. The first federal income tax law, passed in 1894, permitted charitable, religious, and educational organizations to be tax-exempt, and these organizations remained exempt afterward.[65] The revenue acts of the next two decades established other categories of exempt organizations.[66] By 1916, virtually all the categories listed in present § 501 of the Internal Revenue Code had been approved. In 1917 Congress distinguished between organizations that operated free from income taxation and those § 501(c)(3) organizations that were also entitled to provide charitable deductions to their donors.[67]

The Internal Revenue Service for most of the years that followed based its determinations of worthiness for exemption on prior state determinations, together with formal submissions by applicants for exemptions.[68] Determinations of status were supposed to rely on the basis of affirmations or prior determinations by state officers. They were not supposed to involve substantial discretion to determine eligibility on the part of Revenue Service administrators.[69]

For many years the stakes for federal authorities in classifying the eligibility of corporations to receive deductible charitable contributions were small, and the resources deployed to do so were consequently small. Except for the very wealthiest individuals, IRS review of gifts to nonprofits did not generally receive a high priority because the use of charitable contributions in order to minimize federal income tax liability was not widespread. The rates of personal income tax taxation, and also of corporate taxation, rose steeply during World War II and did not return to prewar levels after the war ended.[70] As they remained at high levels, corporations and less wealthy individual taxpayers paid increased attention to tax-avoidance strategies, including the creation of tax-exempt foundations, operating programs, and charitable trusts to defer or reduce tax liabilities.[71] The Internal Revenue Service also began to withhold taxes from employee paychecks during the war, and middle-class taxpayers became adept at using charitable contributions to all types of qualifying nonprofits to minimize what the government kept.[72]

Concern spread in Washington and elsewhere that nonprofit vehicles were being used for inappropriate purposes. Increasingly sensitive to problems of the abuse of tax-exemption rules through the creation of nonprofit forms, and disturbed by the lawful tax-avoidance strategies pursued by citizens, Congress passed the Internal Revenue Act of 1950. It retained the preexisting exemption structure but imposed a tax on revenue that nonprofits obtained from income-producing activities unrelated to their exempt purposes (called "unrelated business income"). In various ways the act also sought to prevent self-dealing by nonprofit officers and directors and to discourage other profit-extracting types of conduct. Violations would—at least in theory—result in the forfeiture of an organization's tax-exempt status.[73]

In 1954, new concerns emerged about the impact of tax-exempt expenditures on the political process, especially by privately endowed foundations.[74] Congress imposed an outright prohibition on campaigning on behalf of any candidate for public office by §501(c)(3) organizations.[75]

Where publicly supported charities were concerned, the Internal Revenue Service began to take a harder look at the record of applicants for recognition of exemption.[76] Without confronting the problem of social value directly, the IRS did begin to pay greater attention to fiscal accountability in deciding whether a tax-exempt organization could keep its exemption. In 1961, the year in which *Association for the Preservation of Freedom of Choice* was decided, the Internal Revenue Service finally developed an audit program to police the activities of tax-exempt organizations for signs of abuse.[77]

By 1965, those who led the federal tax authorities had come to appreciate the fact that more people than ever were contributing more money than ever before to tax-exempt nonprofit organizations, and thereby reducing their tax liabilities. They understood that nonprofit corporations could be formed more easily than ever before and that the stringency of IRS standards for determining whether a nonprofit corporation would receive treatment as a tax-exempt organization affected the stream of federal tax revenue and the financial support given to various causes and charities in America. In light of the tangible subsidies and other direct support that tax exemption provided, it was justifiable for tax authorities to demand more than a superficial review of papers before tax-exempt status would be conferred.

As state supervision diminished, the rationale for federal supervision gained strength. To the extent that persons in the exempt organizations section of the IRS previously relied on determinations made by state officials at the time of an incorporation to decide whether to confer federal tax qualifications, that practice was incompatible with the new conception of a nonprofit charter as an entitlement. The charter proved little about an organization's operation except that its papers were in order.

There was, furthermore, an increasing appreciation that tax exemptions were forms of subsidy. The federal government started to include in its budget analyses the revenues that were foregone because of exemptions as drains on government resources. Officials in the Treasury Department began to argue for "tax expenditure analysis" based on the premise that a "subsidy program that Congress places in the tax code should receive the same type of scrutiny as an equivalent direct spending program."[78] Exempting income, at least as far as Treasury was concerned, *was* equivalent in effect to spending public funds.

The commissioner of Internal Revenue therefore began to subject applications for exemption to more comprehensive scrutiny. Beginning in the 1960s, it regularly issued "provisional" or "advance" letters of tax exemption recognition to §501 (c)(3) groups. "Provisional" letters indicated that determinations of status would not become final until later on in the organization's existence.

In the House of Representatives, antagonism toward large private non-profit foundations mounted. Congressman Wright Patman had provoked legislative concern about whether private foundations served a useful public purpose during the latter 1950s and early 1960s.[79] Congress had set up committees to expose to public view the questionable program and funding activities of certain private foundations. "Goaded largely by these efforts," the Internal Revenue Service initiated new enforcement policies toward the review of nonprofit expenditures, particularly those of foundations.[80]

The cornerstone of changes in the later 1960s involved restrictions on "private foundations," privately funded groups that Patman presumed to be wealthy, politically dangerous, and less susceptible to public control than public charities. In 1965, the Treasury Department advanced recommendations for a comprehensive overhaul of the provisions dealing with private foundations, which led to the major changes effected by the Tax Reform Act of 1969.[81] It included a rebuttable presumption that all the §501 (c)(3) organizations—those organizations authorized to provide their donors and grantors with tax deductions—were to be regarded as *private foundations* unless they could demonstrate otherwise. Most newly organized groups were required to notify the IRS if they wanted tax-exempt status.[82] Penalties for self-dealing and lobbying, in the form of excise taxes of varying degrees of severity, would be imposed on these foundations and those in control of them, rather than lead the IRS necessarily to seek to revoke exemptions. Special reporting requirements were prescribed for private foundations as well. In one action, Congress had imposed sharp new accountability rules on private foundations, while mainly leaving alone publicly supported charities and other organizations.

On a general level of analysis, a principal motive for passage of these special foundation rules was recognition of a flaw in the theory that non-profits were essential for protecting democratic discussion and debate in an increasingly corporate world. Although it might be fair to permit all groups an equal footing in the political process by allowing them a non-profit status, it would not be fair to allow some political speech to be expressed more powerfully than other speech *because* it enjoyed a wealth of sponsorship from private foundations funded by *tax-exempt* contributions from a privileged elite. In such a case, the argument could be made that instead of promoting expressive pluralism, the new conception of nonprofit enterprise at times encouraged unfair competition vis-à-vis the speech of nonexempt organizations.[83]

Federal tax authorities and others who conferred tax benefits appreciated the fact that in addition to private foundations, other nonprofit corporations could be formed more easily than before. With greater necessity, therefore, they required nonprofits seeking benefits to present substantive qualifications for receiving subsidies and advantages. To the extent that tax authorities previously relied on determinations made at the time of incorporation or charter amendments to decide whether to confer tax exemptions, that practice was incompatible with the new conception of a nonprofit charter as part of the "new property." It did not seem incompatible, however, for officials to impose more vigorous prebenefit screening and postbenefit monitoring when groups applied for tax exemptions.

Even accounting for the newer view of First Amendment and Fourteenth Amendment restrictions on corporate supervision, discretionary behavior by government officials would be appropriate and lawful as long as it occurred before due process considerations thoroughly inhibited the revocation of government benefits. In light of the tangible subsidies and other direct support that tax exemption provided, it would be justifiable for more than a cursory review of papers to be demanded by tax authorities before tax-exempt status would be conferred. Taxation officers particularly seemed well positioned to examine organizations for their suitability for exemption.[84]

The Commission on Private Philanthropy and Public Needs explored the operation of the exempt organizations branch of the IRS in 1974.[85] Federal supervision of most nonprofits, its report stated, happened "almost exclusively through administration of the Internal Revenue Code." This presented serious problems, since the mission of the IRS was essentially tax collection, whereas "many provisions [of the Internal Revenue Code] concerning philanthropy have regulatory rather than collection objectives."[86]

The commission reported that the IRS approach to determining whether such groups as segregated schools, abortion rights counselors, and public interest law firms served a "charitable purpose," which qualified them for coveted status as a §501 (c)(3) organization, was less than crystal clear—and that many of its rulings were directed to understanding what was and what was not a suitable charitable purpose entitling a group to an exemption. In recent years the IRS was "undoubtedly delaying recognition of some new charitable concepts longer than their proponents believe desirable and [encouraging] tax-subsidized social innovation more than others believe to be appropriate."[87] Nevertheless, it advised against creating any new federal body to oversee nonprofits or to decide whether applicants for exemptions were meritorious. The Internal Revenue Service, it said, had "a tradition of nonpartisanship and independence."[88] It was uncertain whether a new type of federal agency could do any better.[89]

Although efforts were made to tighten up access to federal tax exemption and to control the conduct of exempt organizations subsequent to their exemption, the view that control over access to exemption provided an adequate surrogate for effective state supervision was shortsighted. None of the screening practices of the IRS directly affected the incorporation process, which generally occurred prior to and separately from the tax exemption process. Most nonprofit organizations for most of the twentieth century could be tax-exempt without having to make an application for recognition of tax-exempt status.[90] When recognition of tax-exempt status by revenue officers was required to be made, their tests were not like the ones state officials used to determine appropriate corporate purposes. And since the IRS for most of the period under study could not discipline most exempt organizations in proportion to perceived misdeeds, but could only revoke or deny an exemption (revocation became known as dropping "the atomic bomb"), sanctions occurred exceedingly rarely.[91]

IRS officers screened nonprofits in order to award them particular tax subsidies for an agency that had, as its objective, curbing abuses in tax avoidance and revenue minimization techniques. They were not second-guessing the determination of states about whether a chartered organization operated in the public benefit. A determination that an organization was not entitled to tax exemption did not cause the automatic revocation of a state charter, since ongoing nonprofit groups received a *presumption* of lawfulness, regardless of whether they were tax-exempt or had lost an exemption.[92] State charters, conversely, were granted without presuming that the corporation would be entitled to any particular exemption, notwithstanding that officials who reviewed applications for tax exemption considered state grants of nonprofit charters relevant to their exemption determinations.[93] A federal exemption would not be granted just because an organization was chartered by a state as not organized for profit, nor would a federal tax exemption be automatically revoked whenever a state nonprofit charter was revoked.[94]

The IRS tax exemption rules were not primarily designed to improve the functioning of nonprofit associations, to appraise the public about their worth, or to encourage some nonprofit activities at the expense of others. The news that a group had lost its exemption because it had violated tax rules might well destroy such an organization if it were widely known—but most often the IRS dealt quietly with nonprofits. In the absence of litigation over fraud or misconduct, discoveries of tax violations seldom were shared with the public. Determining tax-exempt status did not substitute for other forms of state regulation of nonprofit organizations.

Considering the social context in which the IRS rules were being applied, furthermore, tax-exemption determinations were destined to be of limited use for restraining nonprofit subsidies. The incorporation cases ascribed new cultural, political, and legal importance to nonprofits. Non-profit corporations, trusts, foundations, and other entities exercised ever greater power and influence in the economy. Given the expansion of the importance of nonprofits nurtured elsewhere, the IRS was not at liberty to diminish or confine the expressive nonprofit role through administrative regulations.

The difficulties attached to supervising nonprofits through applications for tax relief were greatly compounded as a result of the broader due process and rights of free expression that were extended to nonprofit groups that applied for tax benefits. In the same ways that 1950s legal and political theories argued for special treatment of nonprofit corporations, they also imposed an ever more rigorous mandate on the IRS to be substantially indifferent to diverse points of view about social, political, and economic issues where exemptions were concerned.[95] As the review of tax exemption assumed greater importance as a way of supervising nonprofits, it is ironic that the discretion to reject applications for tax exemption diminished and the procedural protections afforded to applicants increased.[96]

At first, during the Cold War, authorities tried to exclude from exemption people and groups whose views they believed were subversive. In California, applicants for property tax exemptions were required by a state constitutional amendment and revenue rules to sign an oath on their annual tax returns swearing that they did not advocate "the overthrow of the Government of the United States or the State . . . by force or violence or other unlawful means." [97] A number of Californians, including Lawrence Speiser, refused to subscribe to the oath. In a case reminiscent of the New York incorporation case *Lithuanian Workers' Society*, the allegedly subversive nature of Speiser's nonprofit association led to the determination of state officials to disapprove of its application for exemption.[98] Upon denial of the exemption, Speiser challenged the constitutionality of the law under the federal constitution, claiming deprivation of freedom of speech without due process safeguards required by the Fourteenth Amendment.

The California Supreme Court accepted Speiser's argument and compelled the tax assessor, Justin A. Randall, to grant the exemption. The state appealed, and the case of *Speiser v. Randall* reached the U.S. Supreme Court in 1958.[99] Writing for a majority of the Court, Justice Brennan rejected the tax assessor's argument that because tax exemption was a "privilege" or "bounty," its denial did not infringe speech.[100] Denial of tax exemption, Justice Brennan wrote, would have the effect "of coercing the claimants to refrain from the proscribed speech." Since denial was aimed at the suppression of dangerous ideas, the Court defined the problem as ascertaining whether California had chosen a fair method for determining when claimants were persons who engaged in speech for which they might be fined or imprisoned.[101]

Justice Brennan demanded more rigorous and objective methods of discovering subversiveness than California had heretofore employed. He stated that the resolution of the case depended not so much on the lawfulness of the statute but on the process of truth finding used to learn if an organization in question actually fit the bill and contained subversive elements:

> To experienced lawyers it is commonplace that the outcome of a lawsuit—and hence the vindication of legal rights—depends more often on how the factfinder appraises the facts than on a disputed construction of a statute or interpretation of a line of precedents. . . . Since only considerations of the greatest urgency can justify restrictions on speech . . . the procedures by which the facts of the case are adjudicated are of special importance and the validity of the restraint may turn on the safeguards which they afford.[102]

Examining the "summary tax-collection procedure" used by the tax assessor in California, the Court declared that the "separation of legitimate from illegitimate speech calls for more sensitive tools than California has supplied."[103] It was impermissible to place the burden of proof and persuasion on taxpayers who refused to sign a loyalty oath to prove that they were not in violation of California's antisubversion laws as a condition of tax exemption. Concurring, Justice Douglas declared that it was "time for government—state or federal—to become concerned with the citizen's advocacy [only] when his ideas and beliefs move into the realm of action."[104] After 1958, the standards employed to determine whether applicants for tax exemptions could be denied became increasingly sensitive to First Amendment concerns and to due process concerns for procedural consistency.[105]

*     *     *

And so the same conception of the special role of nonprofit groups in American life, which rationalized the demise of pre-incorporation supervision, also turned effective post-incorporation supervision into an intractable problem. Nonprofit corporations even became more difficult to dissolve than ever before. In the 1963 case *California Labor School, Inc., v. Subversive Activities Control Board,* [106] for example, the U.S. Court of Appeals for the District of Columbia decided that a nonprofit corporation that ceased doing business could not necessarily be dissolved by creditors, owing to concerns related to free expression. The permissible ground for forced dissolutions narrowed further over the subsequent years.[107]

Just as the older regime of supervision was falling apart and new constitutional limits were being imposed, the problems caused by inadequate supervision of nonprofits grew even more severe. It became difficult to end a nonprofit corporation's existence even in the face of total inactivity or a wrong to the public. Given the sensitivity to new free expression matters, the question arose, When if ever would it be appropriate for state administrative or judicial officers to challenge the creation, operation, or dissolution of a nonprofit corporation?[108] The answer had been provided by the courts: Only in the most exceptional of circumstances.

## Notes

1. A loose quotation of a description provided by my friend Professor Bernard E. Jacob.

2. *See* James T. Fishman, *The Development of Nonprofit Corporation Law and an Agenda for Reform*, 34 EMORY L.J. 617, 622 (1985).

3. O'Neil, *supra* ch. 1 n. 24.

4. *Id.* at 6–7 (*citing* V. A. Hodgkinson and M. S. Weitzman, DIMENSIONS OF THE INDEPENDENT SECTOR: A STATISTICAL PROFILE (Fall 1988); V. A. Hodgkinson and M. S. Weitzman, GIVING AND VOLUNTEERING IN THE UNITED STATES: FINDINGS FROM A NATIONAL SURVEY [1988]).

5. *Id.*

6. O'Neil, *supra* ch. 1 n. 24; *see also* G. Rudney, *The Scope and Dimensions of Nonprofit Activity*, in THE NONPROFIT SECTOR: A RESEARCH HANDBOOK (ed. W. W. Powell 1987). The average compensation of employees in the nonprofit sector has risen on an adjusted basis.

7. *See generally* Charles T. Clotfelter, WHO BENEFITS FROM THE NONPROFIT SECTOR? (1992).

8. Paul E. Treusch, TAX-EXEMPT CHARITABLE ORGANIZATIONS (1988 ed.) (*citing IRS Statistics of Income for 1984*, 5 SOI BULLETIN, vol. 5, no. 4 at 21–23 [1985–86]).

9. *See* John Kimelman, *Too Charitable to Charities*, FINANCIAL WORLD, Sept. 1, 1994 at 46 (citing recent study by the U.K. Charities Aid Foundation).

10. *See* Information Access Company, *Seven in 10 Households Contribute to Charity: Over Half of Adults Volunteer*, at 1999 WL 22091956, Dec. 3, 1999.

11. It is perhaps indicative of the growth in the practice of tax-exempt and nonprofit law that *Index to Legal Periodicals* did not include a subject heading for tax-exempt organizations until 1955, when it included the heading "Taxation: Exemptions." *See* INDEX TO LEGAL PERIODICALS vol. 11. Prior to that time materials relating to this subject were contained within the heading "Charities." *Id.* Vol. 10. Articles concerned with advising lawyers about or criticizing "tax avoidance" and the tax advantages of charitable giving appear regularly in the Index to Legal Periodicals after 1949. *See* Index to Legal Periodicals.

12. *Id.*

13. *See* James T. Bennett and Thomas J. DiLorenzo, UNFAIR COMPETITION: THE PROFIT OF NONPROFITS (1991).

14. *See, e.g.*, cases noted in TAX-EXEMPT ORGANIZATIONS (Research Institute of America).

15. In early 1969, for example, the New York attorney general investigated fraud within foundations in that state and found "an alarming rate" of cases in which foundation funds had been diverted to personal uses. *See* Howard L. Oleck, NONPROFIT CORPORATIONS, ORGANIZATIONS, AND ASSOCIATIONS (1988).

16. *See, e.g.*, NON-PROFIT LEGAL AND TAX NEWSLETTER (founded in 1962).

17. See, *e.g.*, Commerce Clearing House, THE TAX EXEMPT ORGANIZATION (1969); Marilyn E. Phelan, NONPROFIT ENTERPRISES (1985-); Howard Oleck, NON-PROFIT CORPORATIONS, ORGANIZATIONS, AND ASSOCIATIONS (1988).

18. *Id.*

19. Information provided by Philip M. Sparkes, Bureau of Corporations.

20. Interview with Philip M. Sparkes, director of the Legal Services Division, New York Department of State. Many of these corporations, both commercial and nonprofit, are not active. According to the Business Master File kept by the Extracts Branch of the Input Systems Division of the Internal Revenue Service, the number of all federally tax exempt organizations in New York state as of December 31, 1993 was as follows:

|                        | Brooklyn | Manhattan | Albany | Buffalo | Total   |
|------------------------|----------|-----------|--------|---------|---------|
| All Exempt "Active"    | 17,163   | 31,220    | 9,725  | 19,410  | 77,518  |
| All Exempt "Inactive"  | 8,679    | 16,011    | 4,842  | 10,365  | 39,897  |
|                        |          |           |        | Total   | 117,415 |

There were 42,445 "active" §501 (c)(3) organizations and 15,530 "inactive" §501 (c)(3) organizations, totaling 67,975 such organizations in New York State as of 12/31/93. *Id.*

21. U.S. General Accounting Office, TAX POLICY: COMPETITION BETWEEN TAXABLE BUSINESSES AND TAX-EXEMPT ORGANIZATIONS, BRIEFING REPORT TO THE JOINT COMM. ON TAXATION 14 (Feb. 1987).

22. *Id.* (*citing* Burton A. Weisbrod, THE NONPROFIT ECONOMY 170 [1988]).

23. *Unrelated Business Income Tax: Hearings Before the Subcomm. on Oversight of the House Comm. on Ways and Means*, 100th Cong., 1st sess. 26 (1987).

24. *See* Howard L. Oleck, NONPROFIT CORPORATIONS, ORGANIZATIONS, AND ASSOCIATIONS (1988); Lesley Oelsner, *Tax-Exempt Institutions Asked for Voluntary Payments to City*, N.Y. TIMES, July 21, 1978 at A1.

25. *See* Rebecca S. Rudnick, *State and Local Taxes on Nonprofit Organizations*, 22 CAP. U. L. REV. 321 (1993); Ginsberg, *supra* ch 2. n. 9, at 299–303.

26. *See* A. BALK, THE FREE LIST: PROPERTY WITHOUT TAXES 1 (1971).

27. *See* Gabler and Shannon, *The Exemption of Religious, Educational, and Charitable Institutions from Property Taxation, in* 4 U.S. Dept. of Treasury, RESEARCH PAPERS SPONSORED BY THE COMMISSION ON PRIVATE PHILANTHROPY AND PUBLIC NEEDS 1909, 2535 (1977).

28. *See* Matthew L. Wald, *Connecticut to Reimburse Cities for Tax Lost on Exempt Property*, N.Y. TIMES, May 29, 1978 at A7.

29. *Id.*

30. *Id.*

31. *See* Teresa P. Gordon et al., *Tax-Exempt Organization Financial Data: Availability and Limitations*, ACCOUNTING HORIZONS, June 1, 1999 at 113.

32. John Kimelman, *Too Charitable to Charities?*, FINANCIAL WORLD, Sept. 1, 1994 at 46.

33. Congressional hearings, held by the Subcommittee on Oversight of the House Ways and Means Committee (Cong. Pickle [D. Tx], chair), were held over a series of years to consider the nature of competition between profits and nonprofits. In California and several other states, periodic efforts to toughen or wholly real property tax exemption scheme were made. *See generally* Laura Brown Chisolm, *Politics and Charity: A Proposal for Peaceful Coexistence, 58* GEO. WASH. L. REV. 308, 310 (1990).

34. *See* Amy E. Moody, *Comment: Conditional Federal Grants: Can the Government Undercut Lobbying by Nonprofit Conditions Placed on Federal Grants?* 24 B.C. ENVTL. AFF. L. REV. 113.

35. *See supra,* text at ch. 4 n. 229.

36. Regarding problems with disclosure remedies more generally considered, *see, e.g.,* Harvey P. Dale, *Effects of the Omnibus Budget Reconciliation Act of 1987 on the Disclosure Responsibilities and Lobbying and Political Activities of Tax-Exempt Organizations,* C343 ALI-ABA (1988).

37. *See* Mary E. Phelan, NONPROFIT ENTERPRISES: LAW & TAXATION §§6:01 et seq. (1995).

38. *See* Commission on Private Philanthropy and Public Needs, GIVING IN AMERICA (1975 report).

39. *Id.*

40. *Id.*

41. *See, e.g.,* Michael O'Neil, THE THIRD AMERICA (1989).

42. *See* Symposium, *Introduction,* 39 CASE W. RES. L. REV. 653 (1989); *see also* Henry Hansmann, *The Evolving Law of Nonprofit Organizations: Do Current Trends Make Good Policy,* 39 CASE W. RES. L. REV. 807 (1989).

43. *Id.*

44. Assume, for example, the popularity among large numbers of thieves as well as the effectiveness of a group called Muggers for Darker Streets, whose purpose was to promote efforts to "reduce glare and eliminate unnecessary street illumination." Regardless of its true intentions, such a group might have established its suitability for nonprofit status based on accurately disclosing its success in fund-raising and darkening alleyways. Conversely, a group that promised to be unpopular and small forever—a support group to assist in the rehabilitation of ex-child molesters, for example—might fail to win approval based on market considerations alone.

45. "Charity" is used here to indicate the type of nonprofit endeavor that is publicly supported and designed to serve public health and welfare goals. *See* Hansmann, *supra* n. 42.

46. *See* Leslie G. Espinoza, *Straining the Quality of Mercy: Abandoning the Quest for Informed Charitable Giving,* 64 S. CAL. L. REV. 605, 643 (1991) (referring to solicitation regulations).

47. *n. 42*

48. *See, e.g., Standing to Sue in the Charitable Sector,* 28 U.S.F.L. REV. 37 (1993).

49. See Village of Schaumburg v. Citizens for a Better Env't, 444 U.S. 620, 100 S. Ct. 826, 63 L. Ed. 2d 73 (1980); on recent developments in the law of charitable so-

licitation, *see, e.g.*, John Dziedzic, Comment, *Krishna v. Lee Extricates the Inextricable: An Argument for Regulating the Solicitation in Charitable Solicitation*, 17 U. PUGET SOUND L. REV. 665 (1994).

50. VOLUNTARY HEALTH AND WELFARE AGENCIES IN THE UNITED STATES: AN EXPLORATORY STUDY BY AN AD HOC CITIZENS COMMITTEE (ed. R. Hamlin 1961). According to the committee, the high operating cost of many charities, especially their high fund-raising costs, presented an added disincentive to public giving and threatened the continuation of tax exemptions and the tax deductibility of contributions. In the 1960 *Harvard Law Review*, Professor Karst disputed the assumption that private charity should always be promoted by the law. *See* Karst, *The Efficiency of the Charitable Dollar: An Unfulfilled State Responsibility*, 73 HARV. L. REV. 433 (1960). Private charities, he argued, were frequently less efficient providers of services than government or private firms. Lacking an economic justification, charitable activities might "be absorbed by various levels of government, operated at an overall reduction of cost, and paid for through progressively heavier taxation." While nonprofit charities, especially in the health and welfare fields, had been performing more of the services that the public sector might otherwise have performed, the article suggested that it might be beneficial for the trend to reverse itself. *See* Karst.

51. *See* Espinoza, *supra* n. 46 at 648; *see also* B. Hopkins, CHARITY UNDER SIEGE: GOVERNMENT REGULATION OF FUND RAISING (1980).

52. *Id.*

53. *Id.* at 605.

54. *Id.* at 606.

55. *See* Village of Schaumburg v. Citizens for a Better Env't, 444 U.S. 620, 100 S. Ct. 826, 63 L. Ed. 2d 73 (1980); Secretary of State v. Joseph H. Munson Co., 467 U.S. 947, 104 S. Ct. 2839, 81 L. Ed. 2d 786 (1984); Riley v. National Fed'n of the Blind, 487 U.S. 781, 108 S. Ct. 2667, 101 L. Ed. 2d 669 (1988).

56. *See* Riley v. National Fed'n of the Blind, 487 U.S. 781, 108 S. Ct. 2667, 101 L. Ed. 2d 669 (1988).

57. 357 U.S. 449, 78 S. Ct. 1163, 2 L. Ed. 2d 1488 (1957).

58. *See* Village of Schaumburg, 444 U.S. 620, 100 S. Ct. 826, 63 L. Ed. 2d 73 (1980).

59. Espinoza, *supra* n. 46 at 612.

60. *Id.*

61. *Id.* at 655.

62. Espinoza, *supra* n. 46 at 663.

63. *See also, e.g.*, Tim Darraggh, *Checking on Charities Becomes Difficult Task*, THE MORNING CALL, Oct. 4, 1994 at A2 (difficulty of determining nonprofit activities through available disclosures).

64. There is supervision provided by players other than government, of course. The market represents a discipline upon nonprofits in many situations. *See, e.g.*, Brody, *Agents Without Principals*; Estelle James and Susan Rose Ackerman, THE NONPROFIT ENTERPRISE IN MARKET ECONOMICS (1986). Although standing to challenge nonprofit activity is considerably more restrictive than commercial enterprises, a measure of supervision is nonetheless exercised by boards and members through their standing to challenge improper conduct in court. *See* Brody.

65. *See* Revenue Act of 1894, ch. 349, §32, 28 Stat. 509, 556, later declared unconstitutional in Pollack v. Farmers Loan & Trust Co., 157 U.S. 429, 15 S. Ct. 673, 39 L. Ed. 759 (1895) and subsequently reenacted.

66. Labor, agricultural, and horticultural organizations were added in 1909, Corporation Excise Tax Act of 1909, §38, 36 Stat. 112, 113; mutual cemetery companies, business leagues, chambers of commerce, and social welfare organizations were added in 1913, §2, ¶G(a), 38 Stat. 114, 172 (1913).

67. See Paul E. Treusch, TAX-EXEMPT CHARITABLE ORGANIZATIONS 3–10 (1983).

68. *Id.* at 6 (*citing* §11[a], 39 Stat. 756, 766–67 [1916]).

69. *See* Bittker, *infra* n. 84; Whithorn, TAX TECHNIQUES FOR FOUNDATIONS AND OTHER EXEMPT ORGANIZATIONS (1980); Reiling, *Federal Taxation: What Is a Charitable Organization?*, 44 A.B.A.J. 525, (1958); Chauncy Belknap, *The Federal Tax Exemption of Charitable Organizations: Its History and Underlying Policy*, *in* 4 COMMISSION ON PUBLIC PHILANTHROPY AND PUBLIC NEEDS (Filer Commission), GIVING IN AMERICA: TOWARD A STRONGER VOLUNTARY SECTOR 1909 (Treasury Dept. 1977).

70. *See* Carolyn C. Jones, *From Class Tax to Mass Tax*, 37 BUFFALO L. REV. 685 (1989).

71. *See* Berrien C. Eaton Jr., *Charitable Foundations, Tax Avoidance, and Business Expediency*, 35 VA. L.REV.809, 987 (1949); Peter Hall, INVENTING THE NONPROFIT SECTOR, *supra*.

72. Hall, *Id.*

73. REVENUE ACT OF 1950, §331, 64 Stat. 906, 957–59 (ultimately replaced by I.R.C. §§4941, 4944).

74. *See* House Select Committee to Investigate Foundations (Cox Committee), *Final Report*, H.R. Rep. no. 2514, 82d Cong. 2d sess. (1953); *House Special Committee to Investigate Tax-Exempt Foundations and Comparable Organizations* (Reece Committee), H.R. Rep. no. 2681, 83d Cong. 2d sess. (1954); Hearings Pursuant to H.R. Res. 13 Before Subcommittee no. 1 of the House Select Committee on Small Business, 88th Cong., 2d sess. 1 (1964); *Chairman's Rep. to the House Select Committee on Small Business* (Patman Subcommittee), *Tax-Exempt Foundations and Charitable Trusts: Their Impact on Our Economy*, 87th Cong., 2d sess. (Comm. Print 1962); *Subcommittee Chairman's Rep. to Subcommittee no. 1*, Second Install., 88th Cong., 1st sess. (Comm. Print 1963); Third Install., 88th Cong., 2d sess. (Comm. Print 1964); Fourth Install., 89th Cong., 2d sess. (Comm. Print 1967); Sixth Install., 90th Cong., 2d sess. (Comm. Print 1968); Seventh Install., 91st Cong., 1st Sess. (Comm. Print 1969).

75. *Id.; see also* 68A Stat. 1, 163 (1954).

76. In theory, the IRS does not grant tax exemption, nor revoke the tax exemption of an organization. "Congress . . . by statute has defined the categories of organizations that are eligible for exemption, and it is Congress that, by statute, has determined whether a tax exemption should be continued." For this reason the function of the IRS is said to be to "recognize" tax exemption. *See* Bruce R. Hopkins, THE LAW OF TAX EXEMPT ORGANIZATIONS, sec. 36 at 722 (1992, 6th ed.).

77. *See* Paul E. Treusch, TAX-EXEMPT CHARITABLE ORGANIZATIONS ch. 1-A.03 at 2 (3d ed. 1988) (*citing* News Release IR–534 (Sept. 7, 1962), 1962 Stand. Fed. Tax Rep. (CCH) ¶6503. *See also* Rogovin, *Methods and Objectives of the Revenue Service's Program for Exempt Organizations*, PROC. N.Y.U. SIXTH BIENNIAL CONFERENCE ON CHARITABLE FOUNDATIONS 229 (1963).

78. *See* Donna Adler, *The Internal Revenue Code, the Constitution, and the Courts: The Use of Tax Expenditure Analysis in Judicial Decision Making*, 28 WAKE FOREST L. REV. 855, 860–61 (1993). In 1974, shortly after the enactment of ERISA, the Internal Revenue Commissioner created the separate post of assistant commissioner in charge of employee plans and exempt organizations. *See* IRC §7802(b), Pub. L. no. 93–406, §1051(a).

79. *See* Marts, PHILANTHROPY'S ROLE IN CIVILIZATION (1953); Barney, *The Egg-Head Clutch on the Foundations*, 78 AM. MERCURY 31 (June 1954); White, *What Are Foundations Up To?*, 52 FORTUNE 110 (Oct. 1955); White, *Where the Foundations Fall Down*, 32 FORTUNE 140 (Nov. 1955); Yarmolinsky, *The Foundation As an Expression of the Democratic Society*, N.Y.U. FIFTH CONFERENCE ON CHARITABLE FOUNDATIONS 65 (1961).

80. Treusch, *supra* n. 8 at 10.

81. REVENUE ACT OF 1969, §§101, 121, and 201, adding §§507–509 and ch. 42 (§§4940–4948) to the 1954 Code and modifying §§511–514 and other sections thereof.

82. IRC §508(d)(2)(B).

83. *See* foundation lobbying rules, IRS §4941 et seq.

84. *See* Boris I. Bittker, FEDERAL TAXATION OF INCOME, ESTATES, AND GIFTS, IV, ¶100.1.2 (1981); John Simon, THE TAX TREATMENT OF NONPROFIT ORGANIZATIONS: A REVIEW OF FEDERAL AND STATE POLICIES IN THE NONPROFIT SECTOR: A RESEARCH HANDBOOK (ed. Walter W. Powell 1987).

85. Federal Oversight of Philanthropy: A Study for the Commission on Private Philanthropy and Public Needs (preliminary draft located at Boalt Hall Library) (Oct. 25, 1974), 7.

86. *Id.*

87. *Id.* at 83 (*citing, e.g.*, Rev. Rul. 73–569, I.R.B. 1973–51, 12 (abortion counseling); Rev. Proc. 71–39, 1971–2 Cum. Bull. 575 (public interest law firms); Rev. Rul. 71–447, 1971–2 Cum. Bull. 230 [private racial discrimination]).

88. *Id.*

89. *Id.* at 83, 9.

90. *See* Hopkins, *supra* n. 51 at 723.

91. *See* Monica Langley, *"IRS Gains More-Flexible Power to Curb Excessive Pay at Charities,"* WALL ST. J., Aug. 7, 1996.

92. A key difference between post-incorporation supervision and pre-incorporation screening is that the burden of proof is substantially different. The test is no longer "should an organization that has not yet come into being and in which the public and members have no reliance interest and little constituent support be allowed to enjoy certain prerogatives of status?" The test instead becomes "should an organization that has been receiving benefits continue to receive them?" These two different tests do not necessarily yield different outcomes, but the criteria used to answer them give organizations that already exist receive a strong presumption in their favor.

93. According to the director of the Legal Services Division of the New York Department of State, until 1982, the standard for obtaining an exemption from state income tax was "legal sufficiency." Today it is a clerical matter—if "all the elements are there" the letter of exemption will get filed. It is far easier to receive

an exemption from tax if an organization is corporate as opposed to being unincorporated. Interview with Philip M. Sparkes, director, Legal Services Division, New York State Department of State, 1995.

The Internal Revenue Service will look almost entirely at the organizational documents presented by the corporation when it grants an exemption. Later, as subsequent tax returns are filed, the IRS reviews the operations of the organization from the perspective of a tax collector interested in knowing whether the organization is no longer entitled to exemption. *See* Bruce R. Hopkins, LAW OF TAX EXEMPT ORGANIZATIONS (1992, 6th ed.), §6.1 (organizational test), §35.2 (governing instruments).

94. *See* Treas. Regs. §1.501(a)–1(a)(2).

95. Congress also created several new tax-exempt categories during the period.

96. *See* James J. Fishman and Stephen Schwarz, NONPROFIT ORGANIZATIONS ch. 5 (2000) (presenting revenue rulings and court opinions illustrating difficulties denying tax exempt status to extremist and unconventional organizations).

97. Speiser v. Randall, 357 U.S. 513, 78 S. Ct. 1332, 2 L. Ed. 2d 1460 (1958).

98. *Id.*

99. 357 U.S. 513, 78 S. Ct. 1332, 2 L. Ed. 2d 1460 (1958).

100. *Id.* at 518.

101. *Id.* at 519–20.

102. *Id.* at 520–21 (footnotes omitted).

103. *Id.* at 525.

104. *Id.* at 537. In dissent, Justice Tom Clark argued that the California tax code did not do anything except refuse to provide largesse in the absence of a proof of merit worthiness: "Appellants are free to speak as they wish, to advocate what they will. If they advocate the violent and forceful overthrow of the California Government, California will take no action against them under the tax provisions here in question. But it will refuse to take any action *for them*, in the sense of extending to them the legislative largesse that is inherent in the granting of any tax exemption or deduction. In the view of the California court, '[a]n exemption from taxation is the exception and the unusual. . . . It is a bounty or gratuity on the part of the sovereign and when once granted may be withdrawn.'" *Id.* at 540–41.

105. These standards became increasingly permissive. *See, e.g.,* Rev. Procedure 86–43, 1986 Cum. Bull. 729 (publishing criteria used by IRS to determine when advocacy of a particular viewpoint is considered educational); Big Mama Rag v. United States, 631 F.2d.1030 (1980).

106. 322 F.2d 393 (D.C. Cir. 1963).

107. *Id.*

108. *See* Kevin Sheard, *Forfeiture of Non-Profit Corporation Charters*, 14 Clev. Marshall L. Rev 253, 254 (1965).

# In Search of a New Direction

## Scholarly Assessments

Scholars did not employ the term "nonprofit sector" as a category until the 1970s. "Although there was a vast literature on particular kinds of non-profits—charities, education, hospitals, museums, social welfare, and so on," historian Peter Hall has written, "no effort was made before the 1970s to treat these as part of a unified sector of activity."[1] When they did so, they grouped many different sorts of nonprofit activities together based on one benefit that most of them had in common—tax exemption.

Much of the scholarship that emerged was either in response to campaigns to diminish benefits and to increase government supervision of foundations in particular or to examine various threats to the most significant benefits. Significant work went into attempts to rationalize the standards for federal tax exemption and to understand the centerpiece of the law of tax exemptions and charitable deductions, Internal Revenue Code §§501(c)(3) and 170(b).

Among the scholars engaged in the debate over the justifications for tax exemptions and charitable contribution deductions were Boris Bittker and George Rahdert, who argued in 1976 that nonprofits were exempt from federal income tax because of the difficulty in measuring their income and assessing an appropriate tax.[2] Professor William Ginsberg argued in 1980 that real property exemptions rewarded altruistic behavior in support of communities that might otherwise diminish or fail entirely without a governmental subsidy.[3] A similar approach was taken by the "community benefit" theorists,[4] who suggested that nonprofit organizations contributed to pluralism "by providing the public goods and services that either are undersupplied by the private market or by the government or else not provided in the same socially desirable manner."[5]

Professor Henry Hansmann criticized altruistic explanations for nonprofit activities and suggested in 1980 that the "nondistributional constraint"—the fundamental rule prohibiting officers and directors of nonprofit corporations from sharing in the profits or assets of their organizations—distinguished nonprofit tax-exempt organizations from for-profit organizations in an essential and economically important way.

The necessity for nonprofits to cope with certain theoretical market im-
perfections that otherwise would prevent productive economic activity,
Hansmann suggested, would perhaps justify their tax exemption.[6] Other
analysts deemphasized market-oriented tests and urged that in order to
compensate taxpayers for the benefits conferred by government exemptions, taxpayers should receive a quid pro quo for the exemption,
premised on the view that "in the absence of the exemption, government
would be required to pay the cost of the service or product provided by
the exempt entity."[7] This would require tax authorities to seek direct evidence of need prior to conferring an exemption. Professor John Columbo
reflected one prevalent perspective when he argued that all of these theories suffered from the inability to quantify, in the interests of equal treatment, the particular quality that would result in an exemption being
granted or denied.[8] Professor Evelyn Brody, after reviewing the history of
the charity tax exemption and attempts to justify it, suggested that the
nontaxability of many nonprofits (and presumably their privileged treatment in many other respects) is best explained by understanding them as
part of a "sovereignty," independent of the state rather than subservient
to it.[9] But it is a peculiar sovereign whose power can be given or taken
away, piecemeal, by others. Who should be privileged to anoint these
"sovereigns," if such they be, and on what grounds?

In the course of their work, many of these scholars observed the historically unprecedented amount of tax-exempt giving to an unprecedented
number of exempt entities in recent decades. They suggested various
causes for the expansion, including an increase in governmental giving
and the rising humanitarian, charitable, and altruistic impulses that
emerged in American culture during the 1960s.[10]

These impulses were fueled in turn, according to some views, by middle-class guilt about the disparities between the affluent and the poor.[11]
According to others it was the use of tax-exempt entities as wealth-trans-
fer mechanisms for the rich[12] or dissatisfaction with the profit motive as
an incentive to extract work and induce consumption[13] or a greater abundance in society generally.[14] The gap between rich and poor had been
growing. As the gap widened, demand for public charitable activities
grew commensurately, but the supply of available governmental services
was limited. And so the inability of governmental agencies to provide
services in areas of need was advanced as another reason for broader
willingness to confer exemptions on private groups that might fill unmet
needs.

In 1987, thirty-five years after the first model nonprofit corporation act,
the idea that the nonprofit corporate form should be accessible for "any
lawful purpose," without either enumeration of permissible purposes or
the subjective assessment of state officials, finally became part of pro-

posed model law. In 1979 the Subcommittee on the Model Nonprofit Corporation Law of the Business Law Section of the American Bar Association had begun to revise the 1964 model act.[15] "The committee which drafted the Old Act," wrote Michael Hone, the reporter, did not agree on the nature of nonprofit corporations, and as a result the old act included "nonexclusive examples of corporate purposes . . . to provide some guidance as to the nature of organizations which could be formed . . . without falling into the trap of having an exclusive value-laden list of proper purposes."[16] The revised act, on the other hand, provided that "every corporation incorporated under the Act has the purpose of engaging in any lawful activity unless a more limited purpose is set forth in the articles of incorporation."[17] One dissenting member of the drafting committee complained that the revised model act avoided addressing what nonprofit corporations actually were.[18]

Nonetheless, the free nonprofit incorporation paradigm had been embraced by the bar's leading professional organization and leading practitioners working in the nonprofit sector.

* * *

The story told here illuminates connections between the present contours of the nonprofit sector and the historical evolution of nonprofit legal doctrine. The expansion of the nonprofit sector, the liberalization of its law, and the reconception of the social and political importance of nonprofits were not coincidental. Social, political, and economic changes could and did shape legal doctrines. The law related to nonprofit associations no doubt adapted to broader trends.

Undoubtedly, philanthropic and altruistic motives stimulated the growth in the nonprofit sector to a considerable extent. It also derived from government spending programs, new economic development, and competitive advantages that providers of goods and services could obtain by operating as nonprofits. This growth no doubt created a demand for significant elaboration and refinement of laws that govern nonprofit corporations.

But law also develops relatively autonomously in ways that can shape social action and economic behavior. Trends in jurisprudence and political discourse affect lawmaking and the conduct of legal institutions, which have their own revising effects. A likely explanation for part of the exceptional growth of the nonprofit sector is that the professional training of a generation of young lawyers enabled them to persuade an already receptive judiciary and bar to change the legal rules about the formation and supervision of nonprofits, in response to larger currents of First Amendment and legal process jurisprudence and political thought. The new legal climate attracted many entrepreneurial and advocacy activities that previously would not have been suitable for the nonprofit form and which otherwise might have been established along different lines of organization. In some cases lenient supervision provided an opportunity for fraudulent or abusive conduct. In many cases it provided welcome room for experimentation, innovation, creativity, and the expression of important ideas and actions.

The revision of legal doctrine related to the formation and supervision of nonprofit corporations was only a part of a far broader reconception of nonprofit endeavors. Notwithstanding its flaws, the reconception promoted the enlargement of the nonprofit sector and redefined contemporary understanding of the value of legitimate nonprofit activity. Doors were opened to the easy creation of nonprofit corporations and, more important, I believe, to relaxed cultural, economic, and legal expectations about their operation.

When the legal paradigm of privilege shattered, those who shattered it did not accurately predict the consequences of the new norm that replaced it. In reaction to the preceding years of excessive concern with serving mainstream ideas about permissible purposes, the new line that was drawn during the 1960s left little room for the administrative application of regulatory laws or for determinations about the extent to which nonprofit activity deserved to be subsidized. There developed "no entity in the political process that oversees, regulates, studies (and sometimes promotes) the activities of the nonprofit sector or polices nonprofits on a global scale so as to discourage abuses of nonprofit status." In many quarters the perception spread that the nonprofit sector was "degenerating from an engine of social good into a cloak for private interests seeking privileges to the detriment of the public."[19]

To counter that perception, the states might take steps to reinvigorate the supervision of nonprofit organizations, since the process for determining tax-exempt status has not proven up to that task. It may be time to reconvene a national commission to reconsider, in the interest of governmental economy, public support, and consumer welfare, our system governing nonprofit formation. Broad judicial and administrative discretion to deny charters was buried deeply for good reasons decades ago, but other options have been suggested that are worth considering.

State incorporation procedures might be changed to provide periodic and thorough reviews. An alternative might be to take a page from earlier practices of the Internal Revenue Service and encourage state law to provide for "provisional" or fixed-term, renewable charters, rather than ones with indefinite terms.[20] Upon renewal, corporations might have to report thoroughly on their previous activities and the relation of the activities to the corporate purposes. Groups without tax exemptions would be no less subject to these rules than others. Rules on standing to sue can be liberalized.[21]

Serious intermediate sanctions by state authorities for improper nonprofit corporate activities might be adopted, along with rules and budget allocations that lead to more frequent revocation of nonprofit charters after periodic renewals. These would no doubt produce incentives for more efficient management of the operation of nonprofits. State activities addressed to the imposition of "intermediate sanctions," along the lines of those considered and being applied by the Internal Revenue Service, could be constructive. Tightened national accounting and other performance standards for all nonprofit corporations—not only federally tax-exempt ones—may be useful.[22]

Tailored and standardized disclosure rules could be developed regarding such matters as the use to which funds solicited have been applied, salaries, overhead costs, and other information. This information could be directed in a timely fashion to both consumers of nonprofit services and to donors to nonprofits, and it could be released according to the nature of the corporate form (membership or nonmembership) and the type of nonprofit. One author proposed the creation of private, for-profit monitoring companies that donors or charitable organizations might engage to audit the financial and charitable aspects of nonprofit operations.[23]

As the author of the Columbia Note contemplated, furthermore, the process of administrative consents could and should be broadened to do more than place regulatory agencies on notice that a new corporation has come into existence. It could be redesigned better to trigger regular substantive administrative reviews, as well as adjudication of disputes about the renewal of nonprofit charters.[24] Some scholars have proposed federalizing or otherwise centralizing nonprofit regulation to improve enforcement.[25]

Some such improvements in supervisory apparatus and enforcement appear to be necessary for the nonprofit sector to emerge from its present cloud with a brighter future. Inevitably, the matter is not limited to whether corporations are run efficiently or whether the goals of these groups are being pursued efficiently. The questions that arise are the ones that confronted the early justices of the New York Supreme Court—about the proper purposes of a nonprofit corporation and about the propriety of particular governmental authorities determining whether purposes are suitable.

The discretionary model of supervision worked repressively, capriciously, and with considerable cultural bias. Nonetheless, there is something positive to be said in mitigation of a wholly negative judgment: That model contained a popularly supported mechanism, however flawed, which was widely believed to adequately regulate access to public benefits. It also should be kept in mind that apart from racial bias, ethnic prejudice, class oppression, and other ignoble motives, discretion also was exercised for more legitimate purposes, including consumer protection and the promotion of fair competition.

If nonprofit status itself *is* still a prize worth gaining, then more care should be shown in parceling it out. As access to any substantial entitlement becomes universally available, pressure to reduce the size of the benefit attached to each recipient of the entitlement builds in proportion. The problem, as always, is to determine where to locate discretionary authority to decide about access, how narrowly to contain it, and how to endow it with legitimacy. Changes in cultural and political attitudes toward nonprofits are of course no less important to the problem of legitimacy than legal changes alone.

One barren possibility is that laws might convert the nonprofit status into an insignificant trinket, something like the trinket that the law has treated it as since the paradigm of privilege collapsed. If they did—by making nonprofit corporate benefits indistinguishable from the benefits available to other corporate forms under normal conditions or even by eliminating the benefits entirely—then a decision to choose the "nondistributional constraint" and other unique features of the nonprofit form would define the governance and business arrangements of a group. But it would not do very much else. This is a direction pursued by many of the sector's most severe critics, who challenge not only abuses in the sector but the efficiency and altruistic motivations of most of those within it.

Other approaches, designed to restore some discretion to the system, are possible. Instead of treating incorporation of a nonprofit for any lawful purpose as a right, it might be desirable to recognize that nonprofit corporate status does have some of the characteristics of a welfare entitlement. And, as in the case of the welfare system, some limits to subsidy may be necessary. The corporate typologies currently employed in many states, including New York, to parcel out benefits and supervision activities, could be refined further. Applications for incorporation might be subject to more intrusive administrative scrutiny.

One step that would add legitimacy to expanded discretion in excluding and removing organizations from nonprofit status might be to establish, through legislation or jurisprudence, that nonprofit status is not inherently more protective of free expression than other forms. There has been a dramatic change in the Supreme Court's thinking about the First Amendment rights of for-profit entities, and this could diminish the for-profit/nonprofit distinction.

The denial of nonprofit corporate status might be less stigmatic today than it was decades ago if it became clear that a central premise of the new conception is untrue: that exclusion from the sector does not necessarily deprive a group of the ability to operate corporately and express itself without diminished constitutional protections. A group that loses the largesse available to it as a nonprofit corporation should still be capable of organizing under one or more other corporate forms—general incorporation laws, limited liability corporation laws, partnership laws, or other laws for purposes related to free expression and advocacy.

It would run against the tide of commentary about the nonprofit law to argue in favor of improving the effectiveness of the nonprofit sector by limiting access to nonprofit corporate benefits. Permitting discretion to be exercised in the area of tax-exempt and charitable activities has become decreasingly acceptable. Most analysts continue to search for ways to end all nonlegislative discretion entirely rather than enlarge it.

Professors John Columbo and Mark Hall, for example, not long ago presented a mechanical, "donative" approach to determining eligibility for tax exemption. They suggested rewarding organizations in direct proportion to their receipt of contributions from nongovernmental entities.[26] Such a donative test might provide an objective, quantitative base for allocating charitable contributions in an objective fashion. But in an unadulterated form it would also substitute the values of the donative marketplace for the substantive judgments of exemption grantors. The result would turn the assumption that nonprofit corporations respond to market failures inside out.[27] It might lead some organizations to adjust their priorities and moderate their position in order to maximize their exemption support instead of their social objectives. It would distort the activities of not-for-profit organizations interested in exemptions by inducing them to maximize their commercial fund-raising efforts in the private sector.

Professor George Christie referred to the clash between the desire to arrive at decisions through purely objective, mechanistic means and the desire to be sensitive to essential though unstated differences as "the old struggle between formal rationality and substantive rationality."[28] The reconception of the law of nonprofit corporations effectively declared formal rationality victorious in that struggle; it sacrificed effective state supervision to the imperatives of free expression and due process. "If one seeks objectivity in judicial decision making," Professor Christie wrote, "one may have no choice but to accept a certain simplification, even artificiality."[29] The courts and legislatures that shaped the modern nonprofit sector engaged in just such a trade, shifting from a structure based on discretionary judgments to mechanical rules based on formal universality of access—only to discover that the new structure had weaknesses of its own.

Mirrored in this history of the regulation of the nonprofit sector is opposition between "neoformalists," who insist that rule-based decisionmaking is an essential pillar supporting the goal of the rule of law, and their critics, who have identified unjustifiable reliance on rules as the most significant source of the *corrosion* of the rule of law.[30] Neither of these groups should take comfort from the development of the nonprofit legal regime. Legislatures and courts originally granted great decision-making freedom to judges and bureaucratic officers, and the result was ultimately to diminish confidence in the rule of law. The response, however, was to eliminate all decisionmaking freedom in favor of a formal rule establishing an entitlement; but that, ultimately, did not restore confidence in the effectiveness of the legal regime either.

Frederick Schauer has distinguished two different, difficult tasks connected with the development of an appropriate, rule-based legal regime. He states that "identifying the decision-making freedom that remains after rules have done their work is different from attempting to determine what the rules say in the first instance." [31] Both of these tasks were problematic in the development of nonprofit law. Confusion about what the rules said plagued the discretionary regime, and the identification of broad decisionmaking freedom proved an affront to the rule of law. But the elimination of decisionmaking freedom, once the rules were reinterpreted, threatened, perhaps as severely, the legitimacy of the entitlement regime.

As in many conflicts, the middle ground is the most difficult to hold. Without reverting to the tradition of strong discretion, accepting a smaller dose of artificiality and indiscretion would help restore confidence in the benefits conferred by nonprofit corporations. No amount of skillful judicial interpretation of an exceedingly loose statute can avoid doing social mischief. But even Professor Lon Fuller recognized in his process-glorifying classic *The Morality of Law*[32] that the complexity of the interests served by statutes such as those contained in the corporation laws demands the expression of value judgments in order to interpret rules sensibly. "A statute," Fuller wrote, "does not serve a purpose as simple and as easily defined as a vacuum cleaner."[33]

## Coda

The debate over the efficiency and privileges of nonprofit enterprises took on new meaning late in the 1990s with economic and legal earthquakes in the health care industry and the increasing popularity of for-profit/nonprofit ventures.[34] The metamorphosis of the legal form continued, and many distinctions between profit and nonprofit corporation forms either broke down or were recognized as inherently fictional.[35] By 1996 knowledgeable scholars in the field suggested that the nonprofit and for-profit forms of corporation were merging—that "business corporations are less purely profit-driven than we think, and working for a nonprofit corporation is more like any other job."[36] As a result, the suggestion was made that society might "prefer to subsidize charitable and other social outputs produced by all organizations rather than subsidize nonprofits based on their organizational form."[37] In an age of global communications, when both for-profit and nonprofit enterprises operated on airwaves, through cables, and on the Internet, it became apparent that preserving expressive pluralism was not necessarily a matter of endowing certain corporate forms with subsidies but of preserving the economic viability of a multiplicity of voices. Perhaps antitrust law was a more relevant and appropriate weapon than corporate or tax law to use to preserve a meaningful democratic and participatory democracy.[38]

Ironically, newer evaluations of judicial discretion encouraged judges to assume more and not less latitude in decisionmaking. The "inherent complexity, the situational variability, and the wide array of extrinsic pressures that necessarily define the art and science of judicial decision making," wrote Scott Idleman, pointed to the need to take a "prudentialist" approach to discretion.[39] Even the requirement that judges should tell the truth (or be "candid" about the basis for a decision) could "undermine the judiciary's ability to fulfill its creative lawmaking function."[40] The realists had long ago demonstrated that the line between law and politics was never a very solid one. In the real world, they suggested, the best definition of judicial brilliance was "practical wisdom." "The person of practical wisdom," wrote Lawrence Solum, "knows which particular ends are worth pursuing and which means best achieve those ends. Judicial wisdom is simply the virtue of practical wisdom applied to the choices which judges must make."[41] Under increasing pressure to bend their rulings to popular will and political force, some scholars argued that a space for judges to exercise their personal conscience and conviction was worth preserving.

But the role of judges in nonprofit supervision had long since come to an end. In 1993, New York state legislators finally abolished the requirement that justices of the state's supreme court approve certificates of incorporation. "It is a burdensome ministerial task for the courts, which must process several thousand applications annually," the sponsors wrote.[42] The justices did not protect the public's interest in any meaningful way, the sponsors of the change stated, because judicial review duplicated the ministerial responsibility of the secretary of state, and also the authority of certain executive agencies, to approve the certificates of certain nonprofits.[43] In any event, the attorney general could maintain an action to annul the corporate existence of any nonprofit corporation that was not duly formed.[44]

It was a time of budget austerity. New York groaned under costly spending programs and unmet social needs. General judicial supervision once may have made sense, but no more.[45] And so the last vestiges of judicial discretion fell away, a milestone in the journey from discretion to entitlement.

## Notes

1. *See* Peter Hall, INVENTING THE NONPROFIT SECTOR 244–47 (1992); Barry D. Karl, *Nonprofit Institutions*, 22 SCIENCE 984–85 (1987). *See also* Nygren Bowen et al., THE CHARITABLE NONPROFITS 3–31 (1994).

2. Boris I. Bittker and George K. Rahdert, *The Exemption of Nonprofit Organizations from Federal Income Taxation*, 85 YALE L.J. 299 (1976).

3. *See* Ginsberg, *The Real Property Exemption of Nonprofit Organizations: A Perspective*, 53 TEMPLE L.A. 291 at 342 (1980).

4. *See* John D. Colombo, *Why Is Harvard Tax Exempt? (and Other Mysteries of Tax Exemption for Private Educational Institutions)*, 35 ARIZ. L. REV. 841, 864–68 (*citing* Hopkins, Atkinson).

5. *Id.* The "superior surrogate for government" theories that tried to rationalize tax exemption did not explain convincingly why federal, state, and local governments deemed for-profit, public, or quasi-governmental forms inferior to nonprofit ones as surrogates. They did not indicate why nonprofit organizations that would not have been allowed to form forty years ago became very easy to create and, once formed, could easily obtain tax exemptions. Nor did they explain why the nonprofit sector expanded in areas where the provision of quasi-governmental services was not at issue.

6. Henry B. Hansmann, *The Role of Nonprofit Enterprise*, 89 YALE L.J. 835 (1980); Henry B. Hansmann, *The Rationale for Exempting Nonprofit Organizations from Corporate Income Taxation*, 91 YALE L.J. 54 (1981). Professor Hansmann did not try to establish how or why market conditions became more conducive to nonprofit treatment during the period of greatest nonprofit expansion—a relationship that surely would have lent weight to or diminished the persuasiveness of his thesis. A voluminous literature on the subject of the significance of the nondistributional constraint exists. *See, e.g.*, Richard Steinberg, *The Revealed Objective Functions of Nonprofit Firms*, 23 J. ECON. BEHAV. & ORG. 99 (1994); Evelyn Brody, *Agents Without Principals: The Economic Convergence of the Nonprofit and For-Profit Organizational Forms*, 40 N.Y.L.S. L. REV. 457, 480–90 (1996); Avner Ben-Ner and Benedetto Gui, eds., THE NONPROFIT SECTOR IN THE MIXED ECONOMY (1993); Susan Rose-Ackerman, ed., THE ECONOMICS OF NONPROFIT INSTITUTIONS: STUDIES IN STRUCTURE AND POLICY (1986).

7. *See* Columbo, *supra* n. 176 at 862–63 (citing report of the Filer Commission, in Research Papers Sponsored by the Commission on Private Philanthropy and Public Needs 103 (ed. U.S. Dept. of the Treasury 1977) (stating that the "relief of government burden theory" is "a frequently cited justification for exemption"). *Id.* at n. 127.

8. *See generally Id.*

9. Evelyn Brody, *Of Sovereignty and Subsidy: Conceptualizing the Charity Tax Exemption*, 23 J. CORP. L. 585 (1998).

10. *See* Rob Atkinson, *Altruism in Nonprofit Organizations*, 31 B.C. L. REV. 501 (1990).

11. *See* Michael Harrington, THE OTHER AMERICA: POVERTY IN THE UNITED STATES (1962).

12. *See* Charles T. Clotfelter, FEDERAL TAX POLICY AND CHARITABLE GIVING (1985).

13. *See* Michael Harrington, THE NEW AMERICAN POVERTY (1984).

14. *See* Burton A. Weisbrod, THE ECONOMICS OF POVERTY: AN AMERICAN PARADOX (1965).

15. REVISED MODEL NONPROFIT CORP. ACT ("REVISED ACT"), adopted by the Subcommittee on the Model Nonprofit Corporation Law of the Business Law Section (Michael C. Hone, reporter) (1987).

16. *Id.; see also* Michael Hone, *Thirteen Ways to Look at Blackbirds and Nonprofit Corporations*, 39 CASE WEST. L. REV. 751 (1989).

17. REVISED ACT at xx-xxi; REVISED ACT, sec. 3.01.

18. Lizabeth Moody, response to Michael Hone, *Thirteen Ways to Look at Blackbirds and Nonprofit Corporations*, 39 CASE WEST. L. REV. 751, 766 (1989). ("The subcommittee that drafted the Revised Model Act never really addressed the issue of "what is a blackbird.")

19. *See* Bazil Facchina, Evan Showell, and Jan E. Stone, *Privileges and Exemptions Enjoyed by Nonprofit Organizations: A Catalog and Some Thoughts on Nonprofit Policymaking*, 3 TOPICS ON PHILANTHROPY 110–112 (1993).

20. *See* James J. Fishman and Stephen Schwarz, NONPROFIT ORGANIZATIONS 353 (2000) (discussing provisional letters).

21. *See supra*, ch. 1, n. 13 and accompanying text.

22. *See, e.g.,* FINANCIAL WORLD, Sept. 4, 1994 (*citing* various proposals to improve financial accounting for tax exempts).

23. *See* Geoffrey A. Manne, *Agency Costs and the Oversight of Charitable Organizations*, 1999 WISC. L. REV. 227 (1999).

24. *See supra*, text at ch. 4, n. 57 and accompanying text.

25. *See* Bazil Facchina, Evan Showell, and Jan E. Stone, *Privileges and Exemptions Enjoyed by Nonprofit Organizations, supra* at 112.

26. *Id.; see also* Mark A. Hall and John D. Colombo, *The Charitable Status of Nonprofit Hospitals: Toward a Donative Theory of Tax Exemption*, 66 WASH. L. REV. 307 (1991).

27. *Id.*

28. *See* George C. Christie, *An Essay on Discretion*, 1986 DUKE L.J. 747, 778 (1986); *see also* George C. Christie, *Objectivity in the Law*, 78 YALE L.J. 1311, 1312 (1969).

29. *See* Christie, *An Essay on Discretion*, 1986 DUKE L.J. 747, 778 (1986); *see also* Joseph Raz, *Dworkin: A New Link in the Chain*, 74 CAL. L. REV. 1103 (1986). What is most important for the exercise of discretion to be legitimate, states Raz, is to distinguish the application of the law from its creation so that "it is possible to identify which aspects of [judicial] activities make them law-applying acts and which make them law-creating acts." *Id.* at 1117.

30. See Anthony Sebok, POSITIVISM, FORMALISM, REALISM: LEGAL POSITIVISM IN AMERICAN JURISPRUDENCE (1998); Thomas Grey, *The New Formalism*, Stanford Law School, Public Law and Legal Series, Working Paper no. 4 (SSRN 200732, Sept. 6, 1999). The "apotheosis" of the rule of law has its critics, who have preferred to view lawmaking as a pragmatic normative activity rather than to see the rule of law as an end in itself. *See, e.g.,* Margaret Jane Radin, *Reconsidering the Rule of Law,* 69 B.U.L. REV. 781; Robert W. Gordon, *Critical Legal Histories,* 36 STAN. L. REV. 57 (1984).

31. Frederick Schauer, PLAYING BY THE RULES: A PHILOSOPHICAL EXAMINATION OF RULE-BASED DECISION-MAKING IN LAW AND IN LIFE 222 (1991).

32. Lon Fuller, THE MORALITY OF LAW 87 (1969 ed.).

33. *Id.*

34. Marilyne E. Phelan, NONPROFIT ENTERPRISES: LAW AND TAXATION §11A:05; Evelyn Alicia Lewis, *When Entrepreneurs of Commercial Nonprofits Divorce: Is It Anybody's Business? A Perspective on Individual Property Rights in Nonprofit Corporations,* 73 N.C. L. REV. 1761 (1995); Andrea Castro, *Overview of the Tax Treatment of Nonprofit Hospitals and Their For-Profit Subsidiaries,* 15 PACE L. REV. 501 (1995); Mary Jacobson, NONPROFIT CORPORATIONS: CONVERSION TO FOR-PROFIT STATUS AND NONPROFIT MEMBERS' RIGHTS (1995); M. Gregg Bloche, *Health Policy Below the Waterline: Medical Care and the Charitable Exemption,* 80 MINN. L. REV. 299 (1995).

35. *See* Brody, *infra* n. 221.

36. Evelyn Brody, *"Agents Without Principals: The Economic Convergence of the Nonprofit and For-Profit Organizational Forms,"* 40 N.Y.L.S. L. REV. 457, 458 (1996); Brody, *Hocking the Halo: Implications of the Charities Winning Briefs in Camps New-Found/Owatonna, Inc.,* 27 STETSON L. REV. 433 (1997).

37. *Id.* Brody suggests, however, that we should "hesitate to design changes based solely on the implications from economics." *Id.* at 536.

38. *See, e.g.,* Lee Goldman, *The Politically Correct Corporation and the Anti-Trust Laws,* 137 YALE L. & POL'Y REV. 137 (1995).

39. Scott. C. Idleman, *A Prudential Theory of Judicial Candor,* 73 TEX. L. REV. 1307, 1308 (1995).

40. *Id.* at 1338.

41. Lawrence B. Solum, *The Virtues and Vices of a Judge: An Aristotelian Guide to Judicial Selection,* 61 S. CAL. L. REV. 1735, 1755–56 (1988).

42. Memorandum in support of A. 7098-A, An act to amend the not-for-profit corporation law, in relation to judicial approval of certificates of incorporation, no. 007098 (1993).

43. *Id.;* NPCL §104(e).

44. *Id.; see* NPCL §112.

45. *Id.*

# Index